What reviewers have have said about

HAARP:
THE ULTIMATE WEAPON OF THE CONSPIRACY

"Readers new to the topic will find *HAARP: The Ultimate Weapon of the Conspiracy* to be informative... [Smith] clearly relates the project's history and the technology that preceded it. The chapter on inventor Nikola Tesla is well constructed, as is the description of what HAARP may be capable of—everything from weather modification to mind control."
—Frank Spaith, *Fate Magazine*

"In this comprehensive treatment, Smith analyzes HAARP's background in terms of Tesla technology, the Bernard Eastlund patent for altering the Earth's atmospheric, ionospheric and/or magnetospheric regions, and electromagnetic warfare between the ex-USSR and the USA."
—Ruth Parnell, *Nexus Magazine*

"Jerry E. Smith provides the first full-blown conspiracy analysis of the HAARP project since Nick Begich first brought the subject up...The book provides a wealth of hard data, with graphics and photos, to help readers understand the reality of the facility but complements that with well-documented speculation about even the strangest possibilities. ...*HAARP: The Ultimate Weapon of the Conspiracy* offers quite a tour de force, but readers need not follow the conspiratorializing to appreciate the science presented as well as the basic facts about HAARP."
—Kenn Thomas, *Steamshovel Press*

The Lost Science Series:
The Anti-Gravity Handbook
Anti-Gravity & the World Grid
Anti-Gravity & the Unified Field
The Free-Energy Device Handbook
The Cosmic Conspiracy
The Energy Grid
The Bridge To Infinity
The Harmonic Conquest of Space
Vimana Aircraft of Ancient India & Atlantis
Tapping the Zero Point Energy
The Fantastic Inventions of Nikola Tesla
Man-Made UFOs: 1944-1994

The Lost Cities Series:
Lost Cities of Atlantis, Ancient Europe & the Mediterranean
Lost Cities of North & Central America
Lost Cities & Ancient Mysteries of South America
Lost Cities of Ancient Lemuria & the Pacific
Lost Cities & Ancient Mysteries of Africa & Arabia
Lost Cities of China, Central Asia & India

The Mystic Traveller Series:
In Secret Mongolia by Henning Haslund (1934)
Men & Gods In Mongolia by Henning Haslund (1935)
In Secret Tibet by Theodore Illion (1937)
Darkness Over Tibet by Theodore Illion (1938)
Danger My Ally by F.A. Mitchell-Hedges (1954)
Mystery Cities of the Maya by Thomas Gann (1925)
In Quest of Lost Worlds by Byron de Prorok (1937)

Write for our free catalog of exciting books and tapes.

HAARP

The Ultimate Weapon of the Conspiracy

by

Jerry E. Smith

HAARP:

The Ultimate Weapon of the Conspiracy

by Jerry E. Smith

ISBN 0-932813-53-4

Cover design by Harry Osoff

Thanks to Jennifer Bolm, Nick Begich & Jeanne Manning

Printed in Canada

Second Printing February 1999

Published by
Adventures Unlimited Press
One Adventure Place
Kempton, Illinois 60946 USA
auphq@frontiernet.net

HAARP

The Ultimate Weapon

of the Conspiracy

by

Jerry E. Smith

Acknowledgments

I most especially want to thank Juanita Cox, Citizen Lobbyist, and Bob Sonderfan, researcher extraordinare. Without their unstinting help this book would never have been completed. I also want to thank Jim Keith and Ron Bonds for starting me on this project. Gayla Higgins, George Pickard XIV, Mr. Paul Lee, and Tony are deeply thanked for their invaluable assistance in reading and commenting on problems with the manuscript. Anthony Rodriguez wins two Gold Stars for masterfully helping out as both researcher and computer whiz. Additionally, I owe a great deal to Rich, Ken and David, who also helped keep my antique computers operational long enough to get this out.

HAARP

The Ultimate Weapon of the Conspiracy

CONTENTS

An Aerial View of the HAARP Site

Chapter Zero:
Imagine...

What if you had a single weapon that could destroy all of an enemy's orbiting spy satellites at once? You would have greatly improved your ability to move military forces undetected. This would be invaluable if you were preparing a surprise attack. What if that same weapon could wrap the earth in an impenetrable "shield"? One that would destroy all intercontinental ballistic missiles (ICBMs) attempting to pass through it? Attack, or retaliation, by missile would be impossible. A weapon that could create clouds of electrons moving at the speed of light could accomplish both of these objectives. A ground based radio transmitter of sufficient size might be able to do this.

Such a transmitter could be used to disrupt world-wide radio communications, as well. The ionosphere is used to bounce radio waves around the earth, making long-range communications possible. If this transmitter were used to change the ionosphere at known points, you could jam the rest of the world, while leaving your own messages unaffected. A ground based radio transmitter of sufficient size could easily do this.

One might be able to use this transmitter to do more than merely reshape the ionosphere. What if it could "burn" holes in that protective layer? That would allow deadly radiation from outer space to pour through, searing the earth. You could release a burst of radiation over a target as deadly as a nuclear bomb. There would be no explosion, no damage to buildings and equipment. Yet, every living thing within the area exposed would be dead or dying.

What could a nation at war do with a weapon that could undetectably redirect the jet stream? The weather could be controlled over whole continents, causing floods and droughts as desired. Weather control is food control. Could not such a weapon drive the enemy to his knees without firing a shot? A ground based radio transmitter of sufficient size might be able to do this, too.

What if this amazing weapon also allowed you to see deep into the earth, to find and target enemy underground bases? RADAR uses microwaves sent through the air to detect and identify objects, such as airplanes and missiles. Scientists have similarly seen beneath the earth's surface. The technology is called earth penetrating tomography (EPT). EPT could be used to find buried hazardous waste sites, new sources of oil or even to predict the erup-

tions of volcanos. The U.S. Senate funded an ongoing project called the High-frequency Active Auroral Research Program (HAARP). The HAARP project is building a transmitter of sufficient signal strength to turn the aurora borealis (the "northern lights") into a virtual antenna, rebroadcasting in the extremely low frequency (ELF) range. ELF waves travel deep into the earth, perfect for earth penetrating tomography (EPT). HAARP was funded by the Senate to use EPT to verify treaties prohibiting the spread of weapons of mass destruction.

The United States Navy intends to use the HAARP transmitter to communicate with deeply submerged submarines. ELF radio waves also penetrate deep into the sea. With the aurora used as a virtual antenna to rebroadcast the signal from HAARP, the Navy will be able to direct its submarine fleet, no matter how deeply the subs lie hidden beneath the waves.

What could a nation, or a conspiracy, do with a weapon that can "fry" men's minds? What if you could induce emotions, fear or rage, at will? What if you could do it over a large area, affecting enemy troops on their way to battle? whole cities? even entire continents? If you can tune the aurora to rebroadcast an ELF message, you may have created the ultimate "bio-feedback" machine. The human brain works in the same extremely low frequency range that HAARP will be broadcasting. This may give HAARP's operators the ability to send radio messages directly into the heads of millions of people. HAARP could possibly be used to produce emotions on demand, perhaps even send words. What if your sufficiently large transmitter, the HAARP array or something larger still, could put "thoughts" directly into people's heads? Thoughts like "surrender" or "obey"?

On 23 March, 1983, President Ronald Reagan called upon ". . . the scientific community in our country, those who gave us nuclear weapons, to turn their great talents now to the cause of mankind and world peace, to give us the means of rendering these nuclear weapons impotent and obsolete." This quest for the creation of a technology, of a weapon or weapons system, that would make atomic war impossible, was officially named the Strategic Defense Initiative (SDI). The press lost no time in dubbing it "Star Wars," after George Lucas' trilogy of films.

President Reagan's request sent the United States' military-industrial-scientific research community on the greatest, and costliest, weapons hunt in human history. Thousands of ideas were floated; hundreds of those were funded. Some lines of SDI research have since been abandoned. Some, however, are still being actively pursued to this day.

Not all of these developmental programs are taking place in laboratories of the military and its contractors. Some of these ideas involve technologies or applications that, as weapons, violate international treaties. Others would be repugnant to the ethical and moral values of the majority of Americans. In an effort to avoid public outcry and international condemnation, some of these programs have been "disguised" as civilian science.

This is the true story of one military program that pretends to be a "harmless" civilian research project. It is called HAARP. HAARP is not science fiction. It is a potentially deadly reality. When completed it will be the world's largest radio frequency transmitter. It may well be the "sufficiently large transmitter" of these imaginings.

> The prospect of domination of the nation's scholars by federal employment, project allocations, and the power of money is ever present—and is gravely to be regarded. Yet, in holding scientific research and discovery in respect, as we should, we must be alert to the equal and opposite danger that public policy could itself become the captive of a scientific-technological elite.
> President Dwight D. Eisenhower

> Man has lost the capacity to foresee and to forestall. He will end by destroying the earth.
> Dr. Albert Schweitzer

> I am pessimistic about the human race because it is too ingenious for its own good. Our approach to nature is to beat it into submission. We would stand a better chance of survival if we accommodated ourselves to this planet and viewed it appreciatively instead of skeptically and dictatorially.
> E. B. White

> ... And he doeth great wonders, so that he maketh fire come down from heaven on the earth in the sight of men.
> Rev. 13:13

> In my opinion, the military establishment still believes that the survival of the military organism is worth the sacrifice of the lives and health of large segments of the American population.
> Dr. Robert O. Becker

> By painful experience we have learnt that rational thinking does not suffice to solve the problems of our social life. Penetrating research and keen scientific work have often had tragic implications for mankind,... creating the means for his own mass destruction. This, indeed, is a tragedy of overwhelming poignancy!
> Dr. Albert Einstein

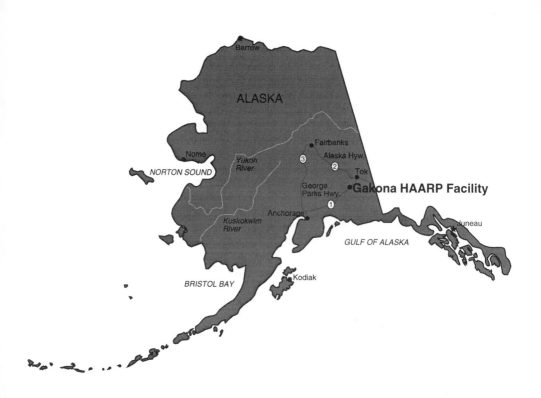

12   HAARP: THE ULTIMATE WEAPON OF THE CONSPIRACY

Chapter One:
The Beast In The Wilderness

WHERE IS HAARP?

Mt. St. Elias, the second highest peak in the United States, is the principal boundary marker between the State of Alaska and Canada. Less than fifty miles inland from the Gulf of Alaska, it rises 18,008 feet. The snow-capped coastal peaks and forested islands of the Alaskan panhandle lie to its south and east. A line, as straight as mapmakers can draw, is penned due north from Mt. St. Elias for nearly 650 miles to the famed North Slope of Alaska and the Beaufort Sea beyond. To the west of that line lies the vastness of Alaska; to the east, the Yukon Territory of Canada.

Mt. St. Elias, 11,000-foot Mt. Miller, and the huge Bagley Ice Field surrounding them, form the southern end of the Wrangell-St. Elias National Park and Preserve. Mt. Sanford, more than one hundred miles to the north, is also in that enormous park. In total acreage it is the largest United States National Park, the size of six Yellowstones. It has been called "the mountain kingdom of North America," as four mountain ranges meet there, with 9 of the 16 highest peaks in the United States. The high country is snow covered year-round, resulting in extensive ice fields and the largest assemblage of glaciers in the country. One glacier, the Malaspina, is larger than the entire state of Rhode Island.

Proclaimed as Wrangell-St. Elias National Monument on 1 December, 1978, it was later re-established as a National Park and Preserve on 2 December, 1980. It has been a "World Heritage Site" under the protection of the United Nations since 24 October, 1979. Along with its southern neighbors, Glacier Bay National Park and Preserve in Alaska and the Alsek-Tatshenshini Provincial Park in British Columbia, this combined 24-million acre wilderness is the largest internationally protected area in the world.

Wrangell-St. Elias stretches for more than a hundred miles from the Copper River in the west to the Canadian border and Klaune National Park in Canada in the east. Beginning in the south at the ice-choked breakers of the North Pacific, the Park runs north and west for 150 miles into the interior of the state. Virtually all of the eastern side of the Copper River Basin is within the Park and Preserve.

The Copper River Basin is also known as the Copper River Lowlands, and is a subdivision of the Pacific Mountain System. The lowlands are an inter-mountain basin flanked on all sides by towering, glacier covered mountains such as 16,208 foot Mt. Sanford. The basin is deeply cut by the valleys of the Copper River and its tributaries, which have steep walls rising up to 500 feet above their frigid waters.

Like much of the Alaskan "bush," the dominant form of vegetation is black and white spruce, although some willow, alder and poplar can be found. As a flier for the Park says:

> …Although the vegetation may seem sparse, especially in the interior, the park contains a variety of wildlife. Dall's sheep and mountain goats patrol the craggy peaks. Herds of caribou feed on the lichen and low woody plants… Moose browse in sloughs and bogs in the coastal lowlands and in brushy areas, which also attract brown/grizzly bears. Black bears roam throughout the park. Many rivers, streams and lakes provide spawning grounds for salmon and other fish. The Copper River drainage and the Malaspina forelands are major flyways for migratory birds and include prime nesting sites for trumpeter swans.

The weather is like that of most of interior Alaska. Summers are cloudy and cool but in July (the warmest month) clear, hot days are not uncommon. August and September tend to be cool and wet, but with mercifully fewer mosquitoes. The weather can be delightfully clear in fall, but the season is short. Winters are extremely cold. With temperatures dropping to 50 below zero, and an average snow cover of two feet, only the hardiest of souls venture out. In spring the skies clear again. Increasingly longer days and warming temperatures break winter's hold on the land with dramatic quickness.

Wrangell-St. Elias National Park's eastern and northern boundary is the Copper River. Alaska State Route 1, known both as the Glenn Highway and as the Tok Cut-Off Highway, follows the Copper River on the opposite side from the park along its northern edge. There the highway passes through the Gakona region, a gently southwest sloping plain with many small lakes and streams. Within the Gakona region are the Gulkona, Gakona, Sanford and Copper Rivers and Tulsona Creek. It is a sparsely populated area with a few small towns like Gakona and Chistochina, and the modest metropolis of Glennallen.

The Copper River 300, an annual dog sled race, is held there on the BLM (Bureau of Land Management) Trail. That trail traverses the Gakona region to the west and north of Wrangell-St. Elias National Park. It also passes through the grounds of that area's most controversial inhabitant: the High-frequency Active Auroral Research Program (HAARP).

THE CONTROVERSY

Like a nest of gigantic TV antennas, four dozen 72-foot-tall metal towers gleamed in the bright fall sunshine, outlined against the brilliant backdrop of Mount Sanford and the Copper River Valley. People wandered among them, gawking at the crisscrossed guy wires and the metal mesh above their heads.

A transmitter built by the Air Force and the Navy to beam radio waves into the ionosphere, the High-frequency Active Auroral Research Program, or HAARP, had opened its gates to general public inspection for the first time. As about 70 people from all over the state visited, scientists touted the transmitter as a potential world-class research station—a tool that would allow them to learn more about the magnetic and physical properties of the outer zone of Earth's atmosphere, the ionosphere.

Others weren't so sure...

So began Doug O'Harra's article of 4 April, 1996, "The Buzz Over HAARP" for *We Alaskans,* the Sunday magazine of *The Anchorage Daily News.*

HAARP is, or will be when completed, the largest and most powerful Department of Defense facility of its kind in the world—just what kind of facility it is, however, is the subject of heated debate. The government says it is a pure science research station, one intended to increase our understanding of the upper atmosphere. Detractors, as reporter O'Harra described, are not convinced. Some think it is a prototype for a "Star Wars" weapons system. Some think it will be used to control the weather. Others think it will be used by the New World Order to take over the world by projecting holographic images into the sky while beaming thoughts directly into our heads, telling us to accept the new "god" of their design. Still others think it is part of a planetary defense system to protect us from invading aliens from outer space. And some have even wilder ideas about HAARP!

This debate over what the heck the darn thing is ranges all the way from finger wagging and head shaking by HAARP's uneasy neighbors in a coffee shop just down the road in Glennallen; to strident and sometimes frightening talk radio shows all across America; to the many documentary and investigative television programs that have aired in the United States, Canada, Great Britain and Japan.

This controversy has surrounded HAARP nearly since the project's inception. Many stories about the mystery of HAARP have been run in the press. These have appeared at every level, from

Glennallen's Copper River County Journal, to *Popular Science Magazine,* to the prestigious international publication, *Jane's Defense Weekly.* Yet for all this publicity, most Americans have never heard of HAARP. *Mother Jones Magazine* cited the construction of HAARP as one of the "Top Censored News Stories of 1994."

Some longterm members of the Alaska State legislature have stated that they have never had so many constituents voice fear and concern over one topic. In response to the concerns of their constituents, several members of the State Legislature have held oversight hearings on HAARP and have stated that they would seek agreement from the Air Force for a thorough, public review of the project. A review that is yet to materialize.

Public debate about HAARP has sprung up in many areas of the globe far from the Alaskan bush that is home to HAARP. For example, a significant debate has played out on the Internet over the past few years. Today there are dozens of websites and discussion groups devoted to the HAARP controversy.

Opposition to HAARP has found adherents on both ends of the political spectrum. Conservatives and liberals alike have joined forces to fight this perceived danger. Liberals, particularly environmentalists, are concerned over the government's bland dismissal of HAARP's potential dangers to living things, especially to migratory species. One such group, Trustees for Alaska, has demanded that the Air Force conduct a new Environmental Impact Study (EIS). Conservatives likewise are disturbed by what they perceive as attempts by the government to cover something up, though they are not sure what.

WHAT IS HAARP?

One of HAARP's distinctions is that it will be the world's most powerful shortwave radio transmitter—only it will not be broadcasting for human ears. Its signal will be sent to the top of our atmosphere where it is intended to heat a portion of the sky, much like a microwave oven warms a frozen burrito. This type of transmitter is called an "ionospheric heater." There are several ionospheric heaters in use around the world today. HAARP, however, will be many times more powerful than all of them combined.

HAARP is jointly managed by the U.S. Air Force Phillips Laboratory, whose

Geophysics Directorate is located at Hanscom Air Force Base, Massachusetts, and two Navy organizations in the District of Columbia: the Office of Naval Research (ONR) and the Naval Research Laboratory (NRL). Although HAARP is funded through the Department of Defense (DOD), the scientific research is coordinated with, and conducted in large part by, educational institutions. Some private business firms are also scheduled to take part in HAARP experiments.

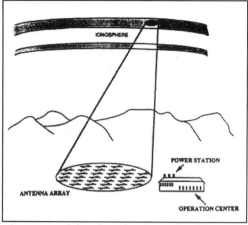

A conceptual drawing of an Ionosphere Heater.

This joint facility is being developed, some official HAARP documents claim, to learn more about how space weather affects communication, navigation and power grid systems. Space weather is the flow of particles from the sun and deep space into the earth's upper atmosphere. Space weather can affect the way the ionosphere propagates radio waves, disrupting world-wide radio communications. Satellites can be affected by space weather, causing damage to their onboard systems and/or degrading communications to and from them. Space "storms" can overload electrical power transmission lines on earth, causing widespread power outages.

When completed, HAARP will be a complex of 180 high frequency (HF) broadcast antennas, called the ionospheric research instrument (IRI), and numerous other scientific instruments. Still under construction, it is being erected a short distance from the Tok Cut-Off Highway (Route 1). The entrance gate to HAARP is located at milepost 11.3 from Route 1's junction with the Richardson Highway (Alaska Route 4), about 260 miles northeast of Anchorage and about the same distance southeast of Fairbanks.

The HAARP site, some 58 acres hacked from virgin forest, is owned by the DOD. Originally the DOD intended the Over The Horizon Backscatter (OTH-B) radar installation to be located there. The DOD made the land available to HAARP in 1991, long after the OTH-B project had been eliminated in the 1980s as the result of federal budget cuts. The facility came complete with an empty power station and a gravel road.

Visually, the antenna array called the IRI is the most striking part of the site. Of HAARP's 58 acres, 22 were wetlands, most of which have been filled in with black gravel to form a level field for the IRI. At project completion, expected in 2002, the final IRI (FIRI) will cover a gravel pad some 33 acres in extent, with 180 antenna towers in a grid of 15 columns and 12 rows. At this writing, the developmental prototype IRI (DP IRI) is comprised of 48 72-foot-high towers on a gravel pad 1,000 feet wide by 1,200 feet long.

The towers of the DP IRI are spaced at 80-foot intervals in a rectangular grid of eight columns and six rows. At the top of each tower are two dipole antennas. One of the dipoles is adjusted to operate in the 2.8 to 7 MHz range, the other in the 7 to 10 MHz range. The two dipoles are mounted horizontally like a large "X" at the top of each tower. Only one of the antennas of each pair can be operated at a time, depending on the output frequency desired. As well as their antennae, these towers support a complex, interconnected structure of wires and beams. A metal screen stretches between the towers 15 feet above the ground. This forms a continuous reflector for the antennas. During transmissions, the screen catches downward-directed radio frequency (RF) energy and re-directs it upward. This intensifies the beam as well as helps to protect people and animals on the ground from the intense RF fields generated when the transmitters are in operation.

On the ground, beneath the antenna array, are 30 transmitter shelters. Each shelter houses 12 diesel-powered transmitters. These can be switched to drive either the low-band or high-band dipoles. Each transmitter is capable of generating 10,000 watts of RF power. Together, these 360 transmitters can send 3.6 million watts of raw RF output to the antennas. HAARP has a unique feature, a patented ability to focus these transmissions into a single point high in the sky. This magnifies the output a thousand times, giving HAARP an effective radiated power in excess of 3.6 billion watts. This makes it more than 72,000 times more powerful than the largest commercial radio station in the United States!

According to the military, the purpose of the HAARP antenna array is to stimulate, on a very small scale, phenomena similar to those that occur naturally when energy from the sun interacts with the earth's upper atmosphere. This could provide scientists and engineers with insights into how these natural phenomena occur and what effects they produce. Official documents describe the government's intention for HAARP to become "a major Arctic facility for upper atmospheric and solar-terrestrial research." The government's official documents on HAARP are often contradictory and seem to be intentionally misleading. Researchers looking into HAARP and related technologies suspect that a great deal is not being told to the American people, much less to Congress who is footing the bill (with our money, of course).

THE CONSPIRACY

The name and location of HAARP may be the only things about this project that we know with complete certainty. "The Purloined Letter," the classic tale by Edgar Allen Poe, tells the story of how something was kept hidden by leaving it in plain sight. The High-frequency Active Auroral Research Program, would appear to be another example of obfuscation by revelation. This scientific project, while located 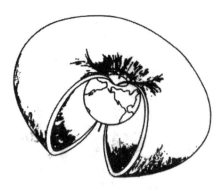 deep in the Alaskan bush, is hardly hidden. The site and many of its documents are open to the public, at least on occasion. HAARP even has its own home page on the Internet (http://w3.nrl.navy.mil/projects/haarp).

HAARP may well be what its supporters claim it is, just another high-tech scientific tool for unlocking the secrets of the universe—in this case, uncovering the mysteries of the upper atmosphere. However, researchers looking into HAARP have found hundreds of clues that there is some hidden agenda, some mysterious, undisclosed purpose lurking behind the academic facade. This book is an examination of the possible clandestine uses for this technology, and of the conspiracy (or conspiracies) that might desire such a tool.

It is hard to imagine how a project that is jointly operated by the Air Force and Navy could be a civilian one, especially one with the astonishing variety of potential weapons systems it embodies. Yet local and federal participants in HAARP have tried at every turn to paint the project as just more civilian science.

As would be proper for a civilian program, they have invited public comment and inspection. Before being granted final approval, HAARP was put through the procedure of public input and environmental impact studies. In the Final Environmental Impact Study (FEIS) one comes face to face with either outrageous lies, or astonishing stupidity.

The FEIS asserts that there will be no impact on the terrestrial (earthly) environment because all the energies broadcast by HAARP will be directed straight up, into the atmosphere and away from the earth. They carefully ignore that even their own documentation discusses that some of this energy would be refracted back to earth. They also pretend that affecting one region of the sky will have no effect on any other regions. This is manifestly untrue.

They conveniently ignore the mounting medical and scientific evidence on the health risks associated with electromagnetic and radio frequency radiation on the grounds that it is "not universally accepted by the large majority of the research community." While that data may not have been universally accepted in 1991 when the Air Force began its studies, things have changed a great deal since.

Indeed, the government is not even able to fool itself on this one: the U.S. Department of Commerce, National Telecommunications and Information Administration, Interdepartment Radio Advisory Committee has ruled that HAARP does present risks to radio communications. These are risks that could have a profound effect on people living in rural Alaska, where reliable radio communication is sometimes a matter of life or death.

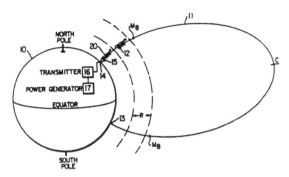

Bernard Eastlund's 1987 patent No. 4,686,605.

As one investigates HAARP one finds a situation not unlike peeling an onion, or opening a Russian nesting doll only to find another doll inside. There are many successive layers of intent and deception here; one hidden agenda hiding behind yet another. HAARP may be a great number of things, few of which are covered in its literature, or in its promoters' smooth lies.

A fact sheet entitled "Purpose and Objectives of the HAARP Program" was posted on the HAARP home page on the Internet. It reads:

> HAARP is a scientific endeavor aimed at studying the properties and behaviour of the ionosphere, with particular emphasis on being able to understand and use it to enhance communications and surveillance systems for both civilian and defense purposes.
>
> The HAARP program is committed to developing a world class ionospheric research facility consisting of:
>
>> The ionospheric research instrument (IRI), a high power transmitter facility operating in the HF frequency range. The IRI will be used to temporarily excite a limited area of the ionosphere for scientific study.
>>
>> Diagnostic instruments that will be used to observe the physical processes that occur in the excited region.
>
> Observation of the processes resulting from the use of the IRI in a controlled manner will allow scientists to better understand processes that occur continuously under the natural stimulation of the sun.
>
> In addition, diagnostics installed at the HAARP facility will be useful for a variety of other research purposes including the study of glo-

SOME RADIO WAVE PATHS THROUGH THE IONOSPHERE

Ionosphere

EARTH'S SURFACE

- Satellite Communication
- Over-The-Horizon Surveillance
- Deep Space Radio Surveys

bal warming and ozone depletion.

The core of HAARP is the IRI. It will be the largest high-frequency radio transmitter ever built. It is designed to concentrate several gigawatts of broadcast power into an intense beam of unimaginable strength. This is done by sequencing the firing of a planar (arranged in a flat plane) array of dipole antennas broadcasting on the shortwave band.

The big difference between HAARP and the dozen or so other ionospheric heaters in the world is that HAARP is a phased-array. This phasing, or sequenced firing, of the transmitters/antenna field allows for the focusing ability that sets HAARP apart from its peers. It also makes it "illegal" if used as over-the-horizon radar (which is precisely what the HAARP site was originally slated for).

Phased-array radar is a very advanced type of radar that can track hundreds of objects simultaneously. The United States and the U.S.S.R. both developed phased-array radar as a way to monitor for evidence of enemy nuclear attacks being initiated. Phased-array radar, however, was restricted by the Anti-Ballistic Missile (ABM) Treaty of 1972, which stipulates that such radars must be deployed only on the periphery of a nation's territory and must point outward, so that their only function would be to warn of an enemy attack. In this way, a phased-array radar could not be used as part of a defensive system to identify and shoot down attacking missiles.

The abandoned "backscatter" program adhered to the stipulations of the ABM Treaty; the only problem was, it didn't work. If HAARP is used as a radar system it will violate the ABM Treaty because of its beam steering capacity, which would allow it to be used defensively. Early HAARP literature openly discussed this use of the facility, while more recent material is strangely silent on this point.

There are three principal stages in the development of a weapons system. The first stage is twofold; first there is the hard science, the fundamental research, that leads

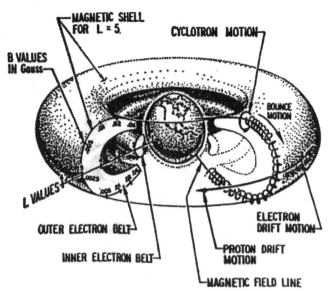

A drawing by Eastlund to illustrate charged particle motion in the earth's geomagnetic field for his global shield patent.

to an increased understanding of natural laws. Then someone gets a bright idea; a "what if..." concept based on trying to apply the hard science discoveries to military needs.

The second stage of the acquisition cycle is called "proof-of-concept." Here scientists, either in universities working under contracts and grants funded by the military or defense contractors, or in the military's or contractor's own labs, develop hardware to test the "what if..." idea. The purpose of this phase is to demonstrate that the concept can be worked up into something that the military could someday use. At this stage the experimental equipment seldom resembles an actual weapon.

It is often not until the third and final stage, the prototype stage, that the idea takes shape as an actual working model. After the prototype is demonstrated, the project would typically move from the lab to the political arena as supporters fight to get the massive funding needed to build and field a new weapons system.

The DOD would have us believe that HAARP is a phase one, pure science project. Many of HAARP's detractors believe it is actually a phase two "proof-of-concept" mockup of a weapons system. Because the field of antennas of the IRI is designed to be built incrementally—some now, more later—these people believe that HAARP is intended to become a full-scale working weapon if the "proof-of-concept" phase succeeds.

Some people believe that there is one over-arching conspiracy, a cadre of incredibly powerful people who want to rule the world. Most of us dismiss such people as paranoid kooks. Still, there is no denying that for over a hundred years a movement has been developing among the world's top intellectuals, industrialists and "global villagers" to end war and solve societal problems (like overpopulation, trade imbalances and environmental degradation) through the creation of a single world government. Whether this globalist movement is a diabolic "conspiracy" of the evil few or a broad "consensus" of the well-intentioned many, in fact matters little. It is as real as AIDS and potentially just as deadly, at least to our individual freedom, if not our very lives. Were this a conspiracy, HAARP could prove invaluable to furthering their plans, as we shall see.

The idea of a "League of Nations" that was floated after World War I was but one embodiment of this movement. Today's United Nations (UN) was built on the League of Nations concept. The UN was created primarily to end war—by ending nations. The logic is that if there are no nations, then there can be no wars between nations. This was clearly stated in the United Nations' "World Constitution" with these words: "The age of nations must end. The governments of the nations have decided to order their separate sovereignties into one government to which they will surrender their arms."

The New World Order (NWO) is but one name given to this push to create a true world government. Many supporters of the NWO espouse a philosophy called technocracy, which is rule by experts, scientists or technicians. It is not democratic in any sense by which Americans understand the term. One very famous advocate of the New World Order is Zbigniew Brzezinski. He was a National Security Advisor to Jimmy Carter and other presidents. He called his version of technocracy "technetronics." In his book, "Between Two Ages," Brzezinski wrote: "The technetronic era involves the gradual appearance of a more controlled society. Such a society would be dominated by an elite, unrestrained by traditional values."

This "technetronic" union of nations would call for the desovereignization of all existing countries. This new ordering would reduce the United States of America to a mere regional government—perhaps the "United States of North America." The North American Free Trade Agreement (NAFTA) is widely seen as one stepping stone to the NWO. Former Secretary of State Henry Kissinger was quoted by the *Los Angeles Times Syndicate* in 1993 as saying: "NAFTA represents the single most creative step towards a New World Order." The Common Market in Europe and the European Union (EU) are similarly seen as bridges to an eventual United States of Europe, which in turn would be just another region of the United Nations' global state (or "global plantation" as some detractors have called it).

The NWO conspiracy/consensus is but one of the possible hidden masters plucking HAARP's strings.

Other candidates include supporters of the Strategic Defense Initiative in the upper echelons of the military-industrial-scientific complex and renegade factions of the intelligence community. The problem with having to guess about something is that there are only a few right answers and a near infinity of wrong answers. The official HAARP material is so obviously contradictory, and seemingly transparent in attempts to misdirect and confuse the general public about the project's real purpose, that it virtually forces one to speculate as to what it is really going on. Clearly, there is something we are not being told. HAARP is almost certainly part of some kind of conspiracy. At this point we cannot know if that conspiracy is something as trivial as a low level plot by a handful of men in the military-industrial-scientific industry to shake America down for a few bucks for a useless big science project. Or, to take the other extreme, if HAARP is part of a plot to destroy America and take over the world. Or, if it is some unimaginable something else entirely.

WHO?

The DOD claims ownership of the land on which HAARP sits. The Air Force's Phillips Laboratory of Massachusetts and the Navy's Office of Naval Research of Washington, D.C. share responsibility for the technical oversight, as well as the management, administration and evaluation of this supposedly civilian project. All three insist that there is nothing sinister about HAARP, that it is just another piece of big science, all open and above board. They are at pains to point out that HAARP literature is unclassified and available to all inquirers, that it can even be downloaded from the Internet. Several universities, private research facilities and corporations, from this and other countries, are involved in the project as well. These include: the University of Alaska, University of Massachusetts, University of California at Los Angeles (UCLA), Massachusetts Institute of Technology (MIT), Stanford University, Clemson University, University of Tulsa, University of Maryland, Cornell University, SRI International, and Geospace, Inc.

This would certainly make it seem like HAARP is outside of the hush-hush, top secret world of weapons development. However, a key DOD document states:

> The heart of the program will be the development of a unique ionospheric heating capability to conduct the pioneering experiments required to adequately assess the potential for exploiting ionospheric enhancement technology for DOD purposes.

Since when has the DOD had non-military purposes?

Another clue that HAARP may not be a civilian activity is found in the current holder of the principal contract to build HAARP—Raytheon E-Systems, one of the world's largest defense contractors.

A key player in the HAARP saga is Senator Ted Stevens (R-Alaska). He has been a staunch supporter of the project both in Washington and in his home state. He seems to view the project as another wonderful piece of political pork barrel for his constituents. He has tried to sell the project as one that would bring jobs and money to the area, and international academic prestige to the University of Alaska. Yet few jobs have developed, and little of the over $58 million spent on the project so far has reached Alaska. Is it pork barrel (which some people would find reason enough to oppose the project), or is the pork a "cover"?

Another strange clue to the real purpose of HAARP is that a top Russian scientist, Roald Zinurovich Sagdeev, was one of the members of a scientific committee who worked on the development of the HAARP concept. This committee, like HAARP, was jointly sponsored by the Air Force's Phillips Laboratory and the Office of Naval Research. This committee was convened by the East/West Space Science Center of the University of Maryland, of which Academician Sagdeev is the Director.

Dr. Sagdeev served for fifteen years as the Director of the Soviet Union's Space Research Institute (comparable to our National Aeronautics and Space Administration (NASA)). While there he directed many high profile multinational projects, including the joint U.S.-U.S.S.R. Apollo-Soyuz program, and international missions to probe Halley's Comet and later Phobos, a moon of Mars. These last two projects were devised and implemented by Academi-

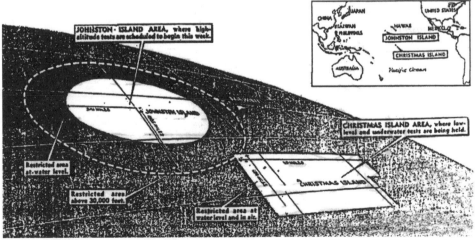

In 1961 a high altitude nuclear test over Johnston Island in the Pacific set off a light show in Hawaii and fried all of America's spy satellites. From a 1961 AP report.

cian Sagdeev in cooperation with more than twelve countries.

Before his appointment to the Soviet's Space Research Institute in 1973, he had an impressive career in nuclear science as a plasma physicist; so much so that he was one of the youngest scientists ever elected to full Academician of the U.S.S.R. Academy of Sciences, for which there is no comparable honor in the United States. He is now Director Emeritus, Russian Space Science Institute, and is in the U.S. as a Distinguished Professor of Physics at the University of Maryland, one of the Universities participating in HAARP. He is also a Foreign Member of the United States' National Academy of Sciences and a Senior Associate at the Center for Post-Soviet Studies.

Academician Sagdeev could well be proof that the "One World" conspiracy has put its roots deep into the soil of Mother Russia, as well as The West. One goal of the New World Order crowd is "convergence," the melding of the United States and the former Soviet Union (FSU) into a single global entity. Dr. Sagdeev has played a significant political role toward that end throughout his career. During the first five years of perestroika he served as an advisor to then Soviet Premier Mikhail Gorbachev at the Geneva, Washington, and Moscow summits.

By the way, "World Citizen" Gorbachev now heads several organizations, such as the Gorbachev Foundation and the Green Cross, all located at The Presidio, a closed U.S. military base in San Francisco, California. Gorbachev's primary occupation these days is to write an ethical platform for the New World Order's ecological edicts. This task was assigned to him by decision of the Earth Summit held in Rio de Janeiro in 1992.

In 1995 Academician Sagdeev was co-recipient, with Evgany P. Velikhov, of the Leo Szilard Award for Physics in the Public Interest: "For their unique contributions to Soviet Glasnost which was a major factor in reversing the nuclear arms race between the Soviet Union and the United States." This award is presented annually by the American Physical Society "...to recognize outstanding accomplishments by physicists in promoting the use of physics for the benefit of society in such areas as the environment, arms control, and science policy." Leo Szilard (1898-1945) was the first American physicist to conceive of building an atomic bomb back in the 1930s. At his urging Albert Einstein (1879-1955) wrote a letter to President Franklin D. Roosevelt in 1940 proposing a project to build a nuclear weapon. That led to the creation of the Manhattan Project that eventually gave us The Bomb.

Velikhov and Sagdeev received the Leo Szilard Award in recognition of their having organized the Soviet Scientists' Committee for Peace

Against the Nuclear Threat in March of 1983. This committee published a physics-based critique of the United States' Strategic Defense Initiative three years later. In Professor Sagdeev we see a very interesting connection between HAARP, SDI, plasma physics (HAARP is alleged to be intended to study the plasma physics of the upper atmosphere), the environment, and arms control. These are subjects that will come up repeatedly in our search for an understanding of what HAARP is about.

Why would a former top Soviet official, scientist, and SDI expert be a part of the birthing of HAARP? Some believe that HAARP is SDI technology coming on-line. President Reagan promised to share "Star Wars" technology with the Soviets. Some thought he was wacky for saying that, others applauded the gesture. The Soviets were convinced that SDI would give the United States "first strike" capability and bitterly opposed it. Are we developing SDI technology? Could we be honoring Reagan's commitment? Was Academician Sagdeev's presence on that committee proof that 1) HAARP is "Star Wars" and 2) that we really are sharing it with the Russians?

WHY?

What if your radar could see far over the horizon, picking up enemy planes and missiles hundreds, even thousands of miles off? What if, once you saw those incoming missiles, you could raise the top of the atmosphere? This would create unplanned drag in space by having "air" where there should not be any. It would probably deflect or destroy the missiles. That is what the original patents for a HAARP-like apparatus said such a device could do. What if you could peer miles deep into the earth and discover all of your enemy's buried secrets? That is exactly what HAARP was funded by the U.S. Senate to do.

What if, as part of manipulating the upper atmosphere, you could turn the jet stream in any direction you liked? What if, with the touch of a button, you could create localized storms, turning routes to potential battlefields into muddy quagmires to stop enemy troop and supply movements in their tracks? The DOD has desired this technology since the Vietnam War. During that conflict they attempted to seed clouds over the enemy's main supply route, the Ho Chi Minh Trail. Thinking bigger, what if you could "dial up" continent-wide storms that would batter down a belligerent nation's food crops with wind and hail or drown it under flood waters? Could you not induce famine at will? These too were part of the original plan for a HAARP-like device.

What if you could direct beams of energy at advancing enemy troops, microwaving their brains like three-minute meals? Would that not be the perfect weapon—your enemy dead or too mentally disturbed to fight, yet nothing else damaged, his equipment still usable, his cities, his industry and yours unblemished by war? This too has been a dream of weapons designers for decades. That was the reason for developing the neutron bomb (which was first tested in the U.S. in 1962). The neutron bomb releases high levels of deadly radiation from a comparatively tiny explosion, causing minimal damage to "assets" and maximal damage to humans.

Could you control people if you could project holographic images into the sky, pictures of the God(s) they worship or of the Demons they fear most? The Air Force thinks so, as they are actively pursuing holographic projectors as a weapons system. What could you do with people if you could transmit words or thoughts directly into their minds? Could you not bend them to do your bidding unawares, or drive them insane with "voices"? Psychologists in the employ of Russia's KGB have been working on radio remote control of people since the 1930s. The CIA has had similar research programs since the 1950s.

All of the above are things that researchers say HAARP (or a device like HAARP) could do, if built sufficiently large and directed to that purpose. As crazy and science-fictional as these may sound, for decades respected scientists have said that it was only a matter of time, and money, to accomplish these things. Is HAARP the next "evolutionary" stage in weapons development?

Who would like to get their hands on such a weapon? Who wouldn't! I am sure you can think of many countries, organizations, agencies and would-be despots who would sell whatever excuse for a soul they had to possess such a weapon. If HAARP truly has these potentials, and some of the evidence says it does, how long do you think it could remain in civilian hands? Even if HAARP today is a purely scientific undertaking, it is hard to imagine it remaining under civilian control for long once its power is proved. The evidence, however, suggests that HAARP has been under the control of some scientific-military conspiracy from the outset. It more than suggests, it positively shouts of a conspiracy—one to further the mysterious aims of some unknown faction at tax payer expense. Discovering who these conspirators might be will be as much a part of this book as understanding HAARP itself.

While supporters point out that the program is unclassified, its "civilian" status may be yet another kind of cover—one intended to circumvent treaties that the United States holds with both the United Nations and the former Soviet Union. As discussed above, HAARP could be a breach of the ABM treaty if pursued by the military. Additionally, HAARP would appear to have tremendous potential to change weather, either over a battlefield or a continent. The United States is signatory to a UN-sponsored treaty banning environmental modification (weather control) as a weapon of war. The military is some-

what restricted in engaging in this type of research, but not civilians.

Perfectly rational and responsible guesses about the truth behind HAARP can sound crazy to the uninitiated. We live in an age where science fiction is becoming fact faster than the futurists can get their visions into print. Control of the weather may, for example, seem like a crazy idea, yet scientists around the world have been developing weather modification technology for over fifty years. In roughly that same length of time, we went from the Wright Brothers at Kitty Hawk to Neil Armstrong on the moon. It is entirely within the bounds of known and accepted scientific principles to say that the HAARP literature shows that some of the experiments planned for HAARP could have profound effects on the weather. What if there is a conspiracy to use this technology offensively? In this book I will direct your attention to some of the most plausible, even if sometimes improbable-sounding, speculations about HAARP and its intended usage.

Some who have made guesses about the reality behind HAARP have come to what I consider to be "inquiring mind," off-the-deep-end conclusions about who is responsible for HAARP and what HAARP will be used for. While I doubt that angels, devils or extraterrestrials are involved, I will share some of those speculations with you as well, just on the off chance that they may be right.

Is there some Big Conspiracy of which HAARP might be a part? Writers before me have written whole libraries in their attempts to answer the question of whether there might be one vast conspiracy of a powerful few to rule the world. Many conspiracy theories have been offered, some very convincing, some obviously the work of disturbed minds. Those of you versed in history and familiar with current events and the forces shaping them have recognized the horrible truth that there is, in fact, a large and powerful movement to create a single, one world government. The New World Order is one name given to this push for world hegemony. The idea of "hegemony" is one nation or central power supreme over many nations, as the Vatican was centuries ago, and the Roman Empire was at the time of Christ. The goal of the "gradualists" who support the New World Order is to make the United Nations, or some other yet-to-be-created organization, the new Rome.

This desire for a unified world government permeates the so-called "Liberal Eastern Establishment." I could give you thousands of citings from books and magazines to support this contention. Hopefully one representative quote shall suffice… Strobe Talbott has been the Deputy Secretary of State (the second highest ranking official in the U.S. State Department) for the last four administrations. In 1992 he said:

> Within the next hundred years nationhood as we know it will be obsolete; all states will recognize a single global authority. . . All countries are basically social arrangements. No matter how permanent and even sacred they may seem at any one time, in fact they are artificial and temporary.

As we will see throughout this book, HAARP embodies several technologies that NWO supporters might desire to use, to put the world into their hands. This includes such covert technologies as beaming microwaves or extremely low frequency radio waves at target populations. Such transmissions could have the effect of disorientation, illness, or mood shifts; and might even be able to put words into people's heads. It is a matter of public record that the CIA and the KGB (and their predecessors) have researched such technology for most of this century. It doesn't take a John Birch Society mindset to be frightened at the prospect of what might happen if those who wish to control and subjugate their fellow man finally got their hands on a working model.

One strange link to HAARP from the ultra-right's outermost fringe is the MJ-12 connection. Some, like Bill Cooper, author of *Behold A Pale Horse* (Light Technology Pub., 1991) and publisher of the newspaper *Veritas,* and John Lear, formerly the CIA's top pilot, have spread tales of the presence of outer space aliens among us. These people maintain that after the crash of a flying saucer near Roswell, New Mexico, in 1947, the government set up an Above Top Secret commission, "Majic 12" or "Majestic 12," to keep a lid on the "truth." MJ-12, they said, eventually took over the government (after inking treaties with the aliens) becoming a conspiracy within a conspiracy, running the NWO conspiracy from deep cover. If this is true, which I doubt, there are many applications of HAARP technology that could be used both by and against MJ-12 and their alien overlords. Some believers in these tales have suggested that HAARP might be intended as a planetary defense shield against alien invasion!

SCIENCE GONE MAD OR STAR WARS?

Beyond the question of who ultimately pulls HAARP's strings, there are two paramount questions about what HAARP really is. Around each of these questions are clustered hundreds more. The first nexus of primal questions is: If it is basic scientific research, is it science gone out of control? What are the dangers inherent in playing around with natural systems and forces of this magnitude? Life on this planet is made possible only because the ionosphere shields us from deadly cosmic rays, much as the ozone layer protects us from ultraviolet light. Will altering the upper atmosphere, the ionosphere and magnetosphere, alter or possibly even end life on earth? Many migratory species, such as salmon and caribou, use some little understood aspect of the earth's magnetic field to guide their migrations. What will happen to them if the magnetosphere is changed as HAARP experimenters intend? As we will be examining, HAARP has the potential  to drastically alter weather patterns over whole continents by moving the jet stream; is this something we want scientists to be tinkering with?

The second set of primary questions is: Is it a weapon? If so, who will it be used on? Does it violate international treaties? Will Star Wars level technology coming on-line destabilize the currently friendly relations between the United States and the former Soviet Union? The U.S. is signatory to a United Nations Convention banning environmental manipulation for military purposes; are we preparing to break that treaty?

Two of HAARP's primary goals (earth penetrating tomography and communicating with subs) will use the production of ELF radio waves in the ionosphere. These ELF broadcasts from the upper atmosphere will blanket most of the northern half of this planet.

Scientific evidence is now pouring in on the medical dangers of ELF exposure. Will HAARP be used to intentionally bathe the northern hemisphere in harmful, possibly deadly, radiation? On a perhaps even more sinister note, the ELF frequencies that they will be using give HAARP a very real potential for mind manipulation. Could the secret plans for HAARP include its use as a thought control weapon against civilian populations, possibly even against the citizens of the United States?

In this book we will examine, and attempt to answer these two principal areas of inquiry. In addition, we will ponder a third question: if it is neither basic science nor a weapon, what else might it be?

For some scientists HAARP offers an exciting step into 21st century technology. For most of the rest of us, it affords a terrifying glimpse into secret plans of the would-be rulers of mankind. I hope you like scary stories, because I plan on scaring the willies out of you. Why? There is a beast in the wilderness of Alaska—one that I hope I can motivate you to help kill.

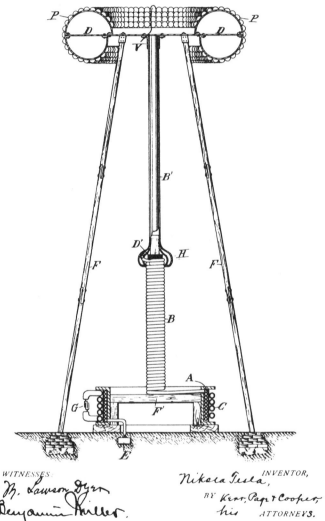

Chapter Two:
The Tesla Connection

Fancy yourself seated in a large, well-lighted room, with mountains of curious-looking machinery on all sides. A tall, thin young man walks up to you, and by merely snapping his fingers creates instantaneously a ball of leaping red flame, and holds it calmly in his hands. As you gaze you are surprised to see it does not burn his fingers. He lets it fall upon his clothing, on his hair, into your lap, and, finally, puts the ball of flame into a wooden box. You are amazed to see that nowhere does the flame leave the slightest trace, and you rub your eyes to make sure you are not asleep.

So spoke Chauncey McGovern, one of the few who were privileged to attend one of Nikola Tesla's famous demonstrations. Tesla gave those shows of the "wonders of electricity" to the rich and famous–to reporters, leading politicians and millionaires–in his New York laboratory in the last two decades of the 19th century. Decades later, the legend of the "mad scientist" with his bizarre lab, sparking and shrieking with electricity, was the basis for the image of Doctor Frankenstein's laboratory in the 1930s Universal Pictures films.

HAARP could be more than merely the scheme of some modern-day mad scientists. Some researchers of the HAARP controversy have traced the program's origin back to the work of the original mad scientist, Nikola Tesla himself. Tesla was no ordinary kook. It was Tesla who discovered and patented the use of alternating current (AC) electricity, the form of electricity that is the very foundation of our electrically powered civilization.

Perhaps the first anti-HAARP researcher to make the connection between Tesla and HAARP was Dr. Nick Begich, co-author with Jeane Manning of *Angels Don't Play This HAARP* (Earthpulse Press, 1995). Dr. Begich is the eldest son of the late U.S. Congressman from Alaska, Nick Begich, Sr., and political activist Pegge Begich. He is a past-president of the Alaska Federation of Teachers. He received his doctorate in traditional medicine from The Open International University for Complementary Medicines of Sri Lanka in

Electrical genius Nikola Tesla.

November of 1994.

In *Angels Don't Play This HAARP*, he explained that his first contact with HAARP came when he read an article in the Australian magazine *Nexus*. After reading that article he went to his local library and pulled up the original patents on a HAARP-like apparatus granted to Dr. Bernard J. Eastlund of Spring, Texas. As Dr. Begich put it:

> A cold chill ran through me as I realized that the diagrams I was seeing were reminiscent of patents issued to Nikola Tesla in the late 19th and early 20th century. I next noted the reference sources in the patent itself, two articles from *The New York Times*. When I reviewed the articles they were about Tesla. The articles referenced in the United States patent were extremely interesting in that they were, in part, the basis for this current technology.

The first article referenced in Eastlund's patent ran in *The New York Times* on 8 December, 1915. It read, in part:

> Nikola Tesla, the inventor, has filed patent applications on the essential parts of a machine the possibilities of which test a layman's imagination and promise a parallel of Thor's shooting thunderbolts from the sky to punish those who have angered the gods... Suffice it to say that the invention will go through space with a speed of 300 miles a second, a manless ship without propelling engine or wings, sent by electricity to any desired point on the globe on its errand of destruction, if destruction its manipulator wishes to effect.
>
> "It is not a time," said Dr. Tesla yesterday, "to go into the details of this thing. It is founded upon a principle that means great things in peace; it can be used for great things in war. But I repeat, this is no time to talk of such things. It is perfectly practicable to transmit electrical energy without wires and produce destructive effects at a distance. I have already constructed a wireless transmitter which makes this possible, and have described it in my technical publications, among which I refer to my patent number 1,119,732 recently granted.
>
> "With a transmitter of this kind we are enabled to project electrical energy in any amount to any distance and apply it for innumerable purposes, both in war and peace. Through the universal adoption of this system, ideal conditions for the maintenance of law and order will be realized, for then the energy necessary to the enforcement of right and justice will be normally productive, yet potential, and in any moment available, for attack and defense. The power transmitted need not

be necessarily destructive, for, if existence is made to depend upon it, its withdrawal or supply will bring about the same results as those now accomplished by force of arms."

The other article referenced in Eastlund's patent ran in *The New York Times* on September 22, 1940. It read, in part:

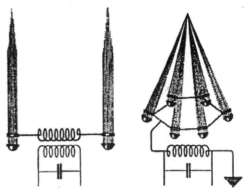

Tesla's "Death-Ray" device as depicted in 1934.

Nikola Tesla, one of the truly great inventors who celebrated his eighty-fourth birthday on July 10, tells the writer that he stands ready to divulge to the United States Government the secret of his "teleforce," with which, he said, airplane motors would be melted at a distance of 250 miles, so that an invisible Chinese Wall of Defense would be built around the country... This "teleforce," he said, is based on an entirely new principle of physics that "no one has ever dreamed about," different from the principle embodied in his inventions relating to the transmission of electrical power from a distance, for which he has received a number of basic patents.

This new type of force, Mr. Tesla said, would operate through a beam one one-hundred-millionth of a square centimeter in diameter, and could be generated from a special plant that would cost no more that $2,000,000 and would take only about three months to construct. The beam, he states, involves four new inventions, two of which already have been tested. One of these is a method and apparatus for producing rays "and other manifestations of energy" in free air, eliminating the necessity for a high vacuum; a second is a method and process for producing "very great electrical force;" the third is a method for amplifying this force; and the fourth is a new method for producing "a tremendous electrical repelling force." This would be the projector, or gun, of the system. The voltage for propelling the beam to its objective, according to the inventor, will attain a potential of 50,000,000 volts. With this enormous voltage, he said, microscopic electrical particles of matter will be catapulted on their mission of defensive destruction. He has been working on this invention, he added, for many years and has recently made a number of improvements in it.

Nikola Tesla, of Serbian descent, proudly became a United States citizen in 1891. He was born in 1857 in the Yugoslavian village of Smiljan, in what was then the Austro-Hungarian Empire. His father was an Orthodox priest and his mother, while unschooled, was highly intelligent and something of an inventor herself. As a youth he was a dreamer with a poetic touch. As he matured he developed the qualities of self-discipline and a mania for precision. In old age he added a remarkable catalog of phobias and weird behaviors to his personality.

From an early age he was fascinated with machines and science. He attended the Technical University at Graz, Austria, and the University of Prague, intending to pursue an engineering career. It was at Graz that he first saw the Gramme dynamo, which worked as a generator in one direction and, when reversed, became an electric motor in the other. Seeing this set him to thinking of ways to turn alternating current to advantage. Later, while visiting Budapest, Hungary, he visualized the principle of the rotating magnetic field and began working up plans for an induction motor based on his vision.

In 1882 Tesla traveled to Paris, France, where he found employment at the Continental Edison Company. The following year, while on assignment to Strasburg, he used his spare time to construct his first induction motor. It was a great technological achievement, though few around him grasped that at the time. His attempts to interest his European contemporaries in his work proved disappointing at best. Going into the 1880s direct current (DC) was all the rage, while AC power was discredited as being unsafe and unworkable. Annoyed with the know-it-all smirking of people he considered fools, Tesla sailed for America in 1884.

The cocky 27-year-old arrived in New York City with four cents in his pocket, a few of his own poems, and calculations for a flying machine (which he patented in 1928). He had little difficulty securing a position in Thomas Edison's organization. Unfortunately, the two inventors were very far apart in background, temperament and methods. Their separation, on decidedly less than friendly terms, was inevitable. In time their intense competition in business and scientific discoveries drew newspaper headlines. Each despised the other. Thomas Alva Edison (1847-1931) thought Tesla was a swaggering snob. Tesla, who saw himself as a real scientist, considered Edison a mere "tinkerer," and a publicity hound at that.

Tesla soon established his own laboratory. Between 1886 and 1898 he received grants for 85 patents from his work, with more still to come. Of the 46 basic patents in alternating current, 45 are held by Tesla! Besides working out the many systems and machines needed to realize an alternating current technology, his interests took him into investigating a wide range of other scientific possibilities.

Tesla experimented with shadowgraphs similar to those that would later be used by Wilhelm Konrad Roentgen (1845-1923), who discovered X-rays in 1895 (for which he received the Nobel prize in 1901). Tesla's countless experiments included work on a carbon button lamp (two patents granted in 1886), on the power of electrical resonance, and on various types of lighting (for which three patents were granted to Tesla in 1891 alone). He worked with globes and tubes filled with gases that gave off light when electrically excited. This led to the creation of fluorescent lighting, so popular in office buildings today. Indeed, his laboratory was brilliantly illuminated with these lamps well before a long-since-forgotten assistant at Edison's lab invented the incandescent bulb—for which the publicity hungry Edison lost no time in taking full credit.

Tesla's Wardencliff Tower.

In the 1880s and '90s Tesla also worked with radio-frequency electromagnetic waves. Despite the claims made by Guglielmo Marconi (1874-1937), it was actually Tesla who did much of the most basic pioneering work in radio frequency technology. A U.S. Supreme Court decision overruled the Marconi patent, awarding it to Tesla. The Supreme Court concluded that Marconi had pirated Tesla's invention, using 14 of his patents.

Tesla also theorized the ability to locate objects in the air or in the ground by using radio waves. Today we call Tesla's idea for finding things in the air with radiowaves RADAR for RAdio Detecting And Ranging (a term coined by Captain S. M. Tucker, U.S. Navy, in the 1930s). Earth penetrating tomography is likewise an expression of Tesla's idea of seeing into the earth with radio waves.

In 1898, two years before Marconi stunned the world with his first wireless telegraph broadcast, Tesla announced his invention of a "teleautomatic" boat, a device powered by radio remote control. When skepticism was voiced, Tesla proved his claim by demonstrating it before a crowd in Madison Square Garden.

Tesla's radio frequency oscillators are still not fully understood. Tesla was a visionary, a mystic, and a genius. His vision was well over a century ahead of his contemporaries'. In many respects it is still far ahead of the thinking in mainstream Western science. In working with radio waves, Tesla created his most famous invention, the Tesla Coil. The Tesla Coil, which he invented in 1891, is widely used in radio and television sets and other electronic equipment today. Tesla might have been remembered as the Father of Radio had not his ambitions run to a far more grandiose scheme—free, universal electrical power for all.

Throughout this period Tesla gave the famous exhibitions in his laboratory. These demonstrations were in part conducted to allay fears of alternating current, and partly because he got a kick out of blowing people's minds. He also become a darling of the lecture circuit, being repeatedly invited to lecture across the United States and abroad.

George Westinghouse (1846-1914), head of the Westinghouse Electric Company of Pittsburgh, Pennsylvania, bought the patent rights to Tesla's polyphase system of alternating-current dynamos, transformers, and motors in 1885 (for which grants of patent streamed in over the next two decades). Tesla developed a friendly and profitable business relationship with Westinghouse. Tesla's interest was in science, not business. The deal with Westinghouse was simple: Tesla, not stooping to soil his hands with Edison-like gadget making, would develop the science while Westinghouse could design and market all the applications that he could dream up. Westinghouse, an engineer and famed inventor in his own right, was well-suited to the task. No doubt some items in your home bear his name.

Among their first collaborations was the contract to illuminate the World's Columbian Exposition at Chicago in 1893. Westinghouse used Tesla's alternating current system to light that early World's Fair, the brilliant success of which was a major factor in winning Westinghouse the contract to install the first power generating machinery at Niagara Falls. The project carried power to Buffalo by 1896, and much of the rest of New York State by the turn of the century.

Railroad magnate and financier John Pierpont Morgan (1837-1913), founder of Wall Street's J. P. Morgan & Co. (and later, in 1901, founder of U.S. Steel, the world's first billion dollar corporation), had been bankrolling Edison for some time before the Columbian Exposition. Seeing great potential in Tesla, he funded his research and put up much of the capitol needed to build the Niagara plant. In doing this, J. P. Morgan effectively cornered the electricity market, buying himself a piece of both Edison and Tesla's pies.

Edison had done all his work with direct current. He had several DC dynamos delivering power to New York City at the time that Westinghouse began construction on the Tesla power station at Niagara. Each of Edison's plants was 10 stories tall by an entire city block and could barely supply power to one square mile of customers. The

Marconi in his Canadian lab, 1901.

Tesla-Westinghouse revolutionary AC system nearly put Edison out of business. General Electric™, nowadays a multinational conglomerate, was formed by Edison to lease the rights to use the AC patents that Tesla-Westinghouse held.

Just before the turn of the century Tesla began his fateful experiments with wireless transmission of electrical power, as mentioned in the first *New York Times* article cited above. He moved from New York to Colorado Springs, Colorado, where he built a new laboratory from the ground up to develop his theories. The Colorado Springs lab contained the largest Tesla Coil ever built. He called it a "Magnifying Transmitter" (today such devices are call TMTs for Tesla Magnifying Transmitter). It was capable of generating some 300,000 watts of power.

Tesla's broadcasting tower in 1904.

The Patent Office often takes a decade or so to process an application. Tesla did not receive a patent on his magnifying transmitter until 1914. He applied for a patent to "Transmit Electrical Energy Through the Natural Mediums" in 1900, for which a patent was issued in 1905. In police investigations, the cops like to find a "smoking gun," an irrefutable piece of evidence linking the criminal to the crime. One "smoking antenna" revealing the connection between HAARP and Tesla is that HAARP is a type of Tesla Magnifying Transmitter (TMT).

Tesla stayed in Colorado Springs from May 1899 until early 1900. It was there that he made what he regarded as his most important discovery, and the one that led to his downfall—terrestrial stationary waves. Simply put, Tesla believed that energy could be pumped into the earth at any node of these waves, and could be extracted at any other. He demonstrated this on at least two occasions. In one experiment he lighted 200 of Mr. Edison's biggest lamps, without wires, from a distance of 25 miles.

His lab pumped electricity into the earth using a 200 foot pole topped by a large copper sphere. With it he generated potentials that discharged lightning bolts up to 135 feet long. Thunder from the released energy could be heard in the town of Cripple Creek, some 15 miles away.

People walking along the streets in Colorado Springs were reported to have been amazed to see sparks jumping between their feet and the ground when Tesla's earth zapper was in operation. All over town, flames of electricity shot from faucets when unsuspecting citizens turned them on for a drink of water. Light bulbs within 100 feet of the experimental tower were reported to

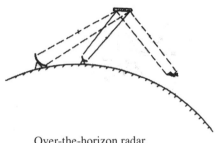
Over-the-horizon radar.

continue glowing long after they had been turned off. Several times during these experiments lightning storms were created, setting hundreds of fires across the state. Horses in livery stables received shocks through their metal shoes and bolted from their stalls. Many other species were affected as well. Years later the local newspaper reported that butterflies had became electrified during these experiments and "helplessly swirled in circles—their wings spouting blue halos of 'St. Elmo's Fire.'"

One of the many unexpected disasters caused by Tesla's experiments occurred at the Colorado Springs Electric Company generating station. The story goes that one day while Tesla was conducting a high power test, the crackling of electricity from inside the laboratory suddenly stopped. An angry Tesla rushed back into the lab demanding to know why his assistant had shut down the coil. The confused and frightened assistant protested that he had changed nothing. He told the bristling scientist that the power from the city's generator just quit. When the angry Tesla telephoned the power company he received an equally angry reply—the electric company had not cut the power, Tesla's experiment had destroyed the generator!

The Electrical Experimenter, carried an explanation of that event in its August, 1917, issue. Tesla had told their reporter that while running his transmitter at a power level of "several hundred kilowatts" high frequency currents were set up in the electric company's generators. These "caused heavy sparks to jump through the windings and destroy the insulation." When the insulation failed, the generator shorted out, melting it to slag in a matter of seconds.

At one point during the experiments in Colorado Springs Tesla became convinced that he had received signals from another planet. At the time the claim was met with derision in many scientific journals. Today it is believed that he had inadvertently discovered radio astronomy. That, along with his claims of having proven the workability of "broadcast power," and his increasingly strange behavior, earned him the dubious distinction of being widely regarded as the archetypical "mad scientist" by the nation's press.

Tesla returned to New York in the spring of 1900. With capital from J. P. Morgan, he soon began construction on Long Island of what was intended to be a world-wide wireless power broadcasting center. There are two major versions of the story from this point. In one version Morgan is the bad guy, ruining Tesla to maintain his monopolistic control of electricity transmitted by wire. The other version has Tesla done in by his own ambitions and bad timing.

In 1900 an article appeared in *Century Magazine* entitled, "The Problem of Increasing Human Energy." In it Tesla wrote that he "…was led to recognize [that] the transmission of electrical energy to any distance through the media [the earth] [w]as by far the best solution of the great problem of harnessing the sun's energy for the use of man."

He believed that a relatively few generating plants located near waterfalls, such as his original plant at Niagara, could supply his very high energy transmitters with all the electricity the world could use. These transmitters, in turn, would send power through the earth to be picked up wherever it was needed. Receiving energy from this high pressure reservoir would require no more than a rod in the ground be connected to a specially designed receiver. As Tesla described it, "the entire apparatus for lighting the average country dwelling will contain no moving parts whatever, and could be readily carried about in a small valise."

There is some question as to how forthcoming Tesla was with Morgan. One story says he told Morgan of his plans for broadcast power; the other says that he lied to Morgan, leading the financier to believe that he would be creating a wireless telegraph device for reaching Europe. With such a station, he could provide Morgan and the world with facilities for sending messages, weather warnings, stock reports, and more. Morgan would certainly have wanted the latter, and very probably would not have desired the former to go forward. Morgan already owned a major piece of pay electricity; why risk those profits with free, broadcast electricity?

We know that Tesla did receive financial backing from J. P. Morgan, enough at least to begin construction on his world electrical energy broadcast station. We also know that he was only given half the amount he had asked for. With the first portion of the money Tesla obtained 200 acres of land at Shoreham, Long Island, to build his transmitter, which site he dubbed "Wardenclyffe." There he began work on a truly astonishing facility—the broadcast tower itself was 187 feet tall (over eighteen stories!) and was topped with a 55 ton, 68 foot metal dome. Ever afterwards, Tesla was referred to by the press as the "Wizard of Wardenclyffe."

Just as Tesla was getting started on Wardenclyffe, investors were rushing to buy the newly offered stock of the Marconi Company. If it was a race to develop radio, Tesla was way too late leaving the starting gate. Adding insult to the injury of Marconi stealing Tesla's radio technology, supporters of the Marconi Company included Tesla's old nemesis, Edison. On 12 December, 1900, Marconi changed the world by sending the first transatlantic signal, the letter "S," from Cornwall, England, to Newfoundland, Canada. Financiers were quick to note that Marconi had accomplished this with equipment far less costly than that envisioned by Tesla.

In 1902 Marconi was hailed as a hero around the world when he successfully transmitted a complete coded message across the Atlantic. All Tesla got that year was bad press. He had ignored a call to jury duty in a murder case (from which he was later excused because of his opposition to the death penalty). Tesla was soundly denounced by the press and public as a shirker.

One version of the Moran-Tesla story says that in 1903 Morgan did send the balance of the money Tesla had requested, but by then it was too little, too late. Whatever the case, Tesla could not cover the amount owed on the Wardenclyffe construction and was desperate for cash. In the version of the story where Tesla had lied to Morgan, it is said that he finally came clean in 1903. Hoping to encourage a larger investment in the face of Marconi's success, Tesla supposedly revealed to Morgan his real purpose was not just sending radio signals, but the wireless transmission of power to any point on the planet. Morgan was either uninterested or decidedly opposed to such a scheme. Either way funding from Morgan ceased after 1903.

In the Morgan-as-conspirator version of the story he is said to have cut off communications with Tesla (when previously they had spoken often), as well. Then Morgan supposedly started a whisper campaign against Tesla; one that all but made the "mad scientist" rap official. When other investors learned that Morgan was no longer talking to his old friend and former "cash cow," and heard the rumors, they too refused to see Tesla, and funding for his project evaporated. Morgan might not have had to do any such thing, of course– Tesla was already well down the road to kookdom, as far as Morgan and media he controlled were concerned. Also, a financial panic hit the fall of 1903, one that rocked the investment world. It, if not Morgan's whispers, put an end to Tesla's hopes for financing by Morgan or any other wealthy industrialist. This left Tesla without enough money even to buy the coal needed to fire the transmitter's electrical generators. Due to all of these factors, the project was unable to go forward. But that does not mean that it was abandoned.

Down, but hardly out, Tesla shifted his attention to turbines and other projects, perhaps to raise quick cash. However, because of a lack of funds, his ideas largely remained in his notebooks. These notebooks are to this day avidly studied by engineers and scientists looking for unexploited avenues of research.

In 1904, despite the lack of financial support, Tesla announced Wardenclyffe's completion to the press. That year Tesla wrote an article, "The 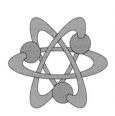Transmission of Electrical Energy Without Wires," for the publication *Electrical World*. In it he attempted to drum up support for his broadcast power technology. Yet another setback occurred that year when the Colorado Springs power company sued him for unpaid electricity used at his experimental station there. Tesla's Colorado laboratory was torn down and sold for lumber to pay the $180 judgment.

The electrical equipment still on site was put into storage.

In 1905 Tesla made a little headway against creditors by manufacturing "electrotherapeutic coils" at Wardenclyffe for hospitals and researchers. It was not enough though, as Tesla was sued by his lawyer for non-payment of a loan and by C. J. Duffner, caretaker at the experimental station

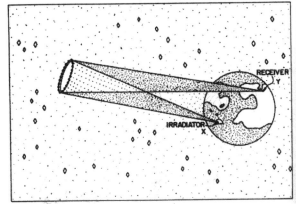

U.S. Patent 5,202,689 describing a power beaming system.

in Colorado Springs, for unpaid wages. In an article that year, Tesla again laid out his plans for energy transmission to any point on the globe. In it he also commented on Peary's expedition to the North Pole, the importance of which will become apparent in a moment.

"Left Property Here; Skips; Sheriff's Sale," was the headline in the Colorado Springs Gazette for March 6th, 1906. Tesla's remaining electrical equipment there was sold to pay a judgment of $928.57.

Workers gradually stopped coming to the Wardenclyffe laboratory when it became obvious that Tesla had no funds with which to pay them; but perhaps Tesla was not left entirely alone. There is circumstantial evidence that the great transmitter was tested, once. The articles referenced in Eastlund's first HAARP-type patent suggest a change in Tesla's thinking, turning his device from peaceful to military purposes.

Oliver Nichelson, in his article, "Nikola Tesla's Long Range Weapon," wrote:

> The difference between a current that can be used to run, say, a sewing machine and a current used as a method of destruction, however, is a matter of timing. If the amount of electricity used to run a sewing machine for an hour is released in a millionth of a second, it would have a very different, and negative, effect on the sewing machine.
>
> Tesla said his transmitter could produce 100 million volts of pressure with currents up to 1000 amperes which is a power level of 100 billion watts.
>
> If it was resonating at a radio frequency of 2 MHz, then the energy released during one period of its oscillation would be 100,000,000,000,000,000 Joules of energy, or roughly the amount of energy released by the explosion of 10 megatons of TNT.
>
> Such a transmitter, would be capable of projecting the energy of a nuclear warhead by radio. Any location in the world could be vapor-

ized at the speed of light.

The secret of how through-the-earth broadcast power [could be achieved] was found not in the theories of electrical engineering, but in the realm of high energy physics.

Dr. Andrija Puharich, in 1976, was the first to point out that Tesla's power transmission system could not be explained by the laws of classical electrodynamics, but, rather, in terms of relativistic transformations in high energy fields. He noted that according to Dirac's theory of the electron, when one of those particles encountered its oppositely charged member, a positron, the two particles would annihilate each other.

Because energy can neither be destroyed nor created the energy of the two former particles are transformed into an electromagnetic wave. The opposite, of course, holds true. If there is a strong enough electric field, two opposite charges of electricity are formed where there was originally no charge at all.

This type of transformation usually takes place near the intense field near an atomic nucleus, but it can also manifest without the aid of a nuclear catalyst if an electric field has enough energy.

Puharich's involved mathematical treatment demonstrated that power levels in a Tesla transmitter were strong enough to cause such pair production.

The mechanism of pair production offers a very attractive explanation for the ground transmission of power. Ordinary electrical currents do not travel far through the earth. Dirt has a high resistance to electricity and quickly turns currents into heat energy that is wasted.

With the pair production method electricity can be moved from one point to another without really having to push the physical particle through the earth—the transmitting source would create a strong field, and a particle would be created at the receiver.

If the sending of currents through the earth is possible from the viewpoint of modern physics, the question remains of whether Tesla actually demonstrated the weapons application of his power transmitter or whether it remained an unrealized plan on the part of the inventor. Circumstantial evidence points to there having been a test of this weapon.

That one test of his great transmitter could have resulted in what is known as "The Tunguska Event," a massive explosion in Siberia which took place on the morning of 30 June, 1908.

One researcher, Marc J. Seifer, a psychologist, believes that Tesla suffered a nervous breakdown in 1906. Such a breakdown could have pushed the normally pacifistic Tesla into acting very uncharacteristically. Seifer believes this breakdown was initiated by the sudden deaths of two men close to Tesla.

One was a partner in the Tesla Electric Company; the other was the shooting death of Stanford White, the noted architect who had designed Wardenclyffe.

Seifer cites as one piece of evidence for this unbalancing of the great mind a letter from George Scherff, Tesla's secretary:

Wardenclyffe, 4/10/1906
Dear Mr. Tesla:
I have received your letter and am very glad to know you are vanquishing your illness. I have scarcely ever seen you so out of sorts as last Sunday; and I was frightened.

From 1900 on, Tesla worked tirelessly to promote his vision of wireless transmission of energy for the betterment of mankind. Surely he must have been under tremendous mental strain by 1906: stung by Marconi's accomplishment, bedeviled by money problems, and spurned by both the financial and scientific establishments. Might he not have made some last ditch effort to save his grand scheme? Could he have tried one desperate high power test of his transmitter—perhaps to show off its destructive potential?

The trail of evidence pointing to Tesla as the cause of "The Tunguska Event" begins a year earlier with the sinking of the French ship *Iena*. The world's media pressed experts for an explanation of the blast that sent her to Davy Jones locker. Many of these experts thought the explosion had been caused by an electrical spark. Naturally, there was substantial discussion over the possible origins of same.

Tesla was immediately implicated by Lee De Forest (1873-1961), the American inventor and pioneer of wireless telegraphy, who invented the audion or vacuum tube used in radio broadcasting and receiving. De Forest recalled to the press that Tesla had experimented with a "dirigible torpedo" capable of delivering such destructive power to a ship through remote control. Tesla had also claimed, De Forrest pointed out, that the same technology used for remotely controlling vehicles, which Tesla had demonstrated a decade earlier in Madison Square Garden, could also project an electrical wave of "sufficient intensity to cause a spark in a ship's magazine and explode it."

Tesla shot a letter to *The New York Times* in response. Curiously, instead of flatly

denying the charge, he admitted, nay bragged, that he had indeed built and tested remotely controlled torpedoes. But, the great scientist insisted, electrical waves would be far more destructive than any mere remote controlled device. "As to projecting wave energy to any particular region of the globe… this can be done by my devices." He also wrote that "…the spot at which the desired effect is to be produced can be calculated very closely, assuming the accepted terrestrial measurements to be correct."

Tesla was on a roll. He repeated the idea of destruction by electrical waves to *The Times* in another letter to the editor dated 21 April, 1908. That letter stated:

> When I spoke of future warfare I meant that it should be conducted by direct application of electrical waves without the use of aerial engines or other implements of destruction… This is not a dream. Even now wireless power plants could be constructed by which any region of the globe might be rendered uninhabitable without subjecting the population of other parts to serious danger or inconvenience.

An explosion of staggering proportions took place near the Tunguska River in central Siberia nine days after that letter was written. The force of the blast has been estimated to have been equivalent to 10—15 megatons of TNT—precisely the amount of destructive force Oliver Nichelson calculated that Tesla's device could deliver. The blast flattened 500,000 acres of pine forest and was heard over a radius of 620 miles!

A scientific expedition was not immediately set out to discover the cause of the catastrophe, however. It was assumed at the time that a meteorite of significant size had crashed to earth. A World War and the Russian Revolution came and went before an expedition could finally be mounted. In 1927 scientists arrived in the area to search for evidence of the presumed meteorite, but no impact crater has ever been found. When the ground was dug and drilled for bits of nickel or iron, the primary constituents of meteorites, none were found down to a depth of 118 feet.

Over the years many explanations have been floated for the Tunguska Event. While no one riddling of the mystery is universally accepted, the official version is that a 100,000 ton fragment of Encke's Comet, composed mainly of dust and ice, entered the atmosphere at 62,000 mph, heated up, and exploded over the earth's surface creating a fireball and shock wave but no crater. Some very wild alternative versions to this telling have been suggested, however, such as a renegade mini-black hole or the aerial destruction of an alien space craft.

Admittedly, trying to make a case for Tesla as the perpetrator of the Tunguska explosion smacks of the worst of tabloid journalism. However, as Mr. Nichelson points out, an unbiased look at the events in Tesla's life prior to the Tunguska Event shows that real historical facts point to at least the possibility that this event could have been caused by a test firing of Tesla's energy weapon. We know that in 1907 and 1908 Tesla wrote about the destructive effects of his energy transmitter. Tesla's Wardenclyffe transmitter was much larger than the Colorado Springs device, and would have been capable of effects many orders of magnitude greater than it.

Nine years later, in another letter to the editor, Tesla stated:

It is perfectly practical to transmit electrical energy without wires and produce destructive effects at a distance. I have already constructed a wireless transmitter which makes this possible... When unavoidable, the [transmitter] may be used to destroy property and life.

Was Tesla admitting that "unavoidable" circumstances had forced him to "destroy property and life"? The Tunguska explosion killed at least two people and wiped out whole herds of Siberian Reindeer, the herd animals of the Siberian natives.

A 1934 letter from Tesla to J. P. Morgan Jr.(the elder Morgan had died in 1913), uncovered by Tesla biographer Margaret Cheney, seems to be final, near-conclusive evidence of such a test. In an effort to raise money for his defensive system (as discussed in *The New York Times* articles referenced by the Eastlund patent) Tesla wrote:

The flying machine has completely demoralized the world, so much so that in some cities, as London and Paris, people are in mortal fear from aerial bombing. The new means I have perfected affords absolute protection against this and other forms of attack... These new discoveries I have carried out experimentally on a limited scale, created a profound impression...

To again quote from Nichelson, he writes:

[T]he evidence is circumstantial but, to use the language of criminal investigation, Tesla had motive and means to be the cause of the Tunguska event. ... His transmitter could generate energy levels and frequencies that would release the destructive force of 10 megatons, or more, of TNT. And the overlooked

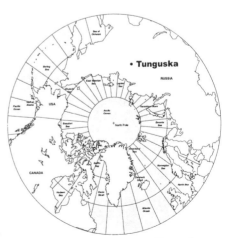

Tesla may have created the Tunguska explosion across the Arctic.

genius was desperate.

The nature of the Tunguska event, also, is not inconsistent with what would happen during the sudden release of wireless power. No fiery object was reported in the skies at that time by professional or amateur astronomers as would be expected when a 200,000,000 pound object enters the atmosphere. The sky glow in the region, mentioned by some witnesses, just before the explosion may have come from the ground, as geological researchers discovered in the 1970's. Just before an earthquake the stressed rock beneath the ground creates an electrical effect causing the air to illuminate.

If the explosion was caused by wireless energy transmission, either the geological stressing or the current itself would cause an air glow. Finally, there is the absence of an impact crater. Because there is no material object to impact, an explosion caused by broadcast power would not leave a crater.

It is hard to understand why he would carry out a test harmful to both animals and the people who herded the animals even when he was in the grip of financial desperation. The answer is that he probably intended no harm, but was aiming for a publicity coup and, literally, missed his target.

At the end of 1908, the whole world was following the daring attempt of Peary to reach the North Pole. Peary claimed the Pole in the Spring of 1909, but the winter before he had returned to the base at Ellesmere Island, about 700 miles from the Pole.

If Tesla wanted the attention of the international press, few things would have been more impressive than the Peary expedition sending out word of a cataclysmic explosion on the ice in the direction of the North Pole. Tesla, then, if he could not be hailed as the master creator that he was, could be seen as the master of a mysterious new force of destruction.

The test... was not a complete success. It must have been difficult controlling the vast amount of power in transmitter and guiding it to the exact spot Tesla wanted.

Alert, Canada on Ellesmere Island and the Tunguska region are all on the same great circle line from Shoreham, Long Island. Both are on a compass bearing of a little more than 2 degrees along a polar path.

The destructive electrical wave overshot its target.

Whoever was privy to Tesla's energy weapon demonstration must have been dismayed either because it missed the intended target and would be a threat to inhabited regions of the planet, or because it worked too well in devastating such a large area at the mere throwing of a switch thousands of miles away. Whichever was the case, Tesla never received the notoriety he sought for his power transmitter.

After that, the days for Wardenclyffe were numbered. Tesla never settled, never became a husband nor a homeowner. He was a stylish man who lived beyond his means. In his affluent youth had he dressed in expensive, trendy clothing. He lived most of his life in posh, upscale hotels, such as New York's famed Waldorf Astoria. As his income dwindled, the quality of the hotels he could stiff for unpaid service eventually declined.

In 1915 Wardenclyffe was deeded over to Waldorf Astoria Hotel, Inc. in lieu of payment for Tesla's hotel bills. In 1917 it was dynamited on orders of the new owners. Per one story, this was done to recover some money from the scrap; in

A drawing of the 1908 Tunguska explosion.

another version it was demolished to foil WWI German submarines which were believed to be using it as a navigational aid. Ironically, Tesla was the recipient of the Edison Medal that same year. It was the highest honor that the American Institute of Electrical Engineers could bestow.

Tesla died penniless on 7 January, 1943, in a cheap hotel in New York City. Aside from a rock band named for him, and a few fans of "out-there" science, Tesla is today largely unknown to the general public. In many parts of this country, people still refer to their electric utility as the "Edison Company," even though it delivers power to their homes using the Tesla-Westinghouse alternating current system, not Edison's direct current. At his original Niagara Falls power generating station, a small statue of Tesla is purposely left unilluminated at night. Tesla himself once commented, "The present is theirs. The future, for which I really worked, is mine."

After Tesla's death the custodian of alien property, a U.S. Government official, impounded his trunks, which held his papers, his diplomas and other honors, his letters, and his laboratory notes. These were eventually inherited by Tesla's nephew, Sava Kosanovich, and later housed in the Nikola Tesla Museum in Belgrade, Yugoslavia.

After WWII it is quite possible that his trunks became a treasure trove for Soviet scientists looking for ideas for possible "super weapons." It has been known for some time that Soviet scientists were investigating Tesla's work.

There is a widespread belief that after the United States detonated two atomic bombs over Japan at the close of World War II, the Soviets panicked and went on a crash program to find a super weapon that was utterly unlike anything the Americans had. One development that could have been a Soviet attempt to replicate Tesla's broadcast power experiments with Tesla Magnifying Transmitters—TMTs—is the infamous "Russian Woodpecker" radio signals, which we will examine in the next chapter.

Hundreds filed into New York City's Cathedral of St. John the Divine for Tesla's funeral services. A flood of messages acknowledged the loss of a great genius. Three Nobel Prize recipients addressed their tribute to "one of the outstanding intellects of the world who paved the way for many of the technological developments of modern times."

Tesla had proposed several applications of his broadcast power research that could have borne fruit as HAARP. HAARP is, if nothing else, a new spin on the broadcast power concept. Here the power is to be broadcast into the atmosphere, not to consumers as Tesla originally intended. One idea of Tesla's that is startlingly similar to HAARP was his idea to light up the night sky by beaming electrical energy into the stratosphere via his magnifying transmitter.

The principal patents for HAARP were granted in the late 1980s, a hundred years after Tesla's first patents on alternating current. U.S. patent number 4,686,605 was granted to Dr. Bernard J. Eastlund (b. 1938) for "Method and Apparatus for Altering a Region in the Earth's Atmosphere, Ionosphere, and/or Magnetosphere." That was the first of three patents he was granted on this idea, all of which he assigned to his employer, Advanced Power Technologies, Inc. (APTI), a subsidiary of the oil giant ARCO, formerly known as the Atlantic Richfield Company. Dr. Eastlund had previously been a physicist at both MIT and Columbia University of New York. It is reported that before joining APTI he had eight years experience with the Atomic Energy Commission.

HAARP seems to be proof that the United States joined the Soviets in attempting to duplicate Tesla's experiments. This could be the real explanation of why Tesla's name has disappeared from American history books. After researching FBI files and other documents, Dr. Marc Seifer, the psychologist mentioned above, stated: "Great support is lent to the hypothesis that Tesla's work and papers were systematically hidden from public view in order to protect the trail of this top secret work, which today is known as Star Wars."

Dr. Eastlund certainly is not trying to hide the connection between his invention and Tesla. Besides the references to Tesla in his initial patent, Eastlund has spoken quite candidly of the connection in interviews. For example, in the BBC/A&E documentary "Masters of the Ionosphere," Eastlund said: "I think Tesla would be very proud."

At a fundamental technical level HAARP is Eastlund's apparatus, and that idea came, if indirectly, from Tesla'a work. HAARP's design clearly sprang from Eastlund's patents. In keeping with Tesla's way of thinking on a colossal scale, Eastlund's proposal was for an antenna array 40 miles on a side! Eastlund is quoted as having said:

> HAARP is the perfect first step towards a plan like mine. Advances in phased-array transmitter technology and power generation can produce the field strength required. The government will say it isn't so, but if it quacks like a duck and it looks like a duck, there's a good chance it is a duck. [end indented quote]

The HAARP project began as a need by ARCO to find a customer for its Alaskan natural gas. This "fact" has been disputed by many "official" voices for the HAARP project as being paranoid conspiracy nonsense. This denial, however, is a transparent attempt to separate HAARP, the "safe" little scientific experiment, from Eastlund's monster.

Natural gas is a byproduct of oil drilling. You pump oil, you get oil and gas. Natural gas does not lend itself well to being shipped from the North Slope oil fields to consumers thousands of miles away. Unable to find a local buyer, ARCO has been pumping the gas back into the earth to keep up pressure in the field. ARCO, however, would much rather sell the gas and pump in sea water as is commonly done elsewhere in the world.

It was ARCO's need to find someone to sell this gas to, right there in Alaska, that was the "necessity" that "mothered" Eastlund's invention. At that time, about the only agency in Alaska it could have been sold to was the government, but the government did not have a need for it. That is when Eastlund got the idea to come up with some government-funded project that would require fantastic amounts of electricity—electricity generated from burning all that gas.

On the television program "Masters of the Ionosphere" Eastlund told the viewing audience:

> …ARCO had a problem of what to do with the natural gas on the north slope. It was too expensive to build a pipeline down to the U.S. They had hired me to think of a non-chemical approach to the use of the gas. The first idea that came to mind was to make radio waves—'cos I had all that energy, I could make a lot of radiowaves. Second idea was it's located in Alaska which is near where the Earth's magnetic field, where the magnetic pole is. And the third idea was I knew that Soviet missiles

would, could come over the pole and I added one piece of physics, which would be the ability in those waves where they hit the upper regions of the magnetic field to make 50 billion degree electrons.

The way these electrons would kill a missile is, if they hit it they would bury themselves in. And if enough buried themselves they could explode it, mess up the electronics, do many bad things to a missile. I came up with a big antenna, big enough to basically fill the Van Allen belts

with energetic particles... the initial thought was to make a complete shield that would put those electrons in all of the paths the missiles might be able to take, and destroy all of them.

Up until the end of that year I worked on the patents and we prepared three very broad patents. Virtually any application we could think of we put in the patents. Besides the global missile shield, we thought of patches of electrons that could shoot down missiles, communications jamming, generation of ELF, VLF waves. The Patent Office brought up a project I, at the time, had never heard of by Nikola Tesla, and they brought out two *New York Times* articles and he was so respected it didn't matter that those weren't patents. Virtually anything he had suggested you have to not be in interference with.

Within a day after the patent was issued, the first patent, *The New York Times* called and wanted to interview me. I provided them an interview and I think maybe ARCO got a little upset about that; and with this big antenna and everything that may, I may, have played a role in my not staying with the operation. One of the reasons given to me was that my ideas were too far out, but they were far out from the beginning and what part of far out do they want to work on?

Eastlund's original patent specifically states that the "invention require[s] large amounts of power..." and that the electricity called for could be supplied by burning:

...certain types of fuel sources which naturally occur at strategic geographical locations around the earth. For example, large reserves of hydrocarbons (oil and natural gas) exist in Alaska and Canada. In northern Alaska, particularly the North Slope region, large reserves are currently readily available...

Eastlund's proposal for an antenna field 40 miles on a side would have called for the creation of an SDI weapons system many magnitudes of power greater than the HAARP array being built near Gakona, Alaska, today. This would certainly have served ARCO's need for an electricity intensive operation to consume vast quantities of natural gas. While the size of the present embodiment of Eastlund's work is measured in acres rather than miles, the basic application is the same. More to the point, the initial HAARP array could be expanded into Eastlund's monster sky zapper—the only limiting factors are the amount of money that the government wants to throw into the project and, perhaps most importantly, public opinion. Public opinion has stopped many previous DOD projects, including the Vietnam War. Fear of negative public opinion became the cross they hung Bernard Eastlund from.

The most important aspect of Eastlund's patent(s) was his discovery of a way to focus a beam of radio frequency energy. Previously, all such transmissions dissipated over distance. Eastlund conceived of a way of overlaying the transmissions, causing them to be focused at a great distance from the transmitter. This permits the HAARP array to concentrate a tremendous amount of power at a precise point, one a hundred miles or more above the earth. While Dr. Eastlund was removed from the HAARP project before it got off the ground, he was rewarded for his work by being promoted to President of ARCO's Production Technologies International Company in Houston, Texas. So, don't cry for him, Gakona...

What did Eastlund envision his apparatus as being capable of? Here are just a few of his ideas of what the big boys could do with such a big science toy. In an interview with *OMNI Magazine* in 1988 he said, "You can virtually lift part of the upper atmosphere... You can make it move, do things to it." In the original patent he wrote:

> This invention has a phenomenal variety of possible ramifications and potential future developments. As alluded to earlier, missile or aircraft destruction, deflection, or confusion could result... large regions of the atmosphere could be lifted to an unexpectedly high altitude so that missiles encounter unexpected and unplanned drag forces with resultant destruction or deflection of same. Weather modification is possible by, for example, altering upper atmosphere wind patterns by constructing one or more plumes of atmospheric particles which will act as a lens or focusing device...

Elsewhere he wrote:

> [This apparatus could] cause... total disruption of communications over a very large portion of the Earth... disrupting not only land-based communications, but also airborne communications and sea communications (both surface and subsurface)... weather modification... by altering solar absorption... ozone, nitrogen, etc., concentrations could be artificially increased.

OMNI concluded that "because the upper atmosphere is extremely sensitive to small changes in its composition, merely testing an Eastlund Device could cause irreversible damage." A growing number of people around the world agree.

From 1987 through 1992 other scientists on APTI's payroll built on Eastlund's concept, patenting various aspects of his method and apparatus. These same scientists, with the too talkative Eastlund omitted, were later listed as key personnel when E-Systems bought APTI, and the HAARP contract, in 1994. By the time APTI was sold it held an even dozen patents that would be vital for the construction of HAARP. But before we look at what has happened since Eastlund received his first patent, let's look at some of the other events of this century that seem to have played a role in creating the High-frequency Active Auroral Research Program.

TESLA, AT 78, BARES NEW 'DEATH-BEAM'

Invention Powerful Enough to Destroy 10,000 Planes 250 Miles Away, He Asserts.

DEFENSIVE WEAPON ONLY

Scientist, in Interview, Tells of Apparatus That He Says . : Will Kill Without Trace.

Nikola Tesla, father of modern methods of generation and distribution of electrical energy, who was 78 years old yesterday, announced a new invention, or inventions, which he said, he considered the most important of the 700 made by him so far.

He has perfected a method and apparatus, Dr. Tesla said yesterday in an interview at the Hotel New Yorker, which will send concentrated beams of particles through the free air, of such tremendous energy that they will bring down a fleet of 10,000 enemy airplanes at a distance of 250 miles from a defending nation's border and will cause armies of millions to drop dead in their tracks.

Times Wide World Photo.

NOTED INVENTOR 78.

Nikola Tesla.

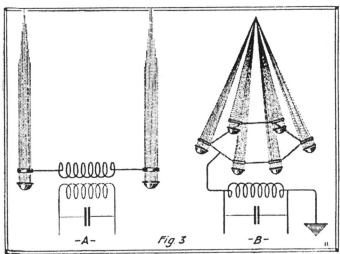

Two Optional Forms of Wireless Antennae Formed of Searchlight Beams—Ionized Atmospheric Streams.

Above: The *New York Times* article on Tesla's Death Ray of July 11, 1934. Below: Two illustrations from an article in the March, 1920 issue of Electrical Experimenter entitled Wireless Transmission of Power Now Possible. The illustrations show his prototype devices for "directed ionized beam transmissions," a "death-ray—searchlight" device. Curiously, powerful searchlight-beams have frequently been reported as part of unidentified discoid and cigar-shaped craft since the late 1800s.

"Death Ray" for Planes

Nikola Tesla, one of the truly great inventors who celebrated his eighty-fourth birthday on July 10, tells the writer that he stands ready to divulge to the United States Government the secret of his "teleforce," with which, he said, airplane motors would be melted at a distance of 250 miles, so that an invisible Chinese Wall of Defense would be built around the country against any attempted attack by an enemy air force, no matter how large.

This "teleforce," he said, is based on an entirely new principle of physics that "no one has ever dreamed about," different from the principle embodied in his inventions relating to the transmission of electrical power from a distance, for which he has received a number of basic patents. This new type of force, Mr. Tesla said, would operate through a beam one one-hundred-millionth of a square centimeter in diameter, and could be generated from a special plant that would cost no more than $2,000,000 and would take only about three months to construct.

A dozen such plants, located at strategic points along the coast, according to Mr. Tesla, would be enough to defend the country against all possible aerial attack. The beam would melt any engine, whether Diesel or gasoline-driven, and would also ignite the explosives aboard any bomber. No possible defense against it could be devised, he asserts, as the beam would be all-penetrating.

High Vacuum Eliminated

The beam, he states, involves four new inventions, two of which already have been tested. One of these is a method and apparatus for producing rays "and other manifestations of energy" in free air, eliminating the necessity for a high vacuum; a second is a method and process for producing "very great electrical force"; the third is a method for amplifying this force, and the fourth is a new method for producing "a tremendous electrical repelling force." This would be the projector, or gun, of the system. The voltage for propelling the beam to its objective, according to the inventor, will attain a potential of 50,000,000 volts.

With this enormous voltage, he said, microscopic electrical particles of matter will be catapulted on their mission of defensive destruction. He has been working on this invention, he added, for many years and has recently made a number of improvements in it.

Mr. Tesla makes one important stipulation. Should the government decide to take up his offer he would go to work at once, but they would have to trust him. He would suffer "no interference from experts."

In ordinary times such a condition would very likely interpose an insuperable obstacle. But times being what they are, and with the nation getting ready to spend billions for national defense, at the same time taking in consideration the reputation of Mr. Tesla as an inventor who always was many years ahead of his time, the question arises whether it may not be advisable to take Mr. Tesla at his word and commission him to go ahead with the construction of his teleforce plant.

Such a Device "Invaluable"

After all, $2,000,000 would be relatively a very small sum compared with what is at stake. If Mr. Tesla really fulfills his promise the result achieved would be truly staggering. Not only would it save billions now planned for air defense, by making the country absolutely impregnable against any air attack, but it would also save many more billions in property that would otherwise be surely destroyed no matter how strong the defenses are as witness current events in England.

Take, for example, the Panama Canal. No matter how strong the defenses, a suicide squadron of dive bombers, according to some experts, might succeed in getting through and cause such damage that would make the Canal unusable, in which case our Navy might find itself bottled up.

Considering the probabilities in the case even if the chances were 100,000 to 1 against Mr. Tesla the odds would still be largely in favor of taking a chance on spending $2,000,000. In the opinion of the writer, who has known Mr. Tesla for many years and can testify that he still retains full intellectual vigor, the authorities in charge of building the national defense should at once look into the matter. The sum is insignificant compared with the magnitude of the stake.

The amazing Wardencliff Tower of Long Island in full action as Tesla envisioned it. The tower is broadcasting power to anti-gravity airships and electric airplanes that hover around it. Note the powerful searchlight-beams on the airships. These were a combination of searchlight and death-ray, as commonly spoken of by Tesla.

The HAARP Developmental Prototype (DP)

The HAARP developmental prototype (DP) is a small portion of the planned Ionospheric Research Instrument (IRI). Its purpose is permit evaluation of the engineering design for the full size IRI prior to beginning final construction.

The DP size was determined based on minimizing the initial cost to prove the validity of the engineering design while still assemblin enough of the antenna array to simulate a true array environment. An array size consisting of 48 antenna elements, arranged in eight rows by six columns was selected as an appropriate size. The following figure shows a plan view of the DP array.

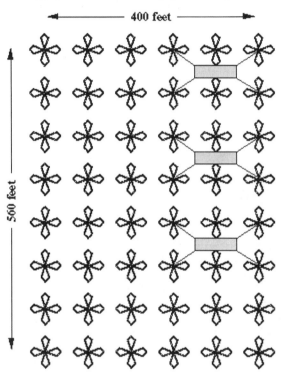

HAARP Developmental Prototype Antenna Array

Each of the 48 antenna elements in the DP array consists of two crossed dipole antennas, oriented approximately North-South and East-West. There are separate crossed dipoles for the low frequency (2.8 - 7 MHz) and the high frequency (7 - 10 MHz) bands. Ea of the crossed dipoles in the IRI will be driven by a dedicated transmitter, two of which are contained in a transmitter cabinet. Thus transmitter cabinet is dedicated to a complete crossed dipole pair. In the DP, only 18 of the 48 antenna elements are actually connect to transmitters, however, and these are shown in red in the figure presented above. All of the transmitters are housed in environmentally controlled shelters, each of which can accommodate six transmitter cabinets. The existing transmitter shelters are shown in yellow in the above figure. Primary power for each of the shelters is currently obtained from independent diesel-generator sets located adjacent to the shelters. None of the power required by the transmitters is obtained from the commercial power grid.

The HAARP DP is intended for engineering evaluation of the IRI design. Some of its expected performance capabilities are shown below.

- Number of active elements: 18.
- Frequency range: 2.8 - 10 MHz.
- Maximum radiated power: 360 kW.
- Modulation: AM/FM/PM.

Chapter Three:
Electromagnetic Warfare:
The Moscow Signal, The Russian Woodpecker, GWEN & HAARP

Perhaps "The Tunguska Event" was not the first demonstration of an electromagnetic (EM) weapon. Certainly, scientists and military strategists since have sought ways to turn the electromagnetic spectrum to advantage in times of war. Curious minds have worked to understand the nature of light, electricity, and magnetism for hundreds of years. Out of this increasing understanding have come ideas for weapons. Many ideas have been put forward, some have even been tried. Radar is one successful application of this knowledge. HAARP may be another.

As mentioned in the previous chapter, Soviet scientists probably investigated Tesla's work for possible weapons. They delved deep into the mysteries of electromagnetism, seemingly getting a sizable jump on the U.S. in this field. The bombardment of our Embassy in Moscow with microwave energy was possibly one development of this research; the mysterious "Russian Woodpecker" radio signal is probably another.

THE ATMOSPHERE AND THE ELECTROMAGNETIC SPECTRUM

If this were one of those "...for Dummies" books there would be a cute drawing of a nerdy looking guy here, warning you that geeky technical stuff was about to follow. Unfortunately, HAARP is a scientific, technical subject. Feel free to skip this section if you are already familiar with basic atmospheric science and the electromagnetic spectrum. If not, here is a quick recap of some of the most important terms and concepts needed to understand the science behind HAARP.

The atmosphere is the envelope of gases that surrounds the earth (or any celestial body). The word atmosphere is made up of two Greek words: "atmos" which means "vapor" (i.e., gas or mist) and "sphaira" which means "sphere" or "the sky," but it also holds the idea of a "realm of influence."

The atmosphere has been divided into several layers by scientists attempting to study it. These layers are never as sharply defined as the terms might imply. These layers are caused by the way the temperature of the atmosphere changes with altitude. The heights and locations of the layers vary tremendously from hour to hour, place to place, and season to season. These layers vary because there is much mixing of atmospheric gases upward and downward, due to changes from day to night; from summer to winter; and because of the different kinds of terrain below; whether sea or land; and especially with the latitude, polar or equatorial.

The three principal layers of the atmosphere are the "troposphere," the "stratosphere," and the "ionosphere." "Tropo-" is Greek, meaning "a turn, change" as that is where most weather is found. "Strato-" is from "stratum," Latin for "layer." The ionosphere's name is again taken from the Greek, in this case from "ienai," meaning "to go." It is the root of "ion," which is an electrically charged atom. Above the atmosphere, entirely out in space, is the "magnetosphere" ("magneto-" from the Greek root that gives us the words magnet and magnetism).

We live at the bottom of the atmosphere in the troposphere. This is where all surface-dwelling life forms are found (as opposed to water-dwelling life forms which live in the "hydrosphere" ("hydro-" for water); or subterranean life forms, which live in the "lithosphere" ("litho-" means "stone"). Collectively, the zones where life is found are known as the "biosphere" ("bio-" for "life"). Officially, HAARP is intended to alter, or "perturb," only the ionosphere; however, it appears to have the ability to affect all the regions of Earth, from the lithosphere beneath our feet, to the magnetosphere, thousands of miles above our heads.

Air close to the ground is warm because the earth itself—the land and the surface of the sea—is warm. Sunlight passing through the air near the surface does not heat the air directly. The earth and sea are warmed by the sun, and that heat is re-radiated from the land and sea into the air, warming the atmosphere. This warming of the air causes weather via convection (hot air rises, cold air falls). The troposphere is the thinnest layer in terms of how many miles thick it is; but, because of the weight of the air above it, squashing it down, the troposphere is the densest part of atmosphere, containing 85% of the mass of the atmosphere.

This warming of the atmosphere by the earth falls off with height, but not exactly. The atmosphere goes through several stages where the warmer air of one layer sits on cooler air below. This causes the so-called inversion layers, responsible for trapping pollution below them over cities.

The principal characteristic of the troposphere, the part of the atmosphere that we live in, is that the air gets colder the higher you go. In the stratosphere, it's the other way around; the air gets warmer the higher you get. In the stratosphere the air gets warmer with height because at that altitude sunlight is energetic enough to directly heat the air. Convection cannot occur in the stratosphere because the warmer air is above, not below. The stratosphere acts as a literal lid on the troposphere, locking virtually all weather into the region below it. The stratosphere averages about 30 miles thick, with its highest and warmest layer being about 50 miles over our heads. The stratosphere contains nearly all of the remaining 15% of the atmosphere not found in the troposphere. Above the altitude of about 25 miles there is less than 1% of the atmosphere remaining.

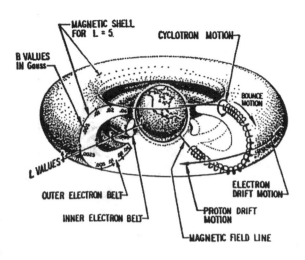

The world famous ozone layer lives in the stratosphere. The ozone layer is caused by the air absorbing ultraviolet radiation from sunlight. A molecule with three atoms of oxygen is called ozone. An oxygen molecule is just two atoms of oxygen bound together. Ultraviolet radiation is energetic enough to knock that binding loose, creating lone oxygen atoms, which are then free to link up with oxygen molecules, creating ozone. This takes place throughout the stratosphere, although the majority of ozone is made near its middle altitudes, at about 30 miles up.

Above the stratosphere lies the topmost layer of the atmosphere: the ionosphere. The ionosphere is hundreds of miles thick and also shows more-or-less distinct layering. Scientists, in turn, have sub-divided the ionosphere into several regions. Some scientists use the Greek and Latin naming system and have called these layers things like "mesosphere" ("meso-" meaning "middle") and "thermosphere" ("thermo-" for "heat"). Other scientists have gone with just referring to the layers with simple letters, "D," "E," "F1," "F2" and so on. As well as not agreeing with the names used, they are rather divided on the altitudes and characteristics of these levels. If HAARP really were used for ionospheric research, it might help to sort this mess out.

An illustration that appeared as part of the HAARP Environmental Impact Statement showed the ionosphere beginning 37 miles above the HAARP site. That chart showed the "D" layer of the ionosphere as being between 37 and 56 miles up, with the aurora indicated as existing in that region. It further gave the "E" layer as residing from 56 to 93 miles up (that would about coincide with the mesosphere). The "F" layer, the top of which is the region that the space shuttle customarily flies in, was listed as from 93 to 620 miles up. Above that is outer space.

Entirely beyond the atmosphere, out in space, is the magnetosphere. The earth is a giant magnet; surrounding it are magnetic lines of force. The Van Allen Radiation Belts are zones of charged particles (protons, electrons and alpha particles) captured by those magnetic lines of force. These particles come from what is known as the solar wind. They stream to earth from the sun and from outer space. The lower Van Allen Belt is about 7,700 km (4,800 miles) above the earth's surface, and the outer Van Allen Belt is about 51,500 km (32,000 miles) above the earth.

These belts were discovered in 1958 during the first weeks of operation of America's first satellite, Explorer I. Most satellites are found in orbital paths called "near-earth," or the much more distant, "geosynchronous." Near-earth orbits are favored by the military for spy satellites. These satellites skim the top of the atmosphere 500 to 1,000 miles up. Like HAARP, NASA's Space Shuttle is an example of a civilian science project built to further a military agenda. The Shuttle was designed under military contract to service low altitude military space "assets." To do real science, however, you need to get your scientific hardware well out of the atmosphere, which is where you will find civilian satellites and where you will not find the Space Shuttle.

The majority of civilian telecommunications and pure science satellites are found from a little below 15,000 miles to nearly 23,000 miles above the earth's surface. A geosynchronous orbit (more Greek, "geo-" for "earth" plus "sunkhronos" meaning "at the same time") keeps a space craft more-or-less parked over one spot on the earth. HAARP, if used to create high levels of electrons in the upper ionosphere, has the potential to knockout satellites and other space assets in near-earth orbit; clearly a potential military objective of the program.

As the name implies, the ionosphere is a region of the atmosphere that has become partially ionized. Atoms normally do not have an electrical charge. They acquire a charge by gaining or losing an electron. An ion is an atom which has become charged. The ionosphere then, is a region of the atmosphere that contains a high percentage of charged particles and free electrons; a place where the atoms of oxygen, and other gases, are constantly losing and gaining electrons. Ionization is the process of producing ions by exposing atoms to radiation with enough energy to dislodge electrons. In the ionosphere this is caused by the sun, daily bombarding the earth with hard radiation from its nuclear furnace, such as with x-rays and gamma rays. The earth is also continuously struck by other forms of radiation from space, called cosmic rays. Radiation that can cause ionization to take place is called ionizing radiation. That's the stuff that atomic bombs spew out, which has made the world so uneasy for over fifty years. It's also what they try to keep bottled up inside nuclear reactors and what makes nuclear waste so deadly.

Life on this planet exists because of the atmosphere's ability to absorb ionizing radiation in the ionosphere and stratosphere. If these layers weren't there, the surface of the earth would be constantly awash in a deadly bath of ionizing radiation. The ionosphere stops the sun's most violent radiation by making ions. The stratosphere filters out most the rest of the sun's weaker radiation, ultraviolet light, by making ozone. That is why a reduction in the ozone layer can pose a threat to life on this planet, and why HAARP's deliberate meddling with the ionosphere is so frightening.

There is also non-ionizing radiation. That is the part of the electromagnetic spectrum that we live in. Electromagnetism is a subject that is still poorly understood by science. They know what it does and how to work with it, but a fundamental understanding of why it exists seems to be still decades or even centuries off. Science knows that a moving electrical current produces a force field which radiates out from it; this is called electromagnetic radiation (EMR), because it radiates away from its source. This field of non-ionizing radiation is both one field and two fields at the same time: one field is electric, the other magnetic, and yet the two are one interrelated electromagnetic phenomena.

There may also be a third field of gravitional waves. These, called "scalar waves," are not yet accepted by conventional science. Many researchers, however, do believe they exist. The Russian Woodpecker, which we will get to in a moment, is believed by some to be a weapon using scalar technology, which would make it far more "advanced" than anything in the West.

Everything electrical, from the wires in the walls and household appliances to high-tech industrial equipment, emits non-ionizing radiation. The air around us is filled with the unseen energies of radio, television and microwaves. The immediate effect of this daily bath of electromagnetic pollution is generally imperceptible, but the long-term consequences can be life threatening, as I will demonstrate shortly. This danger can be seen, for example, in the increase in incidence of cancers and leukemia among people living near high-tension power transmission lines.

We are sometimes also hit with bursts of ionizing radiation. You could get a dose of this deadly radiation if you happen to be unfortunate enough to be downwind of a nuclear weapons test; or downwind when an atomic power plant needs to vent, which occurs all too frequently; or as the result of a nuclear accident, like Three Mile Island or Chernobyl. It does not take a big accident to kill you. On 4 June, 1997, the Department of Energy released the results of a six year study of strategies for the treatment, storage and disposal of radioactive and hazardous wastes generated by American nuclear weapons production. The Final Waste Management Programmatic Environmental Impact Statement came to a startling conclusion: between 11 and 69 Americans would die as the result of transporting this material! Some of these deaths

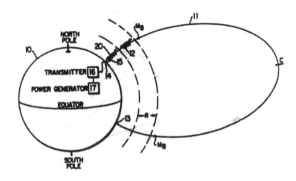

would result from exposure of the transport crew members and the populations along transportation routes to the radioactive and hazardous material being shipped. Others would occur from accidents independent of the waste cargo.

Electromagnetic fields oscillate. These oscillations are measured in terms of how many times they do it per second (referred to as "cycles per second"). The unit of measuring frequency (cycles per second) is the Hertz, named after the short-lived German physicist H. R. Hertz (1857-1894):

one Hertz is equal to one cycle per second
a thousand cycles per second is a kiloHertz (1 KHz)
a million cycles per second is a megaHertz (1 MHz)
and a billion cycles per second is a gigaHertz (1 GHz).

The non-ionizing band of the electromagnetic spectrum runs from zero Hertz, where there are no oscillations, up to and through visible light, where there are trillions of oscillations per second. The electromagnetic spectrum also includes the ionizing radiation above the frequency of visible light: ultraviolet light, gamma-rays, x-rays and so on.

Like the atmosphere, this electromagnetic spectrum has been divided into frequency ranges useful to science. The non-ionizing portion of this spectrum that we are familiar with includes radio, television and microwaves. Of special importance to HAARP are the top and bottom ranges of this portion of the spectrum: extremely low frequency (ELF), from 0 to 1000 cycles per second (below 1 KHz), and the high frequencies just below the realm of visible light.

You probably already know a little about the frequencies immediately below light; collectively they are called the radio frequencies (RF). They range from about half a million cycles per second (500 KHz or .5 MHz) up through 500 million cycles per second (500 MHz or .5 GHz) and include the whole the range of radio transmissions, as well as the broadcast ranges of television (very high frequency (VHF) and ultra high frequency (UHF)) and even include the range your microwave oven works at, which is around 500 million cycles per second (half a gigaHertz). HAARP is a high frequency (HF) transmitter assigned to broadcast in the range from 2.8 to 10 MHz (2.8 to 10 million cycles per second). This is near the bottom of the radio frequency (RF) range, in what radio operators call the "shortwave" band.

As well as being awash in RF energy we also swim through a sea of much,

much lower frequency radiation. Power transmission lines, for example, bath us in 60 Hz ELF waves. It is easy to discover the amount of ambient (background) 60 Hz waves being absorbed by your body. Simply touch the probe of any oscilloscope and you can watch the 60 Hz wave. Your body is acting as an antenna, and the amplitude on the oscilloscope is an indication of the amount of radiation you are absorbing.

David S. Walonick, in his article "Effects of 6-10 Hz ELF on Brain Waves," wrote:

> Electromagnetic radiation may be the most harmful pollutant in our society. There is mounting statistical evidence that cancer and other diseases can be triggered by electromagnetic waves.
>
> ELF pulse-modulated radio waves work at the cellular level. Cancer and birth defects have been increasing in this country since about 1950 (as television became popular). The average resonant frequency of the body is around 82 MHz. It is no coincidence that this is near the middle of the VHF TV band.
>
> Even low intensity 60 Hz fields are capable of causing DNA damage and weakening the immune system. Cancer cells exposed to 60 Hz electromagnetic fields for 24 hours show a sixfold increase in their growth rate.
>
> In our technological society, there are few places to go where you will not be exposed to electromagnetic radiation. Television, radio and microwave radiation are abundant in all metropolitan areas. High voltage 60 Hz power lines crisscross the country. Microwaves (one of the most dangerous) are becoming increasingly common. The FCC has started to grant licenses to use microwaves for cellular phones.
>
> The powers that control the energy and communications industries will stop at no end to prevent the public from learning the truth. Their financial health depends on it. Since the military is one of the largest producers of high power electromagnetic radiation, it is not likely that we can count on government intervention.

THE MOSCOW SIGNAL & THE RUSSIAN WOODPECKER

In 1952, at the insistence of Soviet scientists, a series of secret meetings were held between scientists representing the U.S. and U.S.S.R. at the Sandia National Laboratories in New Mexico. These meetings dealt with a Soviet proposal to exchange information regarding the biological hazards and safety levels of electromagnetic radiation (EMR). The Soviets possessed the greater preponderance of information, by far. The American scientists were unwilling to believe the Soviet's data on the health risks of EMR. At subsequent meetings the Soviet scientists continued to stress the seriousness of the risks, and, all too typically, the American scientists downplayed those risks.

Apparently the Soviets decided to take us at our word, because shortly after the last Sandia meeting, the Soviets began directing a microwave beam at the U.S. Embassy in Moscow. They spent the next four decades using our embassy workers as guinea pigs for their EMR experiments. Washington, D.C., perhaps believing its own scientists, was oddly silent regarding the Moscow embassy bombardment.

Discovered by the Americans in 1962, the Moscow signal was investigated by the CIA. They brought in an outside consultant, Dr. Milton Zaret, and gave his investigation the code name "Project Pandora." Zaret found that the Moscow signal was composed of several different frequencies. He was also startled to discover that the beam was focussed precisely upon the Ambassador's office. The intensity of the bombardment was not made public, but when the State Department finally admitted to the existence of the Moscow signal, over a decade later, it was announced that it was "fairly low."

The bicentennial of the American Revolution was celebrated on 4 July, 1976. The Soviets made some "fireworks" of their own by beginning a series of broadcasts that became known to ham radio operators around the world as the "Russian Woodpecker." The Woodpecker signal seems to have come from an early model of a HAARP-like device using a Tesla Magnifying Transmitter (TMT). The official Defense Department explanation is that it is an over-the-horizon radar system designed to detect enemy missile launches. This is essentially what the Over The Horizon Backscatter (OTH-B) program, the original occupier of the HAARP site, was intended to be. These broadcast-interfering electromagnetic signals were on the 3 to 30 MHz bands and were usually pulsed at an on-off rate of 10 per second, which gave the signal the characteristic tapping which gave rise to its being called the "Russian Woodpecker."

In *The Zapping of America*, (W. W. Norton and Co., 1977), Paul Brodeur wrote:

> A report published in *The New York Times* on October 30, 1976, revealed that in recent months a mysterious broadband, short-wave radio signal had been broadcast intermittently from the Soviet Union. The signal was so powerful that it disrupted radio and telecommunications throughout the world. ... Dr. Zaret is concerned about the Russian signal,... because of its potential hazard to human beings. ... it was very clear that such an encoding impressed onto carrier wavelengths could have a central-nervous-system effect.

It is still not entirely clear just what the Soviets were using this system for.

While the signals have periodically stopped, this system seems to still be operational today. Like HAARP, it could have been erected for a number of possible purposes. Conservative scientists, taking the official line, say it is an over-the-horizon radar system. Other researchers think that it is for environmental modification, that is, control of the weather as a weapon. Still others believe that it is for mental manipulation of target populations. Just as with HAARP, any of these uses are entirely possible.

David Brinkley, on the TV show "NBC Magazine," broadcast on 18 July, 1981, spoke of the Woodpecker signal. He revealed to his audience that the northwestern United States had been continuously bombarded by the U.S.S.R. with low frequency waves set at the approximate level of biological frequencies. On the air Brinkley said:

> As I say I find it hard to believe, it is crazy and none of us here knows what to make of it: the Russian Government is known to be trying to change human behavior by external electronic influences. We do know that much. And we know that some kind of Russian transmitter is bombarding this country with extreme low frequency radiowaves.

If the existence of the Woodpecker program seems hard to believe, let me quote from another credible source. Dr. Andrew Michrowski, Ph.D. was a Technologies Specialist with the Canadian Department of State, as well as the President of the Planetary Association for Clean Energy (PACE). He wrote:

> Since October 1976 the Union of Soviet Socialist Republics has been emitting extremely low frequency signals from a number of Tesla-type transmitters. Their frequencies correspond to brain-wave rhythms of either the depressed or the irritable states of humans—and scientifically tenable tests have shown that the U.S.S.R. signals do lock-in human brain-wave signals. The U.S.S.R. signals have been assessed by the Environmental Protection Agency… to be psychoactive (i.e., liable to produce psychological response and vulnerability in humans). The same agency has noted that the U.S.S.R. ELF signals can be absorbed and re-radiated by 60-Hertz power transmission lines and even be magnified by water-pipe grids.
>
>
>
> The Soviets are on the verge of a breakthrough into a new weapons technology that will make missiles and bombers obsolete. It would allow them to destroy up to five American cities a day just by sending out radio pulses. They could induce panic or illness into whole nations.

Per the Planetary Association for Clean Energy's July 1979, newsletter "At least five USSR installations are operating simultaneously up to 24 hours daily since July 1976, with an intensity of up to 40 million watts."

Pretty wild stuff. If this is even partially right, we could be in a lot of trouble if we allow HAARP to go forward. HAARP rebroadcasting in the ELF band via the aurora could produce many of the same unhealthy effects ascribed to the Russian Woodpecker. HAARP will have an effective radiated power of 3.6 billion watts—nearly a hundred times the broadcast strength of the Woodpecker!

"Entrainment" is the result of external stimulation of the brain by electromagnetic means. An external signal generator can lock on to, or entrain, brain patterns, overriding the normal frequencies of the brain's operation. The outside signal captures, or retunes, the brain to harmonize with the external signal. This causes changes in brain wave patterns, which cause changes in brain chemistry, which then cause changes in thoughts, emotions and physical condition. Used intentionally by the individual it can induce desired states: meditation, calm, even euphoria. Used unknowingly against an individual it is the basic mechanism of radio intracerebral mind control, which will be discussed in depth later.

Over the last few decades a new cottage industry has grown up around producing "bio-feedback" and "brain boost" machines. An excellent introduction to this new technology are the books by Michael Hutchison; such as his: *Mega Brain: New Tools and Techniques for Brain Growth and Mind Expansion;* and *Mega Brain Power: Transform Your Life with Mind Machines and Brain Nutrients.* These cover the possibilities for personal improvement that are opened up by the discovery that the brain can be entrained.

Researchers around the world have opined that the Woodpecker signal could be used to entrain and capture the brains of the people affected by it by placing them in forced sympathetic resonance. It is the concern of many, including this author, that HAARP will be used to do the same.

Dr. W. Ross Adey, then of the University of California's Brain Research Institute, was one of the first to conduct research on EMF (electromagnetic frequency) and brain waves, confirming that brainwaves could be entrained to externally generated signals. His work, which we will be looking at in greater depth later, was funded by the U.S. Navy—another possible link to HAARP.

According to *Mind Wars* by Ron McRae (St. Martin's Press, 1984), "[I]n 1976, the CIA contracted for an exhaustive review of Soviet parapsychology research by outside experts." The report was titled "Novel Biological Information Transfer Systems," by Dr. J. W. Eerkens, et al. Per McRae, Dr. Eerkens "now believes the Soviets are actually building prototype equipment for psychic warfare."

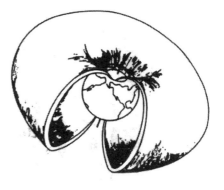

From *Psychic Warfare* by Martin Ebon (McGraw-Hill, 1983) we learn:

> Public evidence for an attempt at influencing U.S. officials during a visit abroad was presented by Dr. Sidney Gottlieb on September 21, 1977, during testimony before a Senate sub-committee. Dr. Gottlieb, then retired, had been the CIA's director of mind-control experiments [MK-Ultra and others]... He told the committee that... several members of President Nixon's staff had shown "inappropriate behavior." ... including "crying without provocation." ... In other parts of his testimony, Gottlieb did include the President himself among those who seemed to be affected by some type of unusual influence. Gottlieb stated, "Not too long ago, in connection with a presidential visit to a potentially hostile country, the President, when he came back, described some unusual feeling he and others had and asked if I would be able to give counsel." (President Nixon visited a "potentially hostile" country, the Soviet Union, in 1972.)

The CIA is reported to have conducted something called Operation Pique in the 1978. This supposedly involved bouncing microwaves off of the ionosphere in an attempt to affect the mental functions of people in selected areas of Europe. Perhaps this was in response to the Moscow Embassy bombardment, the Russian Woodpecker broadcasts, and other provocations. It is not known how successful Operation Pique was. Perhaps HAARP will be more successful.

You may recall Dr. Andrija Puharich's analysis of Tesla's ability to project energy in the preceding chapter. He gives us an interesting angle on the Woodpecker in this transcript of a lecture given by him at an Electromagnetic Conference in September of 1987:

> We were able to develop a hearing device that fit under the cap of a tooth and we could hear very clearly from a small little relay and receiver and transmitter and unfortunately it was promptly classified by an agency of our government. But we did solve the problem in terms of hardware.

About ten years ago in 1976, no I'm sorry early 1977, I made the basic measurements which showed the elf nature of elf coming from Russia and that it was psychoactive, that was my finding and I deduced the chemicals that were released by the frequencies that were being used and I passed that information onto every intelligence agency we have in this country from the president on down and England and Canada and all I got was four years of harassment. My house was burned down, I was shot at, they tried to kill me, they tried to eliminate me, etc., etc., and finally they agreed I was right and in 1981, the U.S. government went into full scale elf warfare and set up all their big transmitters down under in Australia and Africa so on and so on and now they're in business and everything's classified and you can't say a god damned thing about it, a tough situation. And you can't get any real information out of any government agency. And I know all of them that do the work. I know the people who head the projects etc. When they're in trouble, they usually come ask me. And they classify what I tell them. Insanity.

The veracity of Dr. Puharich's statements is somewhat confirmed by an article from *The Washington Post* of 7 Aug. 1977, entitled "Psychic Spying?" The article discussed Dr. Andrija Puharich, saying:

His connections with the military/intelligence communities go back to the early 1950s when he worked in the Army's Chemical and Biological Warfare Center at Ft. Detrick, Md., site of the CIA's now famous shellfish toxin repository. He presented a paper entitled "On the Possible Usefulness of Extrasensory Perception in Psychological Warfare" to a Pentagon conference in 1952 and later lectured the Army, Air Force and Navy on other possibilities for mind warfare. Expert in hypnotism as well as microelectronics, Puharich also invented a miniature tooth radio reportedly for the CIA.

From the PACE 1978 newsletter, Dr. Andrew Michrowski writes:

Potentially, almost anything could be inserted into the target brain mind systems, and such insertions would be processed by the biosystems as internally-generated data/effects. Words, phrases, images, sensations, and emotions could be directly inserted and experienced in the biological targets as internal states, codes, emotions thoughts and ideas.

Hypnotists have long known that when a subject is given a post-hypnotic command to perform some act in his waking state, the subject will do it and rationalize the act as his own idea. In one such example, hypnotists put Robert Kennedy's convicted killer, Sirhan Sirhan, under, then told him to swing from the bars of his cell like a monkey when he was awakened. Sirhan carried out the instruction. When told he had been hypnotized and shown a video of himself acting like a monkey, he insisted that it had been entirely his own idea—he said he needed the exercise! Instructions, thoughts or beliefs transmitted to a target subject could similarly be accepted by the subject as his own thoughts. This is the essence of research into mind control effected through the use of electromagnetic broadcasts.

Dr. Robert Beck, a Ph.D. in nuclear engineering, has done extensive research into electromagnetic effects on humans. At a Psychotronics Association conference in 1979 he read excerpts of a scientific research paper co-authored with Dr. Michael A. Persinger of Laurentian University, Canada, also an expert on ELF radiation. "Human subjects exposed to certain ELF field patterns report sensations of uneasiness, depression, foreboding…" Dr. Beck, a physicist who measured the Woodpecker signal later said: "We found the Soviet signal coming in like gangbusters… right in the window of human psychoactivity." And elsewhere, he said: "The signal was permeating power grids in the United States, it was being picked up by power lines, re-radiated, it was coming into homes on the light circuits…"

Military Review (an official publication of the U.S. Army Command and General Staff College) published an article on "The New Mental Battlefield" by Lt. Col. John B. Alexander, U.S. Army, Ph.D. In it, Col. Alexander wrote:

> [Soviet] mind-altering techniques, designed to impact on an opponent are well-advanced. The procedures employed include manipulation of human behavior through the use of psychological weapons effecting sight, sound, smell, temperature, electromagnetic energy, or sensory deprivation… Soviet researchers, studying controlled behavior, have also examined the effects of electromagnetic radiation on humans and have applied these techniques against the U.S. Embassy in Moscow… Researchers suggest that certain low-frequency (ELF) emissions possess psychoactive characteristics. These transmissions can be used to induce depression or irritability in a target population. The application of large-scale ELF behavior modification could have horrendous impact.

The Russian Woodpecker would appear to be an expansion of the Moscow signal, upping the ante from one building, the U.S. Embassy, to the whole of the United States. It is certainly not too great a stretch of the imagination to think that HAARP could be intended to "return the favor" to our Russian "friends," a la Operation Pique.

The Moscow signal, which had been discovered in 1962, finally became public knowledge in the mid-70s. It then became the subject of heated debate in the media. In 1976 *The Los Angeles Times* reported that the U.S. Ambassador to the U.S.S.R. had informed his Moscow staff that the microwaves that the Soviets were beaming at the U.S. Embassy in Moscow could cause emotional and behavioral problems, as well as leukemia, cancer and cataracts. Even if HAARP is not the "American Woodpecker," it is intended to be used in such a way as to bathe us all in this same energy. Is it really as safe as HAARP's apologists would have us believe?

In the fall of '76, after just a few months of operation, the Soviets completed the first of several expansions of their ELF Woodpecker grid. The second expansion a year later was accompanied by a major piece of curiosity, if not an outright criminal act. In 1977 the U.S. government sold the Soviets a supermagnet knowing that it was going to become part of the Woodpecker program. This magnet was a 40-ton monster capable of generating a magnetic field 250,000 times more powerful than that of the earth's magnetic field. Its purpose was to override, blank out and/or interfere with the earth's natural magnetic field to permit the Soviet Woodpecker signals to penetrate to the United States. The United States not only knew what it was for, they sent a team of scientists to help the Russians install it! With this new supermagnet in place the Soviets completed the second upgrade of the Woodpecker system in the fall of 1977.

This supermagnet was installed at the Gomel site, powered by the Chernobyl reactor. Eleven years later, in 1986, the Chernobyl nuclear reactor outside of Kiev, Ukraine, exploded. Some researchers have speculated that the Chernobyl facility may have been sabotaged by the West to stop the Woodpecker signals; others have suggested that it was shorted out by the Woodpecker transmitter the same way Tesla slagged the generator in Colorado Springs.

Following that second upgrade in 1977, a series of mysterious sonic booms was heard off the eastern coast of the United States. These were very possibly the new enhanced Woodpecker being calibrated. In one United Press International wire story of 22 December, 1977, it was reported that:

...[A] series of mysterious atmospheric explosions were reported along the New Jersey shore last night for the third time this month. ... Police said the explosions were preceded by a series of rumblings. On Dec. 2, there were two similar incidents, but the Federal Aviation Administration, the Civil Aeronautics Board and the Nuclear Regulatory Commission have been unable to offer any explanation for the blasts.

The following month the Associated Press reported that a White House spokesman had informed the press that the Naval Research Laboratory (NRL) would conduct a "measured and prudent" inquiry into the "mysterious atmospheric booms off the East Coast." The NRL never released its findings, yet a little over a decade later it became a member of the HAARP project. Coincidence?

THE GROUND WAVE EMERGENCY NETWORK (GWEN)

The U.S. Air Force began building its system of Ground Wave Emergency Network (GWEN) towers in the early 1980s. The towers are 299 feet tall and have a web of a hundred copper wires, each 330 feet long, radiating out from them in all directions a few feet underground. The towers are 200 miles apart across the northern tier of America. The GWEN system is claimed to be part of Continuancy Of Government plans to keep the government operating in the event of nuclear war. The GWEN communication system uses very low frequency (VLF) ground waves to send messages. Each unit uses about 2,000 watts of power. They send out brief messages at regular intervals; one report I saw said every 20 minutes, another said every hour.

The GWEN system is highly controversial. Currently there are at least 54 operational GWEN towers at a total cost in excess of $235 million. The government plans to build at least 29 more units at a cost of an additional $11 million. The controversy isn't so much over the price of the system. The real questions are whether electromagnetic radiation (EMR) pollution from its transmissions adversely impacts on people and the environment in the vicinity of the towers, and, perhaps more importantly, what the heck are the darned things really supposed to be used for.

Like HAARP, the GWEN system seems to have been built for some reason other than the stated one. It does not look like it has much to do with emergency communications. But it might well be some sort of "science fictional" electromagnetic warfare system, or maybe some sort of weather control system.

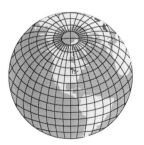

On 1 March, 1987, *The New York Times* reported: "Col. Paul Hanson, GWEN Program Director for the Air Force, said... the towers will not help wage a

nuclear war because they would be destroyed in any protracted confrontation." The GWEN hardware is transistor based, meaning that even if put into "hardened" bunkers it would still be vulnerable to the electromagnetic pulse (EMP) of a nuclear detonation. Also, a nuclear explosion in the vicinity of a GWEN tower would produce major ground currents in the path of the GWEN signals which would decrease their transmission viability. On top of that, all of the GWEN station locations are public record, meaning anyone likely to launch a nuclear war undoubtedly knows their exact locations and so presumably would take them out as part of any first strike action. This leaves us with the uneasy feeling that the government is, again, up to something that it does not want "We The People" to know about.

In *Crosscurrents: The Perils of Electropollution/The Promise of Electromedicine,* (Jeremy P. Tarcher, Los Angeles, 1990), Robert O. Becker, M.D., (author of *The Body Electric* and a two-time Nobel nominee for his work on the biological effects of electromagnetism) wrote of the GWEN system thusly:

> GWEN is a superb system, in combination with cyclotron resonance, for producing behavioral alterations in the civilian population. The average strength of the steady geomagnetic field varies from place to place across the United States. Therefore, if one wished to resonate a specific ion in living things in a specific locality, one would require a specific frequency for that location. The spacing of GWEN transmitters 200 miles apart across the United States would allow such specific frequencies to be "tailored" to the geomagnetic-field strength in each GWEN area.

This resonating of ions within the body is a wild concept, still being debated in scientific circles. Laboratory experiments have shown that a minute quantity of a substance in a living body (an amount too small to cause an effect) can be "excited" by exposure to EMR, through something called "cyclotron resonance," so as to produce effects as though there were up to a thousand times as much of the substance present. The U.S. Naval Medical Research Center, for example, was able to apply external fields in such a way as to affect the brain chemistry of rats in this manner.

This research has clear military applications. An amount of a chemical agent could be introduced into a battlefield at a level far below generally accepted levels for toxic effect (or even detection). Yet, using this technique, a mysterious and deadly level of toxicity could be achieved by washing the "battlespace" with the appropriate electromagnetic frequency. If the levels of the toxic material were below that necessary to set off warning detectors, enemy troops

could be exposed to deadly poisons without their even realizing that an attack was under way.

This technique would make it possible to circumvent treaties prohibiting the use of chemical weapons. A 1982 document prepared for the military by the Southwest Research Institute of San Antonio, Texas, entitled "Final Report on Biotechnology Research Requirements for Aeronautical Systems Through the Year 2000," suggested using this method in time of war. Could the mysterious Gulf War Syndrome be evidence of this suggestion having been acted on—even if "unintentionally."

According to *Defense News,* of 13-19 April, 1992, the United States deployed an electromagnetic pulse weapon in Desert Storm. It was designed to mimic the flash of electricity from a nuclear bomb, the electromagnetic pulse (EMP). Per *The Language of Nuclear War: An Intelligent Citizen's Dictionary* (Harper & Row, 1987):

> An EMP is a burst of radiation released immediately after a nuclear explosion. The EMP is essentially an electric field and a magnetic field moving away from the blast. The electromagnetic pulse burns out electronic circuitry, destroying communications systems, computers, and other sophisticated electronic instruments. The implications of the EMP are uncertain, but some experts assert that the EMP released by one large nuclear explosion over the central United States could cause an electrical blackout affecting the entire country. Further, it is possible that the EMP would damage the circuitry in missiles so that they would be unable to reach their targets. The EMP was first detected during a nuclear test at Johnston Island in 1962.

Gulf War Syndrome could certainly be a side effect of using EM weaponry in the Persian Gulf War with Iraq. Our soldiers were forced to take a number of shots and pills as precautions against chemical and biological attacks. Induced cyclotronic resonance from secret energy weapons might have triggered unexpected reactions to this injected and ingested material.

There is a legitimate fear of what similar harm HAARP could do. We daily consume thousands of chemicals in our foods, and breathe them from our polluted air (cigarette smoke alone contains 600 different chemicals). Early official HAARP literature discussed using HAARP to generate artificial EMPs. If HAARP or GWEN could cause chemicals in our bodies to become "excited" we could have people keeling over by the thousands, maybe even tens of thousands—instant population control! Others trying to guess what GWEN is about have gotten the idea that the towers may be some sort of weather control stations.

HAARP

Dr. Bernard J. Eastlund received the first of his three patents on 11 August, 1987, while working for the ARCO subsidiary APTI. It was but the first of twelve patents that scientists on APTI's payroll would take out over the next few years.

Officially, HAARP was conceived two years later, on 13 December, 1989. A joint Navy-Air Force meeting was held that morning at the Office of Naval Research (ONR) in Washington, D.C. It has since been described as a discussion of their mutual interest in carrying out a DOD program in the area of ionospheric modification. Military and HAARP documents insist that it was at this meeting that the need for a unique heating facility to conduct "critical experiments" relating to potential DOD applications was identified.

The official tale of the birth of HAARP further claims that the Navy and Air Force personnel at that after-breakfast meeting at ONR decided to bring the Defense Advanced Research Projects Agency (DARPA) in on the project. Consequently, Navy and Air Force personnel trooped over to DARPA later that day to present their proposal for a DOD sponsored program. As well as representatives of DARPA, people from the Office of the Defense Director of Research & Engineering (DDR&E) were also present at that second meeting of the day.

This led to an Ionospheric Modification/ELF Workshop held the following month at NUSC on 9-11 January, 1990. It was attended by personnel from a number of government agencies, as well as from several universities and the private sector. The workshop was billed as providing "an opportunity for broad-based inputs concerning research needs in ionospheric modification. In addition, potential systems were defined, and the characteristics of a new, unique, HF heating facility were discussed and identified."

Another joint Navy-Air Force meeting was held at the Geophysics Laboratory at Hanscom AFB on 24 January, 1990, to develop a plan to achieve the "emerging DOD objectives." On 7 February, 1990, a written description of HAARP plans and objectives, under the title "Executive Summary," was circulated to Navy, Air Force, and DARPA personnel for coordination. Another meeting with DDR&E at ONR was held on 12 February, 1990, to present the HAARP plan, and to discuss its implementation.

In a year's time the project moved off of the drawing boards and into reality. Three contracts were awarded to ARCO Power Technologies (APTI) to begin feasibility studies in 1991. In 1992 the principal contract to begin construction was awarded, also to APTI.

At the same time the environmental impact process began. The MITRE Corporation, a non-profit organization, produced the "Environmental Impact Analysis Process #1," the draft environmental impact study proposal for HAARP, in February of 1993. Later, they produced the "Electromagnetic Interference Impact of the Proposed Emitters for the High Frequency Active Auroral Research Program (HAARP)" report, of 14 May, 1993. MITRE was also responsible for the second volume of the Final Environmental Impact Statement, produced in July of 1993.

The Environmental Impact Statement was filed with the Environmental Protection Agency and made available to the public by Federal Register announcement on 23 July, 1993. That statement was approved later that year when James F. Boatright, Deputy Assistant Secretary of the Air Force (Installations) published the Record of Decision, Final Environmental Impact Statement on 18 October, 1993.

In early November 1993 the U.S. Air Force announced, via press release, that the prime contractor on the HAARP program was ARCO Power Technologies, Incorporated (today it is called Advanced Power Technologies, Inc.) owner of the twelve patents granted to Bernard Eastlund and the other APTI scientists. Much later, anti-HAARP investigators discovered that APTI was listed in a Dun & Bradstreet publication ("America's Corporate Families," 1993 Volume I, page 156) as having a President in Los Angeles, California and a CEO and a staff of 25 in Washington, D.C. It was cited as having $5 million in sales a year.

Dr. Nick Begich points out that the HAARP contract was for an amount five times that company's annual sales. He also notes that they were granted several exemptions to the usual military procurement process. This he believes is evidence that APTI possessed proprietary information requiring that they alone were capable of carrying the project forward, i.e., the Eastlund patents. This is important to understanding the government's deception in this affair, as at all levels of HAARP, the government and scientists connected with the project deny any connection between Dr. Eastlund's Star Wars project and their peaceful little scientific experiment. Note also a contradiction between a broadly published Air Force-Navy fact sheet which said that APTI had been granted the contract for HAARP as the result of "a competitive procurement process" and the fact that they were actually granted special privileges and exemptions.

Initial prototype construction began at the Gakona, Alaska site in late 1993 and was completed a year later in late '94. During that time APTI bailed on the project and mysteriously sold it to a major defense contractor, E-Systems of Dallas, Texas. E-Systems reported annual

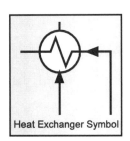

Heat Exchanger Symbol

sales of nearly $2 billion a year and had over 18,000 employees. Also in 1994, the U.S. Senate froze funding for HAARP until planners increased emphasis on earth penetrating tomography uses for nuclear counterproliferation efforts. Despite the funding freeze the first stage of HAARP testing went forward.

The following year, 1995, Raytheon bought E-Systems and all the APTI patents they held. That same year Congress budgeted $10 million more for HAARP in the following fiscal year (FY), FY96. HAARP appeared in the budget under "Counterproliferation—Advanced Development" spending. In the FY 1997 Descriptive Summary of the Counterproliferation Advanced Development Budget, HAARP appears under the sub-heading "Project P539 Counterforce." There it is recorded that "In FY96, Congress added $10 Million to be used for the High-Frequency Acoustic [sic] Auroral Research Program (HAARP) to this project." Elsewhere in that report it states "… [I]n FY96 only, the Congressionally added HAARP program funds will be used to explore the ability of auroral transmissions to detect and locate underground structures of the type where WMD [Weapons of Mass Destruction] can be developed or stored."

The HAARP final ionospheric research instrument (FIRI) is planned to be a field of 180 antennas arranged in a rectangular grid of 12 rows by 15 columns. Initially, a smaller set of elements was constructed so that the predicted performance could be verified before building the entire facility. That initial phase of the program is called the Developmental Prototype (DP) phase. By April of 1995 the DP array of 48 antenna towers arranged as 8 columns by 6 rows had been completed. Thirty additional unpowered and unused towers were also erected at that time.

Official HAARP documents describe the Developmental Prototype phase in this manner:

> Evaluating the prototype is a little like this example: Suppose you are the owner of a fleet of 100 taxis and you want to equip all of the taxis with two-way radios. You have received bids from several companies to provide the antennas to mount on the roof of the taxis, from other companies to supply the radios, and from still other companies to provide the wiring and connectors to connect everything together. Before going out and buying 100 sets of each, you decide to buy 5 of

each with some alternatives to see how they will work together and to pick the best combination of parts. These "prototypes" will be your evaluation models and you buy them and start testing them to see how the individual components work together.

During the DP phase of the HAARP program, the IRI antenna array components are being evaluated prior to completing construction of the facility. When tests are conducted at Gakona, we are studying a certain combination of transmitters, antennas and the wiring that connects them together. Most of the necessary tests can and have been conducted at low power levels and are for the strict purpose of collecting performance data on the components.

The first round of tests of the DP was in April 1995. More start-up tests were conducted in July and November of 1995, while tests of the aircraft detection radar were conducted in September of that year. The aircraft alert radar is intended to automatically shut off "appropriate transmissions" when aircraft are detected within, or approaching a "safety zone" established around the HAARP site.

The first of the annual open houses was held at the HAARP site on 21 September, 1995. The local newspaper, *The Copper River Country Journal*, covered the event, saying:

The HAARP site on the Tok Road held a coffee and Open House last weekend, and over 80 people logged in their names in the visitor guest book. Some were just curious. Others were concerned. There were people there from the immediate Gakona area, from the Copper Valley, and from other parts of the state. Paul Anthoney came up from Anchorage. Anthoney was carrying a copy of a book by Nick Begich called *Angels Don't Play This HAARP*. Begich claims in the book that the HAARP project is "the most incredible weapon yet devised." When he first arrived, Paul Anthoney seemed to be speaking for more than one person when he told the *Journal*, "I'm concerned about concentration camps in America... You don't have to be a scientist to understand the implications of this. By what authority can these experiments be conducted that have such far-reaching effects..."

Some of the other visitors expressed other concerns, including fears of weather control, concerns about somehow "amplifying" energy, fears of injuring the ionosphere, and concerns that the project is somehow "a decoy." Several even expressed a fear the HAARP will be used for mind control.

Doug O'Harra of *We Alaskans*, the Sunday Magazine of *The Anchorage Daily News*, also covered the event, as quoted in Chapter One. In describing the scene at the open house he wrote:

Some [attendees] wandered about the grounds with expressions of polite curiosity and admiration, their children playing under the antennas as they might at a local park. Several ham-radio buffs questioned officials about technical characteristics. But some visitors were tense and distrustful, reflecting a growing opposition to the project fueled by national magazine articles, new books and talk shows. HAARP's ability to broadcast radio signals into the sky scared them.

Inside the control building—where computers will record measurements from 19 radio and optical instruments—people crowded around tables with books, charts and pamphlets. Some munched chocolate chip cookies and sipped juice. Others cornered scientists who had gathered to explain the project.

Among them was Anchorage business owner Lucille Clark. Surrounded by a half-dozen physicists, electrical engineers and HAARP officials, the petite Clark unflinchingly announced that HAARP was a dangerous military device capable of harming people and the Earth with concentrated beams of radio energy.

"What we have here is a 'Star Wars' nonlethal weapon that is capable of mind control," Clark told them. "This is a mind-control and weather-control station. ...What I'm hoping is that one of you is going to tell me I'm wrong."

For several minutes, three or four physicists and engineers tried...

Listening to the exchange was HAARP project manager John Heckscher, a scientist with the Air Force's Phillips Laboratory at Hanscom Air Force Base in Massachusetts. "I don't know where people get these things," he said, exasperated, turning away.

Later, Heckscher said he was frustrated by accusations that the project is sinister. "This is not an instrument of war—this is a research facility," he said. "We're interested in the ionosphere and what it's like in the auroral zone."

He doesn't know how to refute charges that HAARP is aimed at mind control or weather disruption or some other exotic military goal—especially with critics usually dismissing his explanations as lies or disinformation.

"The only thing we can do is show what we're doing," he said.

"That's why we're having this open house."

HAARP documents claim that the facility was shut down at the end of the last set of initial low power tests on the DP on 21 November, 1995. Officially, no testing was conducted from that time until the HAARP facility was at last put to scientific use for the first time, over a year later.

This claim of being "dark" from November 1995 to February 1997, however, contradicts other evidence presented by Dr. Begich. He claims that inside sources told him that a series of full power tests had been conducted in December of '95 and March of '96. My research team and I have not been able to independently verify this. Richard Hoagland and Dr. Nick Begich both claim that clandestine experiments were conducted during this period of alleged non-activity. These alleged experiments will be discussed at length later in this book.

The HAARP literature calls for the array to be used in two week blocks of intensive activity called "campaigns." Officially, the first such campaign was 27 February through 14 March, 1997. In addition to science experiments, this two week period included several visits from tour groups; participation in a lecture series by HAARP personnel at the nearby community college; a public talk on ionospheric research and the HAARP facility; and the first HAARP-Amateur radio listening test. HAARP documents claim that all testing of the IRI prior to that first campaign was to test the components of the DP array only.

From 15-25 May, 1997, more tests were run on the DP. Some official documents say the next series of tests was not until 11-27 August, 1997, but this is again contradicted. Tests may have been run in June—tests that could have bathed some or all of North America in deadly gamma radiation!

Researcher Michael Unum has posted the following startling data on the Internet:

> One of the most impressive uses for the HAARP device is as an indirect fire energy weapon. The HAARP can create a steerable beam which can burn temporary holes in our protective ionosphere layer. This can cause a predictable corridor for the Sun's Gamma radiation pulse to get through this protective layer.
>
> Evidence of this capability was obtained through the internet sights [sic] that measure gamma radiation around the Nv. [Nevada] test sight [sic]. These monitors all spiked on the same day at the same time! I have run a real time comparison of the EPA [Environmental Protection Agency] meter data and discovered that the time of the spikes on the gamma meters are timed closely together even though these meters are some distance [apart]. This is due to a large gamma pulse in the region. This could almost be perceived as a nuclear weapon with out [sic] the

bomb or the explosion.

Just before this Gamma event took place there was a massive electromagnetic event registered in the University of Alaska magnometer sight [sic] sensors. All of the readings were off the chart. The HAARP sight [sic] was registering that it was in use at this same time as well! All of this information was collected from many different unconnected sights [sic].

When the information is analyzed together it creates a picture that seems to state that the HAARP can be used as a weapon. What we are seeing is a weapons test in the area of the test range.

If my conclusion is correct this device could be employed in secret. Targeting any point on earth with a massive Gamma Radiation pulse. Causing destruction with no sound or any obvious attack. Making this the ultimate sneak attack device.

The date of the test was June 09 and 10 [1997]. Look at the before and after readings on all the sights [sic]. You will notice the background levels return to normal fairly quickly after the test.

He gives the Internet addresses for these sites:
1. Gamma meter sites: http://newnet.jdola.lanl.gov/snvmap. html
2. Magnetometer site: (http://maxwell.gi.alaska.edu).

Michael Unum believed that HAARP had been used to create a "hole" in the ionosphere that rained deadly gamma radiation over the Nevada Test Site (NTS—the U.S. nuclear weapons testing facility in the desert north of Las Vegas). Gamma ray detectors in Alaska and Nevada spiked off the scale at the same time. The event that caused the spike(s), according to Unum, was a test of HAARP. Gamma rays are a high-energy radiation that is extremely dangerous to living cells. They cause severe cell mutations. Protection from gamma rays is very difficult because they penetrate even thick concrete. If HAARP actually was used to conduct such a clandestine experiment, this evidence makes it clear that HAARP is deadly dangerous; far more so than any government official or project scientist is willing to admit.

During the early part of the August 1997 testing period, several experiments were performed with the NASA WIND satellite which was at a favorable position in its orbit. The WIND satellite project is part of the International Solar Terrestrial Physics program, the goal of which is said to be the measurement of near-earth, solar induced phenomena; particularly the solar wind (particles that have been ejected by the sun). WIND was launched on 1 November, 1994. Per NASA documents, WIND supports several related research programs in-

cluding efforts in:

Hot Plasma and Charged Particles
Transient Gamma Ray and EUV Spectroscopy
Magnetic Field Monitoring and Characterization
Plasma and Radio Waves
Solar Wind Studies
Energetic Particle Acceleration, Composition and Transport Studies, and
Gamma Ray Burst Detection.

A document posted on the Internet entitled "Transionospheric Measurements Using HAARP as a Signal Source for the WIND Satellite" gave some details on the HAARP/WIND experiment:

During engineering evaluations of the HAARP High Frequency (HF) transmitter in November [sic], a scientific experiment-of-opportunity was conducted in conjunction with the NASA WIND satellite, which carries on-board, a channelized HF receiver as part of its diagnostics suite to measure near-earth, solar induced phenomena in space. For the experiment, a signal from HAARP at the 300 kW level was transmitted in the direction of the WIND satellite, as it passed from perigee [point nearest the earth] on the outbound portion of its trajectory at a distance of 18 earth radii. Five hours of HF data were recorded on-board the WIND satellite. The data set includes separate, hour-long recordings of HAARP transmissions at three frequencies within the 4-10 MHz band.

Calculations prior to the test indicated that the ionospheric cutoff frequency for the geometry associated with propagation toward the WIND satellite could be high enough to significantly affect received signal levels. The low levels of observed signal strength indicate that this was the case. The variations in signal are, in part, indicative of the rapidly changing path from HAARP to WIND at the time of this test. The spacecraft was travelling at approximately 1 km/sec at the time of this experiment and, during a 30 second HAARP transmission, WIND covered about 30 km. ...The temporal and spatial variations observed in the data will be used to characterize electron densities and structures in the ionosphere and the magnetosphere and to provide insight into the degree of homogeneity of the ionosphere-magnetosphere paths associated with the propagation of the HAARP HF signals to the WIND satellite. The data will also be correlated with complementary data obtained on the WIND satellite from observations of HF signals from the Russian SURA ionospheric research facility, which also took part in this novel, international, scientific experiment.

The third annual HAARP open house was held 23-24 August, 1997. Program personnel were present to discuss the project and to give demonstrations and tours of the facility. Several experts in ionospheric physics were also present to discuss the research plans and the physics of the earth's upper atmosphere.

As of September 1997, the HAARP facility was shut down for the winter, with the exception of some "continuously running observatory instruments." Official documents claim that no transmitter testing nor similar operations have taken place between the completion of a series of antenna impedance measurements on 27 August, 1997 and the time I wrote this in February 1998.

We know where HAARP is and what it physically is, but, what can HAARP actually do? What about those "other concerns, including fears of weather control, concerns about somehow "amplifying" energy, fears of injuring the ionosphere... even... a fear the HAARP will be used for mind control..."?

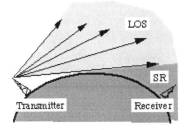

Figure 1. Areas in the light blue region are within the radio "Line of Sight" (LOS). The receiving antenna is in the shadow region (SR) and cannot receive a signal directly from the transmitter.

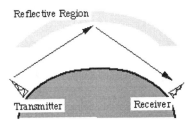

Figure 2. A conductive region at high altitude would "reflect" radio signals that reached it and return them to Earth.

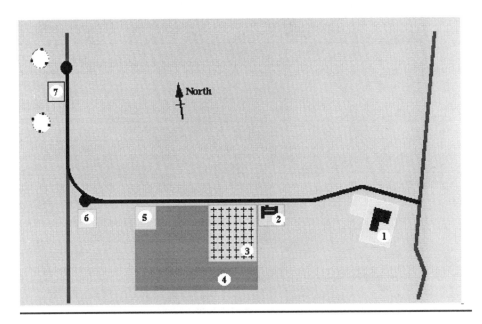

A map of the HAARP facility from the home page.
Map Key:
1. Power Plant Building
2. Temporary Operations Center
3. FDP 6x8 Antenna Array
4. The Final HF Transmitter Antenna Array (when completed)
5. VHF Radiometers
6. Aircraft Alert Radar
7. Ionosonde Site
8. Land and Access Roads

Good Afternoon and Welcome to the Home Page of the
HIGH FREQUENCY ACTIVE AURORAL RESEARCH PROGRAM

What's New ▷
General Information ▷
Technical Details ▷
Data from the Site ▷
Photo Index ▷
Safety Index ▷
News Articles ▷
Research Activity ▷
The Ionosphere ▷
Table of Contents ▷
Search ▷

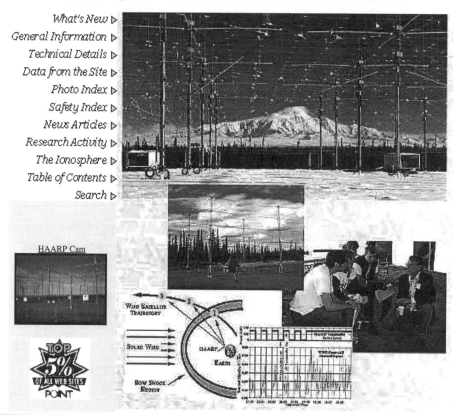

HAARP Cam

Questions of a technical nature can be sent to askhaarp@itd.nrl.navy.mil Use the feedback page to send a comment or a suggestion. Please read the cautionary message . You may freely copy material from this site or distribute it without modification, subject to any indicated copyright restrictions and normally accepted procedures for properly crediting original sources.

HAARP

The HAARP web server has been in continuous operation since February 1995.

HAARP Home Page-> http://w3.nrl.navy.mil/haarp.html

The HAARP world-wide web home page, operated by the U.S. Government.

CHAPTER FOUR:
Science Out Of Control Or "Star Wars"?
Part One: Earth Penetrating Tomography

Most of the scientific and technical areas planned for HAARP to examine are potentially dangerous: some may be illegal and others could be considered immoral (though I doubt if any are fattening). In the four parts of this chapter I will examine several of the alleged scientific research goals for HAARP and in the process will address the two coupled questions I posed in Chapter One. Those questions were 1) is HAARP science gone out of control? and 2) might it be "Star Wars" technology coming on-line? By the end of this examination I believe you will agree with me that it is, in fact, both.

In 1995 the U.S. Senate appropriated $10 million in the 1996 budget to build HAARP. They did this only after insisting that the DOD's project give stronger emphasis to developing a technology called earth penetrating tomography (EPT). EPT is a lot like "CAT scanning" the earth; its purpose is to see deep into the earth, perhaps as deep as several miles. The Senate was led to believe that if the United States had the ability to detect hidden underground structures, it could more effectively prevent the spread of nuclear weapons (and chemical and biological ones as well) by detecting their hidden underground manufacturing, storage and/or launch facilities.

EPT, I hasten to point out, has nothing to do with "characterizing" the ionosphere, which is what DOD scientists claim to be HAARP's purpose. EPT is, however, an example of utilizing what is already known about the ionosphere to accomplish military goals. We are supposed to believe that HAARP is all about "discovery," yet EPT is clearly in the realm of "application." This at least hints that HAARP may not be what its operators say it is.

By using HAARP to conduct EPT scans of the earth, scientists hope to be able to see far deeper than with any currently existing technology. HAARP's supporters have promoted EPT as an ideal technological use for HAARP. The HAARP facility could become a significant force for world peace by being able to locate underground facilities, tunnels, and so forth. Do I need to point out that EPT, when used for counterproliferation measures, is not exactly a civilian use?

The environmental group Trustees for Alaska has correctly noted that, at the very least, the military has not acted in a "confidence building" way in its handling of this affair. In their letter to the Air Force requesting a new Environmental Impact Study (EIS) they say:

...[I]t is incongruous for the Air Force to conclude that no significant effects will flow from HAARP (with the exception of electromagnetic and radio frequency interference which the Air Force has pledged to mitigate...) when an EIS is required only for those federal actions which have a "significant impact on the quality of the human environment." 42 U.S.C. Sec. 4332(2)(C); compare 40 C.F.R. Sections 1501.4(b), 1508.9 (1988) (EIS unnecessary for major federal action that does not significantly affect the environment). Certainly, the Air Force should recognize this incongruity and realize that it provides a reasonable basis for the public to question the accuracy of other assertions made by the Air Force.

In any event, plentiful evidence exists that raises questions about HAARP and its current and intended uses and effects. In 1994, for example, the Senate Committee on Armed Services stated the following in a report attached to its passage of the National Defense Authorization Act for Fiscal Year 1995:

> The committee is aware of the promising results of the high frequency active auroral research program (HAARP). This transmitter in Alaska, besides providing a world class research facility for ionospheric physics, could allow earth-penetrating tomography over most of the northern hemisphere. Such a capability would permit the detection and precise location of tunnels, shelters, and other underground shelters. The absence of such a capability has been noted as a serious weakness in the Department of Defense plans for precision attacks on hardened targets and for counterproliferation. 103d Congress, 2d session, Report 103-282 at 86 (June 14, 1994).

The Armed Services Committee went on to state that it would condition future funds for a "full-scale HAARP facility" on the Department of Defense's commitment to exploring the counterproliferation possibilities of HAARP. Id.

The very next year, the Committee on Appropriations recommended passage of the Department of Defense Appropriation Bill for 1996, with specific recommendation that the Senate  include substantial monies for HAARP. 104th Congress, 1st session, Report 104-24 at 190 (July 28, 1995). This appropriation appeared under the heading "Counterproliferation support-advanced development." Id.

Nowhere in the HAARP Final EIS does the Air Force so much as mention, much less evaluate, the earth-penetrating tomography aspects of HAARP or its use for counterproliferation purposes. Indeed, the Index to the Final EIS does not even contain a reference to these terms. See Final EIS Vol. I at 8-1.

In response to a letter from a concerned citizen who raised this issue, the Air Force admitted that earth-penetrating tomography was "not specifically documented in the EIS" yet stated that this use is "within original design and operating parameters which have been identified in the Final EIS." Letter from John Heckscher, Air Force, to Arthur Gray, NTIA (November 17, 1994).

Given the total lack of reference to earth-penetrating tomography and counterproliferation in the Final EIS, this statement does not appear supported by the record. See 40 C.F.R. Sec. 1502.8 (Environmental Impact Statements "shall be written in plain language... so that decisionmakers and the public can readily understand them"); 40 C.F.R. Sec. 1502.13 (agency shall "briefly specify the underlying purpose and need" of the proposed action). Indeed, given the attention focused on this specific application of HAARP and the substantial federal monies apparently dedicated to it, the Air Force should not so easily dismiss this issue.

Dr. Nick Begich told radio talk show host Art Bell:

I've never believed this to be a purely scientific research project. It just smells to high heaven when you research the data, when you look at the material, you know, it's just not there. In looking at the operators of this system, and how they've developed the technology—it's too big to hide, so you develop the mask behind which you hide—and that's exactly what they've done by characterizing it as a purely scientific research project.

He stated his belief that the reason HAARP received funding at all was because the head of the Senate Defense Appropriations Subcommittee is Senator Ted Stevens of Alaska. There is more than a little evidence that this is the case.

A press release dated Monday, 4 December, 1995, under the heading "New Defense Law Contains Alaska Projects" reads:

The $243 billion defense appropriations bill that became law late last week contains several Alaska-specific items. At the request of Senator Stevens, Chairman of the Defense Appropriations Subcommittee, the bill continues the local hire provision for Department of Defense service and construction projects in Alaska. The Alaska joint military exercise, Northern Edge, will receive $5 million, and $15 million is included to continue the High Altitude [sic] Auroral Research Program (HAARP), at Stevens' request.

Stevens, Begich said, hyped HAARP in his home state during the 1995-6 election year as some great godsend. Stevens makes HAARP look like good old-fashioned pork barrel. Senator Stevens may even believe in the project. When emotionally defending HAARP before his committee, he said:

> I could tell you about the time when the University of Alaska came to me and said it might be possible to bring the aurora to Earth. We might be able to harness the energy in the aurora… No one in the Department of Defense, no one in the Department of Energy, no one in the executive branch was interested in pursuing it at all. Why? Because it did not come from the good old boy network. So I did just what you say I should do. I got Congress to earmark the money, and the experiment is going on now. It will cost $10 million to $20 million. If it is successful, it will change the history of the world.

Frankly, I am mystified by this statement. Nowhere in the HAARP documentation, official or otherwise, is there any indication that HAARP originated with the University of Alaska or Senator Stevens. Indeed, everything that I and my research team have been able to unearth points to the project originating with APTI and Bernard Eastlund. This, however, is denied and covered up by all involved. Officially, HAARP was conceived at an after breakfast meeting at the Office of Naval Research in December of 1989. The quote from Senator Stevens is attributed to 1990. By that time the ball was already rolling in military circles. Lies, and more lies? The price tag he gives for the project in this quote is also rather far off the mark. Most official estimates for the cost of the completed final ionospheric research instrument is in the neighborhood of $150 million (and upward).

Begich thinks that HAARP is far more sinister than merely big government looking for a cool new way to blow tax dollars, and decidedly less altruistic than changing human history for the better. In 1996, on the *Art Bell Radio Show,* he expressed that he suspected the tomography angle of being a gimmick the military wanted to use to sucker the Alaska State Legislature into signing onto the project.

Begich found it interesting that the newspaper with the largest circulation in Alaska printed only stories on HAARP that focused on this particular application. Early on, he said, they ran puff pieces extolling the value of this technology to the State of Alaska. The paper claimed to support the project because it believed that HAARP would also have the potential of locating underground oil deposits, natural gas deposits, and the like. HAARP may be able to do this because the porous strata that such deposits are formed in are so different from the surrounding rock.

One aspect that Begich finds telling is that the location of HAARP is within twenty or thirty miles of the Alaskan oil pipeline. In 1996 that pipeline was running at about 65% capacity. Additionally, the HAARP site in Gakona is situated within a potential oil basement that was defined by the U.S. Geodetic Survey a couple of decades earlier. HAARP's value in this regard is seen in that Alaska in the mid-1990s was in a financial crunch because its oil revenues had declined.

According to reports posted on the Internet, Dr. Begich had sources inside HAARP who revealed to him that HAARP had run full power EPT tests in December 1995 and again in the first week of March 1996. There is no acknowledgement of such testing on the HAARP home page nor from HAARP spokesfolks on the Internet. As of the 7 March, 1996, interview on the *Art Bell Show,* Begich seemed convinced that his sources were credible. He found it especially telling that they were conducting EPT tests at the same time that the Alaska legislature was in session. He speculated that if they could have told the state legislature that there was a strong indication of oil reserves located near the HAARP facility, they may have been in a position to co-opt the Alaskan legislature into supporting the project as opposed to standing against it.

HAARP, Dr. Begich noted, is in an excellent location for development as an oil revenue producer. Not only is it located close to a pipeline that is not running at capacity, it is on Alaska's primary highway system. The logistics would be extremely good for developing a field there, if they could discover one. It would seem that if they were running secret tests, HAARP failed to find oil under its own feet. Or, if Dr. Begich was right about HAARP running full power tests, his sources might have been wrong on where or why.

WHAT IS EARTH PENETRATING TOMOGRAPHY?

Considerable interest has been expressed in recent years in both military and civilian circles to use radar-like waves to detect and identify a variety of underground features and objects. There are, of course, the obvious military uses of locating hidden targets, from objects as small as anti-personnel mines to as large as deeply buried nuclear, chemical or biological facilities.

Another area of keen interest is in detection and mapping of hazardous waste sites. Both government and private industry have produced untold billions of tons of environmentally dangerous wastes. These products all too often have been introduced into the environment by simple carelessness (like consumers pouring used motor oil down a convenient drain), by shipping accidents (from train derailments to the "Exxon Valdiz") and by receptacle failures (leaking, and sometimes exploding, tanks). Environmental contamination has also occurred through deliberate undocumented burial (toxic dumping in the dead of night) and purposeful abandonment (just shutting down a contaminated site and walking away).

Still another need for nondestructive evaluation techniques has emerged in civil engineering applications; such as inspecting bridges for damage or for potential failure, before or after earthquakes. Other scientific uses for underground and undersea radar mapping include the previously mentioned oil and gas exploration, sounding lake bottoms and coasts, and in archeology.

Another somewhat disturbing use for this technology has been discussed in the militia/constitutional restoration movement press. Some fear that if it comes down to an armed conflict between patriotic Americans and the multinational forces of the New World Order and/or United Nations (i.e., the Conspiracy) EPT could be used to detect their buried caches of guns, food, valuable coins and so on.

While that may sound as "out-there" as Paul Anthoney's reported fear of the New World Order erecting concentration camps, a la Jim Keith's book *Black Helicopters Over America: Strikeforce for the New World Order* (IllumiNet Press, 1994), one should not dismiss it out of hand. After all, the United States did build concentration camps during World War II and did intern its own loyal citizens (of Japanese descent) in those camps. Such niceties as laws and Constitutional rights mattered little then. There should be little doubt that the government would do it again, should it consider such measures necessary. Statutes are on the books making "hoarding" illegal in times of emergency. Survivalist stockpiling of food and medicines, much less guns and gold, would surely be considered hoarding in a declared emergency. Doubtless the defenders of public interest would seek to confiscate such stores if they could.

Earth penetrating tomography is an extremely new science, originating in the 1980s. A variety of systems have been tried in this attempt to peer into the earth, from mobile vehicles, helicopters and man-portable systems, all the way up to satellites. Much of the current research has focused on airborne radar systems. The Swedish National Defense Research Establishment, of Linkoeping, Sweden, is one organization in the forefront of this research. They designed an airborne system called CARABAS, which stands for "Coherent All Radio Band Sensing." They began construction of CARABAS in 1987, with the first radar tests taking place in 1992.

The Russians, as could be expected, have also experimented with a number of earth penetrating sensor systems. One paper by Igor V. Cherny of the Center for Program Studies, Moscow, describes the results of shipboard and airborne studies of some oceanic processes by means of EPT techniques.

In the United States several series of research projects were undertaken by the Massachusetts Institute of Technology's Lincoln Laboratory of Lexington, Massachusetts. These were undertaken in conjunction with the Swedish National Defense Research Establishment and the Institute for Defense Analyses, of Alexandria, Virginia. One such experiment was conducted 4-15 June, 1993, in the desert near Yuma, Arizona.

Several private sector researchers have also jumped on the earth penetrating band wagon, such as Airborne Environmental Surveys, of Santa Maria, California. Since 1992 they have used airborne radars in locating manmade objects in landfills, hazardous waste sites (some of which have contained unexploded ordnance), and tank farm leakage into underground water. Another private sector player is Coleman Research Corp. of Florida. They have developed a system they call EPRIS (Earth Penetration Radar Imaging System) which is also intended to find buried objects, contamination, and geological or hydrological features. They have been working with the Department of Energy.

Another of the many private firms working in this field is XADAR Corp. of Springfield, Virginia. Using their equipment, a team of archaeologists mapped out a subsurface prehistoric Indian village in Ohio; a survey crew in New York located buried containers of toxic chemicals before excavating; and mining engineers in several states have probed subterranean rock to identify hazardous formations.

One use that XADAR is focusing on is in the area of coal mining safety. Safety regulations require that core-hole drillings be taken at regular intervals so that the electrical, chemical and structural properties of the ground ahead can be determined. They hope that their radar profiles will prove at least as accurate in identifying water—or gas-filled cavities and in determining the structural integrity of mines, which could improve safety as well as substantially reducing costs and downtime for mine owners.

Lawrence Livermore National Laboratories of Livermore, California, also has gotten into the act by developing a variety of gadgets and processes. One airborne device was developed specifically for locating buried landmines. They also developed equipment and techniques for seeing through the concrete of bridges to judge their structural integrity.

NASA, too, has seen the value of this technology. Their LightSAR project is in the very earliest phases of development. As of 6 March, 1997, they had only reached the "studies" stage. A joint press release of that date from NASA Headquarters, Washington, D.C., and Jet Propulsion Laboratory (JPL), Pasadena, California, announced that this proposed satellite based system would:

...[P]rovide high-resolution images on a nearly continuous basis, giving the project considerable capability to map changes in land cover, generate topographic maps and provide long-term mapping of natural hazards such as earthquakes, floods and volcanoes.

The NASA/JPL press release stated that potential commercial applications for data collected by LightSAR could include: mapping and cartography, crop monitoring and health assessment, forestry management, resource exploration and environmental monitoring, including oil spills, and coastal zone monitoring.

Other nations are looking at using their satellites for EPT. In 1997 British scientists used satellite imaging to find an unexploded World War II 450 ton "block buster bomb" buried nine feet in the ground.

The severely underfunded Sandia National Labs of Albuquerque, New Mexico, is also trying to develop their own earth peepers. One system they have touted is called SISAR, for Subsurface-Imaging Synthetic-Aperture Radar. They appear to be attempting to get funding to go forward with designing a device that would be equally applicable to a diverse suite of uses, from nuclear weapons counterproliferation programs to environmental monitoring.

Sandia's research seems to indicate that VHF and UHF, perhaps as high as 1 GHz, are the most promising for their general purpose SISAR system. This is most interesting in view of the fact that HAARP can produce those same extremely high frequencies, yet the Air Force and Navy say they will not be operating in this range. They make this claim, perhaps, because that is the same radio frequency (RF) range that would be utilized for creating artificial ionospheric mirrors which could be used for over-the-horizon radar and intentional weather modification, both subjects being studiously avoided in HAARP literature.

As described in the February 1990 "Executive Summary" of the HAARP project:

> The use of very high power RF heaters to accelerate electrons... opens the way for the creation of substantial layers of ionization at altitudes where normally there are very few electrons. This concept already has been the subject of investigations by the Air Force (Geophysics Lab), the Navy (NRL), and DARPA. The Air Force, in particular, has carried the concept, termed Artificial Ionospheric Mirror (AIM), to the point of demonstrating its technical viability and proposing a new initiative to conduct proof-of-concepts experiments. The RF heater(s) being considered for AIM are in the 400 MHz-3 GHz range, much higher than the HF frequencies (1.5 MHz-15 MHz) suitable for investigating the other topics discussed in this summary. As such, the DOD program (HAARP) will not be directly involved with AIM-related ionospheric enhance-

ment efforts.

Maybe, maybe not. Because of HAARP's ability to up-convert frequencies (which I will explain in a moment), they can definitely achieve this range, if they so desire. Note their mention of the Air Force's desire to move forward with a proof-of-concepts design. Despite this denial, many researchers believe that HAARP is a proof-of-concepts mock-up—and a great deal more.

As you can see from the above thumbnail sketch of this emerging 21st century technology, there is a definite overlap of civilian and military uses for concrete and ground penetrating radar. This blurring of the distinctions between "sword" and "plowshare" gives the Conspiracy an exquisite means for hiding their purposes in plain sight.

While the majority of labs engaged in the development of EPT techniques have been pursuing research in high frequencies, a few have delved into the possibilities of using the other end of the spectrum: very low frequency (VLF) and extremely low frequency (ELF) for ground penetrating sensors. HAARP planners have decided to use the bottom of the electromagnetic spectrum, ELF, to do EPT.

American scientists associated with the HAARP project have already successfully demonstrated using ELF to do EPT. Some readers may have seen the BBC/A&E television program "Masters of the Ionosphere" which deals at length with HAARP. Dr. Dennis Papadopoulos was mis-identified by that TV show as a "chief scientist" on the HAARP project, which he is not. He is, however, a physics professor at the University of Maryland (one of the Universities involved in HAARP) and was a science consultant to APTI.

On the show he spoke enthusiastically of the first successful testing of atmospherically generated ELF for earth penetrating tomography. The show made it seem like he was talking about HAARP. He was not. His experiments were conducted using another ionospheric heater, HIPAS, the High Power Auroral Stimulation Observatory. One can think of HIPAS as an "older brother" of HAARP.

The HIPAS facility is run by the UCLA Plasma Physics Laboratory, and like HAARP, is engaged in the study of the ionosphere through the use of high power transmissions. It is located 25 miles east of Fairbanks, Alaska. HIPAS consists of eight 150 kW transmitters broadcasting from an eight element circular crossed-dipole antenna array. HIPAS operates at 2.85 and 4.53 MHz with an effective radiated power (ERP) of 84 megawatts at 2.85 MHz. Like HAARP, the site also includes several diagnostic instruments. Current projects at HIPAS include experiments in double frequency ELF/VLF (extremely low and very low

frequency) generation and in ion cyclotron excitation.

Dr. Papadopoulos told the show's reporter: "There was an experiment in which there was a particular old mine which was about 30 meters underground and we were trying to see whether we could really image it..." The HIPAS transmitter was used to produce ELF/VLF waves in the ionosphere. These waves were picked up by sensors as they returned from deep underground. After interpretation, they clearly revealed the old mining tunnel.

Dr. Papadopoulos told the camera:

> This was really the first test of the concept in the world and we were, I was actually amazed because usually a first experiment always fails. This experiment succeeded beyond our imagination. It is a fantastic remote sensing tool. I can do remote sensing of the ionosphere, of the ground, of the underground, of the seas. I can measure the temperature of the water. I think, you know, dreams that I have dreamt for the last, you know, 25 years are becoming reality and the first one happened two weeks ago. That was really, a sweet moment.

ELF and VLF are generated in the ionosphere naturally by lightening. Natural ELF/VLF has been used for some time to do EPT in searches for vast underground targets, like oil deposits. This experiment with HIPAS involved two novelties. One, it found a narrow tunnel, something far smaller than had previously been accomplished, and two, it used man-made ELF/VLF. It is expected that HAARP will be able to generate this same sort of ELF/VLF. HAARP does not need to affect the aurora to accomplish this. The real reason for having HAARP modulate the electrojet is the military purpose of communicating with submerged submarines. Ionospherically generated ELF/VLF can be used for EPT but not for sending messages. It is just "noise." To send submarines coherent messages the signal has to be coherent. Only an antenna, or a "virtual" antenna, can send messages.

The difficulty with broadcasting in the ELF range is the necessary length of the antenna. An antenna must be at least as long as the wavelength of the radio waves it is used to broadcast. Roughly, the wavelength is 10 meters for 30MHz waves, 100 meters for 3MHz waves, 10 kilometers for 30KHz waves, and 1,000 kilometers (600 miles) for 30Hz waves. The folks working on HAARP want to turn the aurora (that Senator Stevens is so enthusiastic about harnessing) into a virtual antenna thousands of miles long.

The earth is a giant magnet surrounded by invisible lines of force. Some of the incoming cosmic and solar radiation (such as from the solar wind) is trapped between these magnetic lines of force in the Van Allen Radiation Belts. Electrons also spiral around those magnetic lines of force. Most of these electrons are bounced back before entering the atmosphere, pulsing back and forth in space from one end of the earth to the other. This creates a flow of electrical current of tremendous power. Some of this flow does escape from the magnetosphere to stream down on the earth at the poles. This stream of electrons pouring to earth is called the electrojet. The electrojet is what causes the aurora, or Northern (and Southern) Lights. As these electrons cas-

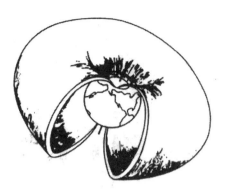

cade from space they heat the gases in the atmosphere to temperatures where they give off photons (light), creating the breath-taking displays of the aurora borealis in the northern hemisphere and the aurora australis in the southern.

"HAARP Research and Applications," an executive summary dating from June of 1995, produced by the Technical Information Division of the Naval Research Laboratory in Washington, D.C. said of the electrojet: "the auroral electro-dynamic circuit carries towards the earth .1 to 1 million mega-watts of power, equivalent to a hundred to a thousand large power plants." The power potentials that HAARP will attempt to tap into are truly enormous.

That document goes on to state what the HAARP high frequency (HF) transmitter should be able to do:

> ...[B]y exploring the properties of the auroral ionosphere as an active, non-linear medium the primary energy of the HF transmitter which is confined to a frequency range of 2.8 to 10 MHz can be down-converted in frequency to coherent low frequency waves spanning five decades, as well as up-converted to infra-red and visible photons. As a result the HAARP HF transmitter can generate sources for remote sensing and communications spanning sixteen decades in frequency.

This shows the deliberate misdirection of the current HAARP literature, which does all it can to downplay the true power of this transmitter in terms of what it can affect. By being able to rebroadcast anywhere in the non-ionizing (non-radioactive) segment of the electromagnetic spectrum, with a potential re-radiated broadcast power equal to, if not greater than all the TV and radio stations of the world combined, the HAARP array is utterly in a class of its own. Frankly, its potential exceeds the imaginations of many science fiction writers working today.

This sci-fi-like plan for HAARP to turn the electrojet into a virtual antenna is the primary method by which they plan to communicate with deeply submerged submarines. It has the added benefit of potentially producing far higher levels of man-made ELF/VLF with which to conduct nuclear counterproliferation studies (and targeting) using EPT. To use this application of HAARP, the signal broadcast from HAARP is beamed into the electrojet in an attempt to get the aurora to resonate, to match its vibrations, frequency, to that of the signal being sent from HAARP.

Most of us learned a little about radio in school. We daily use the phrases "AM" and "FM" to distinguish between the two most common bands of long wave radio transmission. Broadcasts from commercial radio stations use two different signals, one modulating the other. First is the carrier wave, the base frequency that the station operates at, the second wave is the message (voice or music) that modifies the carrier. AM (amplitude modulation), for example, changes the shape of the carrier wave. Radio stations with names like "Magic 104" or "Power 106.7" are referring to their assigned carrier frequency.

HAARP also has a range of carrier frequencies that it has been assigned by the National Telecommunications and Information Administration, a branch of the Department of Commerce. HAARP has been assigned to operate in the shortwave band between 2.8 and 10 MHz. Just as you hear a message of words or music that rides on the carrier wave, the HAARP HF signal is also modulated, sending a "message" to the aurora. The HAARP carrier wave will be modulated by a message in the ELF range.

HAARP Program Manager, John Heckscher, said in a phone interview with the authors of *Angels Don't Play This HAARP,* in February, 1995, that for the purposes of earth penetrating tomography, HAARP would use "in terms of frequency, like 10 or 20 Hertz, or maybe one Hertz, one cycle per second type waves." As Dr. Begich and Ms. Manning repeatedly pointed out in their book, and I feel compelled to do the same, this is the same frequency range at which the human brain works (0.5-40Hz). This broadcasting in the same range as we think opens the lid to a virtual Pandora's Box of possibilities for side-effects and abuse.

If they can get the electrojet to go into resonance with the signal being beamed from the HAARP transmitter, then the aurora will rebroadcast that

message, whatever it might be. The ultimate owners of HAARP would have a tool that "...can generate sources for remote sensing and communications spanning sixteen decades in frequency." Note that they specify "communications" as well as "remote sensing." This is how they plan to broadcast to deeply submerged submarines—and perhaps covertly into the heads of humans.

Were this rebroadcasting from the aurora to be used for civilian purposes, HAARP has more to offer than just scientific wisdom. It could add a great deal to the coffers of the U.S. Treasury through broadcast licensing, for example. This technology could be used to increase the number of transmission bandwidths (frequencies available for new TV and radio stations) by thousands of times. This, in fact, is one of the carrots being dangled before the civilian scientists at various universities to get them to participate in the program.

This is not the Navy's first try at using ELF to direct its submarine fleet. An earlier attempt to use ELF to talk to deeply submerged submarines was Project Sanguine, back in the 1960s. It was the baby of Nick Christofilos, a leading DOD scientist in the 1950s and '60s. He has been compared to Tesla both in intellect and in the bigness of his thinking. In Sanguine he intended to cover a good portion of the state of Wisconsin with wires, about 8 inches under the ground, creating an antenna 26,000 miles long to broadcast in the ELF range. An aggressive anti-ELF campaign blocked the construction of Christofilos' monster antenna system. The Navy did eventually get a drastically scaled-down version in 1988, but at the time it had only limited ability to communicate with submerged submarines. The failure of Sanguine is no doubt part of the Navy's desire to push forward with HAARP.

In 1968 Soviet scientists made public what they had known about ELF since the mid-50s. They announced that they had pinpointed which pulsed magnetic field frequencies help mental and physiological functioning and which do harm. As a result, in 1973, a Congressional subcommittee recommended that the Navy study the biological effects of Project Sanguine. The Navy declined. Keep in mind, the Navy is a co-operator of HAARP. The evidence is overwhelming, as I shall show, that the Navy is fully aware of the health risks of this technology and is blithely going forward with HAARP in spite of that knowledge.

Since the human brain works in the ELF range, there is a serious potential for this ELF technology being used in time of war to induce debilitating mental states or even disrupt mental function entirely in a target population, whether soldiers on a battlefield or civilians in a population center. Spooks, as agents of the intelligence community (spies) are called, are keenly interested in this technology, as well. It is possible that it may be capable of putting words directly into the heads of targeted individuals or even whole populations. If spooks or other minions of the Conspiracy do pull HAARP's strings, and, if it can modulate the electrojet into rebroadcasting their message, either down-converted into the ELF range or up-converted into the microwave range, then they can put their plans for screwing with people's heads to the ultimate test.

Operatives of the intelligence community have a driving passion to bend others to their wills, and have engaged in a continuous and ongoing search for tools to intellectually cripple and/or enslave humans, both as individuals and as whole populations, for decades, as I will attempt to prove in the upcoming chapter on mind control. Some have experimented with ELF and ULF mind control techniques, others have used microwave technology. Either way, HAARP would be a fabulous windfall for them. If only one of these two technologies panned out, they would be sitting with their collective finger on a button as potentially devastating as the President's nuclear launch button.

Using a smoke screen of euphemized terms, former CIA Director Richard Helms described that research, during Congressional hearings, as developing "sophisticated approaches to the 'coding' of information for transmittal to population targets in the 'battle for the minds of men'…" He admitted that scientists working on the CIA payroll were using "an approach integrating biological, social and physical-mathematical research in attempts… to control behavior." He described the "use of modern information theory, automata theory, and feedback concepts… for a technology for controlling behavior… using information inputs as causative agents." He was describing the CIA's mind control program MKUltra, which will be reviewed at greater length later.

Perhaps it is unpatriotic of me to suggest that the American intelligence community might use HAARP as a weapon against "We The People." Certainly the multinationals of the One World Conspiracy would have no such qualms. Dare we allow this technology to be developed by anyone, for any reason? Is this one of those weapons that is just too horrible to use, no matter how just the cause? One might ask, "What if it gets into the wrong hands?" But I wonder if it might not already be in those hands.

ELECTROMAGNETIC RADIATION AND HEALTH

In this use of the electrojet to rebroadcast in the ELF and/or microwave ranges we can clearly see an area where there is a significant potential medical danger in the HAARP project. Even if HAARP is not a CIA/DOD black project, if it really is just a scientific experiment, it is no less dangerous. A literal mountain of documentation has been generated by medical researchers in the last two decades showing unmistakable health hazards associated with electromagnetic radiation (EMR) exposure.

HAARP, if "just" science, clearly is science out of control. How dare they ignore the health risks to the people (and other life forms) living above the underground targets they plan to irradiate? What about all those who will receive the fallout of this EMR meant to penetrate to submarines? Even if they are not deliberately trying to fry our brains, they might still succeed in turning our grey matter into three-minute meals.

Literally hundreds of scientific papers have been produced showing health risks associated with EMR in the United States alone. One such, a 1971 report issued by a Presidential advisory council, stated "electromagnetic radiations emanating from radar, television, communications systems, microwave ovens, permeate the environment" and warned that "the consequences of undervaluing or misjudging the biological effects of long-term, low-level exposure could become a critical problem for the public health, especially if genetic effects are involved."

In 1975 U.S. Senator Gaylord Nelson forced the Navy to release research that showed that ELF transmissions can alter human blood chemistry. The following year, in 1976, Drs. Susan Bawin and W. Ross Adey showed that nerve cells are affected by ELF fields.

On 15 December, 1976, a seminar was convened in Washington, D.C. by the Electromagnetic Radiation Management Advisory Council. Dr. William M. Leach, chief of the experimental studies branch of the Bureau of Radiological Health's Division of Biological Effects, told the assembled scientists and government representatives about discoveries from a study conducted during the first six months of 1976. This research involved "easily demonstrable and easily quantified microwave effects on the lymphocytes and lymphocytic systems of mice, rabbits, and guinea pigs which had been exposed to low doses of radiation." Dr. Leach told them that up to 20% of the normal lymphocyte cells (white blood cells) in the irradiated animals underwent "blastic transformation," which means that the cells grew in size then divided into two. Dr. Leach then told the audience, "We have a word for that; the word is cancer."

In 1979 evidence on the dangers of EMR from power transmission lines made news when an epidemiological report by Nancy Wertheimer and Edward Leeper was released, linking possible health problems in humans to proximity exposure to power lines. Similar stories have appeared in the Australian press. The newspaper The Australian reported that "A British electricity authority is being sued over the death of a boy who allegedly developed cancer as he slept near high-voltage power cables." A Melbourne occupational medicine consultant, Dr. Bruce Hocking, found that "children living within about four kilometres of Syndney's main television towers had more than twice the rate of leukemia than children living outside the four-kilometre radius."

The Environmental Protection Agency released a summary of scientific reviews in December of 1990 which concluded that scientific evidence "suggests a causal link" between ELF electromagnetic fields and leukemia, lymphoma, and brain cancer. And, taking a conservative stance, it stated that ELF EMR is "a possible but not proven, cause of cancer in Humans."

This "possible but not proven" statement was in fact, a lie. This was revealed by Time, in its 30 July, 1990 issue under the heading of "Technology," on page 53. The article "Hidden Hazards of the Airwaves, An obscure newsletter uncovers the perils of the information age" read in part:

In the current issue of *Microwave News*, [Louis] Slesin has printed what may be his greatest scoop: the key paragraph of a two-year Environmental Protection Agency Study recommending that so-called extremely low-frequency fields be classified as 'probable human carcinogens' alongside such notorious chemical toxins as PCBs, formaldehyde and dioxin [was deliberately omitted].

The recommendation to classify ELF as a probable cancer causing agent could have set off a costly chain of regulatory actions. *Time* reported that the recommendation was deleted from the final draft after review by the White House Office of Policy Development. *Time* further stated:

Louis Slesin's [*Microwave News*] stories have a tendency to shock. Like the one about the 23 workers of the Bath Iron Works in Bath, ME, who got "sunburns" one rainy day when someone on a Navy frigate flicked on the ship's radar. Or the trash fires that start spontaneously from time to time near the radio and TV broadcast antennas in downtown Honolulu. Or the pristine suburb of Vernon, NJ, that has both one of the world's highest concentrations of satellite transmitting stations and a "persistent" and unexplained cluster of Down's syndrome cases.

Why have these stories not made front page news? Is this evidence of a conspiracy to manage the news we read? Why have scientists failed to speak out? As "Microwave News," an industry trade paper, expressed it:

...[T]he atmosphere in this field has been corrupted by dependence on industry and the military for funding. In such an environment, there is great pressure, both explicit and silent, to be a "team player." Those who never offend the patrons of research become known as responsible and objective—part of the scientific mainstream. Those who follow the data wherever it goes can be marginalized, and find it harder to get grants.

This leads to silence, even in the face of blatant attacks on scientific inquiry. When Dr. Gilles Theriault of McGill University reported a tenfold increase in lung cancer risk among utility workers with the greatest exposures to high-frequency transients, the study's sponsor, Hydro-Quebec, blocked his access to the data. Imagine what would happen if Dow Chemical reacted that way to a pesticide study. Yet not a single member of the EMF [electromagnetic frequency] community publicly condemned Hydro-Quebec's outrageous behavior.

Research can be sabotaged in other, less obvious ways. For example, studies of EMF health effects are rarely followed up, even when they point to significant risks. Dr. Eugene Sobel of the University of Southern California has linked EMF exposure to three- to-fourfold increases in the risk of Alzheimer's disease in four different worker populations. Dr. Anthony Miller of the University of Toronto has found that when both electric and magnetic fields are taken into account, EMF exposures on the job are linked to a leukemia risk up to 11 times higher than expected. In both cases, interest in funding further study has been less than overwhelming.

With good reason, scientists trust a result only after it has been independently replicated. Studies that had not been repeated were ignored by the NAS-NRC [National Academy of Sciences-National Research Council] EMF panel. So without funding for replication, Sobel's and Miller's work can be ignored.

Of course, lip service is paid to the need for follow-up. The president of EPRI declared that Dr. Genevieve Matanoski's results on cancer among telephone line workers "clearly warrant further study." Yet when Matanoski, of Johns Hopkins University, sought funding for such research, EPRI's checkbook stayed closed.

Criticizing the powers-that-be is not considered a smart career move. You can find yourself labeled an ideologue, or even a purveyor of "junk science"—when, in fact, this better describes those who want to shut down EMF research.

Bioelectromagnetics researchers believe they have little to gain by taking part in public disputes. Many honest researchers just keep their heads down and get funding wherever they can. Other talented scientists have quietly left the field.

This practice of having one's findings not rock the boss' boat is hardly a new situation. Over a century ago, in 1873, Lord Jessel wrote:

> Expert evidence... is evidence of persons who sometimes live by their business, but in all cases are remunerated for their evidence... Now it is

natural that his mind, however honest he may be, should be biased in favor of the person employing him, and accordingly we do find such bias.

A few brave scientists have come forward with evidence that the establishment (industrial and scientific) would rather not see. One such is Dr. W. Ross Adey, a neurologist from the

Veterans Affairs Medical Centre in Loma Linda, California. He told *New Scientist* magazine that there is now a "powerful body of impressive evidence" to suggest that very low exposure to EMFs has subtle, long-term effects on human health. "The sensitivity of the brain and its mechanisms to these fields is the key to understanding this issue."

In the 440-page HAARP Final Environmental Impact Statement (FEIS); the 17-page Record of Decision, HAARP Final Environmental Impact Statement; and in all the official public releases since, the government has consistently ignored the old adage "what goes up must come down." Their favorite technique is the old confidence game misdirection dodge of overexplaining the obvious in hopes of the subject of the con missing the obscure.

An example of this is from the March 1996 HAARP Fact Sheet where, under the heading of "Are these transmission [sic] harmful?," they answer:

> Because the IRI beam will be directed upward, rather than toward the horizon, radio field strength at ground level, including directly under the antenna array, are calculated to be smaller than Radio Frequency Radiation (RFR) standards allow for human exposure. This is possible because the individual transmitters are spaced apart over 33 acres so that the concentration of radio fields never exceeds the RFR standards. Radio field strengths on the ground around the array were measured during the April 1995 tests of the Development Prototype, and show good agreement with the calculations. At the point of closest public access on the Tok Highway, the measured fields are ten-thousand times smaller than permitted by the RFR standards and one-thousand times smaller than typically found near AM broadcast station antennas.

Okay, what about the energies rebroadcast from the aurora? No mention.

What about possible changes in the density of the ionosphere "accidentally" letting cosmic radiation through? No mention.

The FEIS admits that "80-90 percent of the experiments would employ the IRI in modes that refract fundamental radio frequency energy Earthward from the ionosphere." What will be the impact of this EMR returned to earth? No mention. What about those RFR standards, how safe are they really? No mention.

From another official HAARP document, "HAARP Frequently Asked Questions" comes:

Are there any health hazards due to fields produced by HAARP?

The health and safety of the public (and of the scientific researchers who will be present at the site) has
been a primary focus in the design of the HAARP
IRI. There are no locations on-site where the E-M
fields exceed standards for RFR exposure as defined
by the IEEE and adopted by the ANSI (C95.1-1991).
In fact, the E-M fields measured at the closest public
access to the site are lower than those existing in many
urban environments.

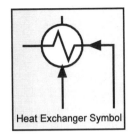

Heat Exchanger Symbol

Will HAARP be used to generate ELF?

Previous experience at other facilities has shown that it is possible to
generate a small but useful ELF signal through ionospheric heating. This
field will be more than one and a half billion times weaker than the
Earth's background field and about one million times weaker than the
level where researchers have reported biological effects in the literature. The field is so weak, in fact, that sophisticated instruments must
be used to observe it, yet it is still quite useful for many applications.

Health, or hype? Here, I believe, they are speaking of ELF generated in
regions of the ionosphere excited by RF heating, such as in the above mentioned experiment using HIPAS, and not the aurorally rebroadcast ELF transmission of vastly greater magnitude that would be used to communicate to
submarines.

An amazing case of parallel lies is seen in the cellular phone industry. A
mobile, or cellular, phone is a mini-radio transmitter that sends microwaves
to a receiving point—usually a tower 50 to 300 feet tall—a few hundred yards
to a few miles away. That industry uses a nearly identical script to tell local
officials how safe their transponder tower's emissions are. They use that same
"hundreds to thousands of times" below standards set by the appropriate
federal agency crap.

Cell towers are so new that, of the many studies being done, no studies
have yet measured the long-term health effects. Much less have they studied
the effects of the combined wash of EMR we are bathed in daily. We live in a
soup of non-ionizing radiation coming from hundreds of radio and television
broadcasts; the electromagnetic grids of the power lines in the walls of our
homes and above and below our streets; and from home and work electronics
like TV sets, personal computers and microwave ovens. Individually, each
unit meets some arbitrary Threshold Limit Value (TLV) set by some government engineer in some federally funded lab. However, we know zip about
their combined effects. Much less does anybody have a clue as to what will
happen when HAARP is added to this EMR stew.

On 3 June, 1996 the *London Times* of London, England, in an article cap-
tioned "Mobile phone users 'face cancer risk'" reported that scientists work-

ing in Australia, America and Stockholm would be presenting evidence of the health risks associated with cellular phones that night on the BBC 1 television program *Watchdog HealthCheck*. They reported that the experiments conducted by these scientists indicated a link between the microwave transmissions of cell phones and such diseases as asthma, Alzheimer's disease and cancer. Among those interviewed on the program were neuroscientists from the University of Washington, Seattle, who observed damage to DNA in the brain cells of rats as a result of exposure to microwave radiation similar to that emitted by mobile phones.

Two of the six scientists presented on the show said they had stopped using mobile phones and the rest said they did so "only when essential." As I write this, there are several American citizens bringing personal injury claims against mobile phone companies. Perhaps as a way out, a telephone industry group has put up a $25 million fund for research into the health effects of microwaves and cell phones—do you think these scientists will discover things their employers do not like?

In the same news story, *The London Times* reported that Volkswagen UK has issued a warning to each new car buyer not to use a mobile phone inside the vehicle because the company had concluded that the electromagnetic fields generated by cell phones were injurious to health.

A year later *The Sunday Times* reported on 21 September, 1997 that "[m]obile phones can be [a] cause of memory loss." Scientists at the National Radiological Protection Board (NRPB), the British government agency responsible for researching radiation hazards, were reported to have "accepted [that] mobile phone radiation could alter the way human brain cells worked."

Dr. John Stather, Deputy Director of the NRPB was quoted as saying: "Until recently we believed any harmful effects from microwaves were due to their heating effects, which would be negligible at the low powers used by mobile phones. Now there might be another effect at work and we are much less certain." The *Times* article ended with this chilling observation: "The findings that low-level microwave radiation of the kind emitted by mobile phones can damage short-term memory and concentration could explain why the devices are so often associated with road accidents."

The Air Force, like the Navy, is aware of the biological effects of EM fields, at least at some levels. For example, Dr. Cletus Kanavy, chief of the biological effects group of the Phillips Laboratory's Electromagnetic Effects Division at Kirkland Air Force Base in New Mexico, has stated that "the entire issue of human interaction with electromagnetic (RF & microwave) radiation is... a major national population health concern."

Dr. Kanavy noted that there is a "large amount of data, both animal experimental and human clinical, to support the existence of chronic, nonthermal effects." These effects include behavioral aberrations (mental disorder), fetal (embryonic) tissue damage (inducing birth defects), cataractogenesis (causing the formation of cataracts, i.e., blindness), altered blood chemistry, metabolic changes and suppression of the endocrine and immune systems (artificial AIDS).

More than ample experimental evidence exists from credible researchers from well-established and highly regarded institutions, both in government and at the university level, to justify a national research program into the full spectrum of biological effects of electromagnetic radiation. The Air Force's reliance on standards established by the Institute of Electrical and Electronics Engineers (IEEE) to downplay the likelihood of adverse bioeffects is seriously misplaced. In discussing the IEEE and the issue of bioeffects, Dr. Kanavas states:

> The United States has lagged behind badly in this kind of research. Initially, the principal concern for human exposure to microwave radiation was that of thermal heating of the tissues. Permissive exposure limits were based on such criteria. These limits... are... derived by the... IEEE. Under IEEE, a blue-ribbon panel of experts periodically reviews the research database and assesses the need to revise the standards. Until 1991, these standards did not consider the possible biological effects of "pulsed" microwaves. The 1991 standards do address the pulse condition (rather shabbily, I believe), place [some] restrictions... and continue to use the continuous wave time averaging technique for thermal criteria. The existence of non-thermal effects is essentially denied by omission... The literature published in the late 1980s is abundant with information on nonthermal effects which are produced at levels below the [IEEE-derived] standards.

As Trustees for Alaska put it:

> Perhaps the Air Force rejected full consideration and analysis of the biological effects of ELF fields in 1993 (when the Air Force issued its Record of Decision (ROD) for HAARP) due to the rather cutting-edge nature of then-available information. This excuse no longer exists. Scientific understanding of bioeffects has evolved now to the point where the Air Force can no longer deny its existence or simply dismiss this information as "not universally accepted by the large majority of the research community." Final EIS Vol. I at 3-147. This is especially true when the Air Force's own expert states that bioeffects are a "major population health concern." NEPA [The National Environmental Policy Act] regulations mandate the preparation of a supplemental EIS when there "are significant new circumstances or information relevant to environ-

mental concerns and bearing on the proposed action or its impacts." 40 C.F.R. Sec. 1502.9(c)(1). The scientific information on the bioeffects of ELF fields, coupled with the fact that HAARP causes ELF fields, mandates that the Air Force supplement the HAARP EIS.

For decades the government has acted as though it knew all there was to know about the health issues associated with what ever new technology they were fiddling around with. As ridiculous as that may seem, even more absurd is the general public's unquestioning acceptance of such nonsense. The government told us DDT was safe. They told us above ground nuclear testing was safe. They told us tobacco cigarettes were safe. Now they claim that blanketing us in EMR is safe. Do you feel safe from these assurances?

OTHER CONCERNS

Nor is health, physical and mental, the only area of concern with HAARP beaming gigawatts of energy into the ionosphere, and from there back to earth. As noted in a HAARP fact sheet:

> ...[S]ince the sun's radiation creates and maintains the ionosphere, sudden variations in this radiation such as those caused by solar flares can affect the performance of radio systems. Sometimes the changes are sufficient to induce large transient currents in electric power transmission grids, causing widespread power outages.

HAARP is designed to duplicate solar phenomena. It is certainly not inconceivable that it, too, will cause power outages. For some, a power outage is merely an inconvenience. For others it can mean damaged electronic equipment, particularly computers; doctors forced to operate by flash light; and, as in the infamous blackouts of New York City, it often means rape, burglary and murder. Are you prepared to let some scientist tinkering with the aurora turn out your lights?

A widely recognized military potential of HAARP is that it could be used to jam all enemy (and non-belligerent) nations' radio communications, while keeping the DOD's own secret bands open. Changes in the shape of the ionosphere, alter its ability to propagate radio waves. This has been known for many decades. Scientists have been using high power transmitters to deliberately "perturb" the ionosphere for nearly as long. Fear of possible disruption of regular radio communications has folks out in the Alaskan bush in an uproar over HAARP. There, sometimes hundreds of miles from the closest road (or even near a road made impassible by winter snow), being able to get a radio message through to a medical emergency air ambulance service literally means life or death. While HAARP's operators claim to have taken elaborate precautions, there is still a very real possibility of accidental jamming. What if they plan to do it on purpose?

There is yet another important environmental question left unanswered by HAARP literature and its botched EIS—what about migratory species? They threw up a fence around the site to keep out animals (including humans). But what about birds flying through HAARP's intense RF beam? The HAARP site was nearly half wetlands, in a vast stretch of nearly flat, wet "bush." The wetlands were filled in, the "dispensable" spruce cut down. HAARP is located in the heart of a prime waterfowl migratory path! The FEIS acknowledges this. It states that HAARP "lies within the Copper River Basin, which is one of Alaska's more important migration corridors." And yet it insists that "no significant impacts to birds would result from the construction of the HAARP facility." The most they did was to propose putting some colored streamers on the antenna masts to help reduce the number of birds flying into them!

Salmon, caribou and other migratory species may be affected by HAARP as well. That is because altering the electrojet may cause alterations of the earth's magnetic field. This little noted side effect of modulating the electrojet may have profound and unseen consequences for "spaceship" earth and its passengers. The magnetically-sensitive material magnetite has been found in salmon and caribou brains and in a special organ for sensing direction in the noses of some waterfowl. It has also been found in the human brain.

There may already have been deaths attributable to HAARP, or perhaps to its "cousin," the Russian Woodpecker. Thousands of individuals of a migratory species of turtle "forgot" to migrate south in the fall of 1995 and died in the frigid North Atlantic; something that has never happened in recorded history.

The February 1994 issue of the Alaskan monthly *Bush Blade* carried comments by the late geomagnetic researcher Lloyd Zirbes, who strongly opposed HAARP. He wrote:

> [D]isruption of the Earth's magnetic field will complete damages done by the nuclear bomb blasts in the natural radiation belts. Earth's magnetic field keeps the planet in balance.
>
> Projected results of the HAARP project may include disturbance of the circadian rhythms of human beings and increased exposure to radiation as the magnetic field is attenuated.

The May 1992 issue of *Discovery Magazine* discussed what might result from disrupting the Earth's internal "dynamo" and altering the upper atmosphere's magnetic belts, saying:

[HAARP could] create a premature reversal of the magnetic poles, worsen the newly discovered wobble of the Earth, and possibly create a total polar reversal or Earth shift. During at least one [previous] reversal, magnetic north may have changed direction by as much as 4 to 8 degrees in a single day.

In 1988 scientists at the U.S. Naval Observatory and at the Jet Propulsion Laboratory announced that the earth had developed a wobble in its spin. The cause of that wobble is still unknown. Some suspect that it was caused by the Russian Woodpecker signal. What effect, if any, HAARP may have on the magnetic pole or that wobble are equally unknown. Do we want the DOD to get that answer the hard way?

During a reversal of the magnetic pole the strength of the earth's magnet field would collapse, then rebuild in the opposite polarity. During the period of collapse and rebirth of the field, the earth would be without the protection of the magnetosphere. The only living things to survive would be deep in the earth or the sea. Humanity, and virtually all species that live exposed to the sky would be wiped out by the flood of hard radiation from the sun and space. Changes in the earth's interior are known to affect the magnetoshpere. If the reverse is also the case, the magnetosphere affecting the interior, then ignorant or intentional misuse of HAARP has the potential to virtually wipe out life on earth.

Clare Zickuhr is a former ARCO employee, ham radio operator, and the founder of the Alaskan group No-HAARP. In speaking of the HAARP scientists and what their experiments with the ionosphere will accomplish, he said: "They don't know what it will do." He further commented that what they want to do with their sky zapper is "kick the atmosphere real hard and watch what happens."

Of course, fears about damage to the atmosphere are unfounded according to John Heckscher, of the Air Force's Phillips Laboratory, who is the principal government spokesman for HAARP. Heckscher is reported to have told *Microwave News* in a telephone interview that "It's not unreasonable to expect that something three times more powerful than anything that's previously been built might have unforeseen effects, but that's why we do Environmental Impact Statements."

The only problem is, HAARP's EIS is pretty much "doo-doo" because, while it very carefully covers the effects broadcast out from the HAARP transmitter, it largely ignores any effects returning to earth from the atmospheric regions affected by HAARP. This is either incredible stupidity or carefully planned misdirection.

If it is just ignorance, then we need to wake them up. Every 4th of July several people are killed because some bean-brained people fired their guns into the air, forgetting that their bullets have to come down someplace. We need to act before HAARP can accidentally drop EMR bullets into our brains.

If it is a lie, as I suspect, we need to find out why they are lying and what it is they don't want us to know. Contrary to the old adage, what you don't know can sometimes kill you. Remember Michael Unum's discovery of gamma ray detectors spiking off the scale during an (alleged) test of HAARP, washing the Nevada Test Site (at the least) with deadly gamma radiation.

HAARP literature and spokesfools insist that HAARP is not a weapon and will not be used as a weapon. Yet, in 1994 the Senate Committee on Armed Services stated that:

> The committee is aware of the promising results of the high frequency active auroral research program (HAARP). This transmitter in Alaska... would permit the detection and precise location of tunnels, shelters, and other underground shelters. The absence of such a capability has been noted as a serious weakness in the Department of Defense plans for precision attacks on hardened targets...

Perhaps the scope on a sniper's rifle is not a weapon, either. HAARP has many potential military uses, as we shall see in upcoming chapters. We have seen in just this one application of HAARP several serious threats to health and liberty. Unfortunately, we have just scratched the surface of the threat posed by HAARP.

Part Two:
"Non-Conventional Weapons"

In the Senate Report referencing the counterproliferation purposes of HAARP, the Senate also recommended substantial appropriations for HAARP under the heading "advanced weapons" (104th Congress, 1st session, Report 104-24 at 190 (July 28, 1995)). The Committee provided no explanation for this appropriation.

"Advanced weapons" is certainly not within the purposes claimed for HAARP by the DOD. In several public forums, the Air Force and other project participants have repeatedly assured the public that there is no "classified" component of HAARP. Thus, if indeed there were an "advanced weaponry" aspect to HAARP, and if the Air Force's statements about HAARP being an "open-project" are true, then the Air Force would have to tell us about its being an advanced weapons system, wouldn't they? Well, they are not telling us any such thing, so there must be a lie there somewhere. If HAARP is an advanced weapons project then they must be lying about being open and unclassified, no? If it is an "advanced weapon," what type of weapon is it?

Today there is a growing "directed-energy weapons" (DEW) arsenal. This technology is generally discussed in the media under the heading of "nonlethal" weaponry. The most recent push to develop this technology began at the very end of the 1980s as military strategists began to re-think warfare in the post-Cold War era.

Several major publications have discussed American behavior control weapons, such as Barbara Opall's article "U.S. Explores Russian Mind-Control Technology," in *Defense News*, January, 1993, or Sam Walker's "'Nonlethal Weapons', James Bond Style," that appeared in the *Christian Science Monitor*, 6 Sept., 1994. However, this technology is described in only the broadest detail. Research is highly classified and scientists face prison terms and other penalties for disclosing classified weapons research.

With the breakup of the Soviet Union, however, international and Russian newspapers have published many articles on this developing technology. Take for example Owen Matthews' article "Report: Soviets Used Top-Secret 'Psychotronic' Weapons," which appeared in the *Moscow Times* on 11 July, 1995. It reported on the work of journalist Yury Vorobyovsky, who for three years, had been investigating a top secret program of "psychotronic" brainwashing techniques developed by the KGB. These techniques included "debilitating high frequency radio waves, hypnotic computer-scrambled sounds and mind-bending electromagnetic fields, as well as an ultrasound gun capable of killing a cat at fifty meters..." These techniques had originally been developed for medical purposes, Vorobyovsky claimed, but had since been adapted into weapons.

"Official confirmation," Matthews wrote, "was first hinted at in the 1991 Soviet budget, which mentioned that 500 million rubles of the State Security Budget had been spent on 'psychological warfare technology' over an unspecified period of years..." Matthews also reported that Former State Security and Interior Minister General Viktor Barannikov, who had been sacked for supporting the 1993 coup attempt, warned in an Interior Ministry memorandum that he had information that the Russian Mafia had acquired the technology.

Matthews reported that the Russian parliament, the Duma, was taking the matter seriously enough to draft a law on "security of the individual," which will impose state controls on all equipment in private hands that can be used as "psychotronic weaponry." This would make Russia the second country to outlaw such equipment specifically; the only other one is Bulgaria.

"The law is pre-emptive," said Vladimir Lopatkin, chairman of the drafting committee. "The equipment that now exists in laboratories must be very strictly controlled to prevent it from being sold to the private sector."

Stolitsa, a major Russian newspaper, reported that Victor Sedletsky, a scientist from Kiev, claimed that the practical testing of "new kind[s] of weapons based on the impact of certain frequencies on the human body" occurred back in 1965. In what may be a reference to the Russian Woodpecker, *Stolista* reported that "...the development of an entirely new radar system allowing one to control any place on the globe began in 1982. Such equipment could be used for creating a 'psychotronic field' for brain-control."

The Soviet Union is known to have invested huge sums of time and money into investigating exotic technology. A search of the Soviet technical press has turned up that there was a consensus among Soviet EMR researchers that a beam, such as the one focused on the U.S. Embassy in Moscow, could produce blurred vision and loss of mental concentration. In 1976, *The Boston Globe* reported that the U.S. Ambassador to the U.S.S.R., Walter Stoessel, "developed a rare blood disease similar to leukemia and was suffering headaches and was suffering bleeding from the eyes. Two of his irradiated predecessors, Ambassador Charles Bohlen and Ambassador Llewellyn Thompson, died of cancers."

Project Pandora went beyond merely detecting the bombardment of our embassy in Moscow. Monkeys were brought into the embassy and exposed to it. They developed blood composition anomalies and unusual chromosome counts. Embassy personnel were found to have a 40 percent higher-than-average white blood cell count. While Project Pandora's data gathering proceeded, embassy personnel continued working in the facility and were not informed of the bombardment until 10 years after the signal was detected. Embassy employees were eventually granted a 20 percent hardship allowance for their service in an unhealthful post.

Not being the sort to pass up a good thing when they saw one, the CIA apparently considered the Soviets to be doing them a favor in providing them with test equipment at no cost and unwitting test subjects. In shocking disregard for the health and safety of fellow Americans, the CIA used the Moscow signal as an opportunity to gather data on the psychological and biological effects of microwave beams on the embassy personnel throughout the period of bombardment (which was still ongoing as of 1992).

After the bombardment of the American Embassy in Moscow became headline news, other agencies of the U.S. government began their own examinations into the effects of the Moscow signal. One such agency was the Defense Advanced Research Projects Agency (DARPA). DARPA, you may recall is one of the original members of the HAARP team and is now heavily involved in developing electromagnetic weaponry.

The 1987 issue of *Soviet Military Power*, a Pentagon publication, warned that the Soviets might be close to "a prototype short-range tactical RF weapon." *The Washington Post* reported that year that the Soviets had used such weapons to kill goats at a range of one kilometer. The U.S. military it turns out, has been pursuing similar devices since the 1960s.

Daniel Brandt, in his 1996 article "Mind Control and the Secret State" wrote:

Nonlethal technology becomes important in a discussion of mind control, as it involves something very close to it, in a form which might be used to control large populations. The propaganda aspect of "humanitarian warfare" is merely a sideshow; it's the technology itself that enlists the enthusiasm of Pentagon planners and law enforcement officials. Much of this "friendly force" technology involves electromagnetic fields and directed-energy radiation, and ultrasound or infrasound weapons—the same technology that's currently of interest in brain-stimulation and mind-control research.

A partial list of aggressive promoters of this new technology includes Oak Ridge National Lab, Sandia National Laboratories, Science Applications International Corporation, MITRE Corporation, Lawrence Livermore National Lab, and Los Alamos National Laboratory. In the 1996 defense authorization bill, Congress earmarked $37.2 million to investigate nonlethal technologies.

Note that MITRE Corporation, which prepared portions of HAARP's Environmental Impact Studies is involved in this research. Another smoking antenna?

Oak Ridge National Laboratory was one of the prime locations for the development of the atomic bomb and is today one of the "aggressive promoters" of nonlethal weapons mentioned above. They produced the following press release:

PHYSIOLOGICAL RESPONSES APPLICABLE TO DEVELOPMENT OF LESS-THAN-LETHAL WEAPONS
Sponsored by National Institute of Justice
Oak Ridge National Laboratory
Less-than-lethal weapons have a variety of applications in law enforcement, including rescuing hostages, stopping fleeing felons, and quelling prison disturbances. The National Institute of Justice is sponsoring a broad program to develop new techniques for "friendly force" as an alternative to the use of deadly force. As part of this program, Oak Ridge National Laboratory (ORNL) is examining approaches based on

known physiological responses to certain types of stimuli. These "weapons" would temporarily incapacitate an individual or a group with no lasting physiological damage. These concepts are based on ORNL's experience and expertise in biological-based systems and biophysical responses, particularly in evaluating the physical responses of humans to a variety of chemical, physical and radiological agents. ORNL also has extensive experience and expertise in risk analysis and in risk assessment and modeling.

The ORNL less-than-lethal weapons project sponsored by the National Institute of Justice began in September 1993. The following tasks are being performed:

Locate and compile data from tests, accidents, medical literature, etc. on biological and biophysical responses to energetic stimuli (such as electromagnetic fields). Analyze the information and identify promising candidate mechanisms for further development for a friendly force application. Evaluate the applicability of the proposed approaches to several realistic scenarios (such as hostage rescue or riot control).

ORNL has already examined several possible concepts for less-than-lethal weapons based on known physiological responses to energetic stimuli, including a thermal gun, a seizure gun, and a magnetophosphene gun. A thermal gun would have the operational effect of heating the body to 105 to 107°F, thereby incapacitating any threat, based on the fact that even a slight fever can affect the ability of a person to perform even simple tasks. This approach is built on four decades of research relating radio frequency exposure to body heating. A seizure gun would use electromagnetic energy to induce epileptic-like seizures in persons within the range of a particular electromagnetic field. The magnetophosphene gun is designed around a biophysical mechanism which evokes a visual response and is thought to be centered in the retina, known as magnetophosphenes. This effect is experienced when a person receives a blow to the head and sees "stars." This same effect can be produced with electromagnetic energy. While there are a number of technical challenges to be overcome in building devices of these types, less-than-lethal weapons based on physiological responses to energetic stimuli would provide a safe and effective means of dealing with a number of law enforcement situations where use of deadly force is not desirable.

Each military branch has its own labs working up nonlethal weapons as well. For example:

ARL [Army Research Laboratory] is the designated leader for the

Army's rf directed-energy weapon (DEW) technology based program. This includes both high-power microwave (HPM) and non-nuclear EMP [electromagnetic pulse] (NNEMP). ARL has a continuing interest in a broad spectrum of research in these areas, including: (1) a better understanding of the susceptibility of developmental and fielded systems to attack by an rf DEW threat; (2) improved methods and technologies for hardening systems against that threat; and (3) the development of new components (sources, pulsers, and antennas) for possible future application in an rf weapon system. Such weapon systems can cause an electronic kill by coupling sufficient energy into a system to damage critical electronic or electro-optic components.

Studies on this subject have come from outside military circles as well. In 1993, for example, ARPA (Advanced Research Projects Agency) provided grant money to regional business alliances (comprised of civilian-sector businesses and government organizations) to develop new technologies, including non-lethal weaponry.

Civilian think tanks have also gotten into the act. One example of such was a white paper published in 1991 by the U.S. Global Strategy Council—a Washington-based organization, under the chairmanship of Ray Cline, former Deputy Director of the CIA, who maintains very close ties with the U.S. intelligence community. This "white paper" describes the foreign and domestic uses foreseen for laser weapons, isotropic radiators, infrasound, non-nuclear electromagnetic pulse generators, high-powered microwave emitters, and similarly exotic sounding toys.

The Congressional Research Service of The Library of Congress periodically prepares reports at the request of Congress Members and Congressional Committees. One such was report number 95-974 S, dated 14 September, 1995, "Nonlethal Weapons and Operations: Potential Applications and Practical Limitations." It was prepared by John M. Collins, a Senior Specialist in the National Defense Office of Senior Specialists. In it he said:

> Nonlethal weapons and operations (NLW), whether employed for offensive or defensive purposes, usually supplement rather than replace lethal instruments. They are designed to minimize fatalities among belligerents and non-combatants as well as unplanned damage to property during wars and so-called operations other than war. One important purpose, which accommodates policies of restraint with overwhelming power, is to expand options, complicate enemy decision making, and thereby promote greater freedom of action in the gap between relatively benign pressures (diplomacy, economic sanctions, military posturing), and deadly force. This brief report summarizes technological progress, potential operations, and practical constraints... (A few non-

lethal weapons now are available for use by U.S. Armed Forces or could be in short notice, but a rich variety of innovated additions deliverable by manned aircraft, missiles, remotely piloted vehicles, motor transports, ships, and/or individuals is under development (see table).

NONLETHAL WEAPONS
Selected by Types and Characteristics

Categories	Typical Types	Primary Field Targets(1)	Land Mobile(2)	Testing Feasible(3)
Biological Biodegrading	Microbes	I,M	Variable	1-4 yr
Chemical Irritants	(CS; Pepper Spray)	P	Yes	Complete
Calmatives; Tranquilizers		P	Yes	1-4 yr
Adhesives	("Stickums")	M,P	Variable	1-4 yr
Antitraction	("Slickums")	M,P	Variable	1-4 yr
Binding Agents	(Fibers, Polymers)	I	Variable	1 yr
Combustion Modifiers		I,M	Yes	1-3 yr
Metal Embrittle-ments/Caustics		M	Yes	> 5 yr
Odiferous Agents		P	Yes	1-4 yr
Specialty Foam		P	Variable	< 1 yr
Electro-magnetic High-powered Microwave		I,M	Variable	1-4 yr
Nonnuclear Electro-magnetic Pulse		M,I	Variable	1-4 yr
Conductive Ribbons		M,I	Variable	Complete
Directed Energy Particle Beams		M,I	Variable	3-5 yr
Thermal Counter-Sniper Counter Mortar		P,I,M	Yes	1-4 yr
Barriers		P	Yes	1-4 yr
Acoustics High Intensity Sound		P	Yes	Complete
Infrasound, Ultra-sound	(VLF, VHF)	P	Yes	< 1 yr
Electric Stun Stun Guns; TASERS		P	Yes	Complete;<1yr
Water Cannons		P	Yes	Complete
Kinetic Nonpenetrating Projectiles		P	Yes	< 1 yr
Optical Low Energy Lasers		M,P	Yes	< 1 yr
Strobe Lights		P	Yes	< 1 yr
Holographs		P	Yes	1-4 yr
Directional & Omni-directional Flares		M,P	Yes	2 yr
Informational Computer Software Corruption		M,I	Unnecessary	Now
Voice Cloning		P	Unnecessary	2 yr

---

1. I = Infrastructure; M = Material; P = Personnel 2. Land Mobility varies with models. Weight, volume, distance to target, and enemy defenses are key considerations. 3. Feasible test dates may a bit optimistic. Availability commonly depends on complexities and funding.)

Nonlethal antipersonnel weapons such as malodorous substances, nonpenetrating projectiles, stun guns, water cannons, and ear-splitting noises need no explanation. High-powered microwaves can melt electronic components; strobe lights may disorient individuals; holograms may confuse them; aqueous foams can fill enclosures and form barriers. Voice cloning makes it possible to simulate radio broadcasts by enemy officials as a specialized form of psychological operations. Embrittlements that break down molecular bonding in metals, super caustics that attack many otherwise immune materials, biodegrading bacteria that "eat" products such as petroleum, and low energy lasers that blind hostile sensors typify nonlethal weapons that primarily attack inanimate targets. Multipurpose implements like "slickums" and "stickums" could engage personnel and property. Each type, if and when perfected, will possess unique strengths and weaknesses compared with other lethal and nonlethal tools.

U.S. Armed Forces have as yet put few sophisticated nonlethal weapons to practical tests. Marines, for example, deployed with a small assortment during the February withdrawal of U.N. peacekeepers from Somalia, but use was limited to a little sticky foam. Nearly all NLW, however, hypothetically may be applied under conditions short of armed combat and to deter, defend against, or defeat military aggression of any kind, sometimes independently, but most often as ancillaries to other arms (lethal means might often constitute essential "insurance policies").

NLW would be politically attractive during humanitarian operations and are potentially valuable in other situations short of war, because they avoid military bloodletting that could strengthen enemy resolve and precipitate domestic/international censure. The U.S. Government might enhance economic sanctions by conducting nonlethal blockades or clandestinely employing computer viruses to cripple the offenders' financial system. Psychological operations specialists able to "capture" enemy radio and television frequencies would posses a powerful lever with which to influence public perceptions and attitudes during crises.

Peacekeepers might profitably employ acoustic "barricades" to help keep hotheads apart during crises. Peace enforcers would welcome nonlethal weapons to disperse or otherwise control crowds and deny them access to sensitive areas such as embassies, arsenals, power plants, and telecommunications centers. Lasers that temporarily dazzle, but do not permanently blind, could discretely disable snipers who use noncombatants as human shields. Nonlethal weapons also could simplify the evacuation of U.S. citizens and close associates from unfriendly soil.

Counterterrorists might apply adhesives, antitraction substances, and combustion inhibitors to isolate hostage rescue sites, then tranquilize captors without jeopardizing captives. Special operations to neutralize enemy nuclear, biological and chemical warfare facilities could benefit from high-powered microwaves to suppress enemy defenses; super caustics and metal embrittlements could disable nuclear reactors, other processors, and finished weapons; compact particle beams in the hands of special operations forces could irradiate and neutralize nuclear, chemical, and biological munitions; aqueous foams could fill storage rooms thereafter.

Large-scale combat operations offer opportunities to employ nonlethal weapons independently or as complements of lethal power. Strategically significant warfare against enemy officials, their supporters, and infrastructure theoretically is feasible on a grand scale. High tech sabotage might insert biodegrading bacteria into petroleum storage tanks and use high-powered microwaves to disable fuses in ammunition depots. Adhesives or superlubricants liberally applied on seaports, air base runways, highway intersections, steep railway grades, key bridges, and other bottlenecks could impede enemy military traffic or bring it to a standstill. Missiles and aircraft might deposit conductive ribbons (fine carbon fibers) on power grids to short-circuit switches and transformers, as they did during Operation Desert Storm.

Nonlethal weapons also could be tactically advantageous. Counterinsurgents, whose main aim is to win hearts and minds, could minimize collateral damage and noncombatant casualties if armed with incapacitants. Foes in custody rather than body bags could furnish valuable intelligence as a bonus. Various nonlethal implements could favorably influence urban combat by blocking avenues of approach and escape, channel enemy formations into ambushes, flush out strong points while preserving sites of great cultural value, and simplify reconstruction problems after armed conflict ceases.

Policy limitations affect the choice of nonlethal weapons as much as (perhaps more than) technological constraints and costs. "Department of Defense Instruction 5000.2: Defense Management Policies and Procedures" specifies that U.S. weapons and munitions must undergo legal reviews during development, procurement, and deployment to ensure compliance with laws of war and moral/ethical obligations. No other nations save the United Kingdom and the Federal Republic of Germany seem to have similar stipulations.

The mention of biological and chemical warfare weapons raises red

flags among arms control specialists and on Capitol Hill. Law enforcement units may use riot control agents against U.S. citizens, whereas "Executive Order 11850" of April 10, 1975 forbids first use, "in war except in defensive military modes to save lives such as: ...situations in which civilians are used to mask or screen attacks... or to protect convoys from civil disturbances, terrorists and paramilitary organizations..." The benign use of biodegrading bacteria to clean up oil spills is permissible, but actions to contaminate enemy petroleum reserves might not be if narrow interpretations of the Biological Weapons Convention prevail. Dr. Matthew Meselson, Professor of Biochemistry at Harvard University, represents many who believe it would be unwise for nonlethal weapons to blur the line between use and non use of chemicals by U.S. Armed Forces, regardless of purposes. An independent task force sponsored by the Council of Foreign Relations, however, expressed a different opinion: "It would, of course, be a tragic irony if nations used lethal means against noncombatants because nonlethal means were banned by international convention."

Note the question of the legality of such weapons. HAARP, as a civilian science project, neatly side-steps the legal review process that admitted weapons systems must undergo. This is probably a leading factor in the DOD's making HAARP a civilian rather than military research project. HAARP, used as an advanced weapons system, poses several possible violations of the laws of humanity and the laws of armed conflict, both specifically and in general, as we shall examine in the final chapter.

Several acknowledged weapons of this type already exist, as the above table shows. Of particular note are lasers used to temporarily, or permanently, blind enemy soldiers. Prototypes of such weapons were considered for tryout when U.S. troops intervened in Somalia. An article in *U.S. News and World Report* stated:

In early 1995, some U.S. Marines were supplied with so-called dazzling lasers. The idea was to inflict as little harm as possible if Somalis turned hostile. But the Marines' commander then decided that the lasers should be "de-tuned" to prevent the chance of their blinding citizens. With their intensity thus diminished, they could be used only for designating or illuminating targets.

On March 1, 1995, commandos of U.S. Navy SEAL Team 5 were positioned at the south end of Mogadishu airport. At 7 a.m., a technician from the Air Force's Phillips Laboratory, developer of the lasers, used one to illuminate a Somali man armed with a rocket-propelled grenade. A SEAL sniper shot and killed the Somali. There was no question the

Somali was aiming at the SEALs. But the decision not to use the laser to dazzle or temporarily blind the man irks some of the nonlethal-team members. "We were not allowed to disable these guys because that was considered inhumane," said one. "Putting a bullet in their head is somehow more humane?"

Some humanitarian organizations, like The International Red Cross and Human Rights Watch are deeply concerned about the use of weapons that would induce permanent effects. The United States signed a treaty that prohibits the development of lasers designed "to cause permanent blindness" in the fall of 1995. The treaty does not forbid dazzling or "glare" lasers, like those sent to Somalia, however, if their effects are temporary. Seemingly undaunted, U.S. military labs are reported to be continuing research in blinding lasers; and several commercial contractors are currently marketing both types of laser weapons to police around the world.

Some researchers note that these NLWs are the "logical" outgrowth of weapons types that are already in the arsenal. We have numerous weapons in use, for example, that are designed to disable the delicate electronic systems of aircraft, computers, and/or missiles. "Once you are into these antimateriel weapons, it is a short jump to antipersonnel weapons," says Louis Slesin, editor of *Microwave News*.

The term "nonlethal," used to describe this technology, is highly misleading. The energy emitted from most of these weapon types can kill people when appropriately amplified. At lower power levels they can cause extreme forms of pain and debilitation. In "The Soft Kill Fallacy," published in *The Bulletin of the Atomic Scientists,* Sept, Oct 1994, Steve Aftergood with Barbara Hatch Rosenberg, wrote:

> Many of the non-lethal weapons under consideration utilize infrasound or electromagnetic energy (including lasers, microwave or radio-frequency radiation or visible light pulsed at brain-wave frequency) for their effects. These weapons are said to cause temporary or permanent blinding, interference with mental processes, modification of behavior and emotional response, seizures, severe pain, dizziness, nausea and diarrhea, or disruption of internal organ functions in various other ways.

The Department of the Army (DA) identifies these same weapons as "nonconventional." They were so identified in an exhibit at a DA-sponsored symposium on "The Soldier As A System," held in Crystal City, VA, on 30 June, 1992. Mr. Vernon Shisler was the manager of the DA's exhibit there. He is the Army's delegate to NATO in matters pertaining to "The Soldier As A System." Mr. Shisler acknowledged that directed energy weapons are in the

DOD's arsenal. Additionally, he emphasized that the American soldier is currently vulnerable to their effects, should they be employed on the battlefield.

The above mentioned U.S. Global Strategy Council has recognized the issue of vulnerability, as well, urging ongoing research into effective countermeasures. You can send for the U.S. Global Strategy Council's complete project proposal on this subject, "Nonlethality: Development of a National Policy and Employing Nonlethal Means in a New Strategic Era," prepared by Janet Morris. The Council's address is 1800 K Street, N.W., Washington, D.C. 20006. A number of references in this proposal to unidentified, elusive "enemies" of the U.S. government and the potential domestic applications of this mis-labeled "nonlethal" technology invite serious consideration by the public at large, and by supporters of the "patriot movement" in particular.

In her article, "Another Arms Race With The Former Soviet Union? What the Public Should Know About Electromagnetic Frequency Weapons" Cheryl Welsh originally published in *Newspeak* in 1996, (welsh@calweb.com) wrote:

The U.S. public has a right to know about a currently classified weapons program. There are many corroborating articles to confirm the existence of electromagnetic frequency (emf) behavior or mind control weapons in the U.S. and Russian arsenals. There is also evidence that there has been a secret race between the two superpowers to gain an upper edge and control the use of this revolutionary technology. Like the atomic bomb, the technology will change the perception of the world.

The U.S. public also has the right to determine the policy and use of this technology. They have the democratic right to express their opinion on issues that deeply affect their lives, but unfortunately mind control weapons are classified and are being developed without public input. Like nuclear war protesters who expressed their views and significantly affected arms control policy, there is a need for public debate on emf technology.

The best proof of this ongoing emf arms race would be from the U.S. government, but it is classified under the National Security Act.

The U.S. public was told about the secret development of the atomic bomb after it was dropped on Hiroshima in 1945. It is inevitable that history will repeat and the U.S. public will learn about the emf arms race when the weapons are used or leaked to the press. In all likelihood, only public protest can alter this course.

There has been a quantum leap of technology and many articles confirm that the technology is capable of computer-brain interface and control of every nerve in the human body. The mind control technology is as mind boggling as the landing of the man on the moon. The physics and functioning of the brain is known on a biomedical level and can be highly controlled. The implications of its use as a weapon are as serious as the consequences of the use of the atomic bomb. The motive of superpowers to develop and control the use of mind control technology becomes obvious.

Weapon technology is advancing rapidly. ...The next weapons in the history of warfare will include the complicated emf and behavior control technologies. The mind control arms race winner has the capability to control the world. Therefore, if the opponent develops behavior control weapons, then the U.S. or Russian government would be negligent to its citizens if they did not also. The picture of why, how and who would develop the mind control weapons becomes clear, in spite of the National Security Act.

Possible remedies include the revision of the National Security law so that radiation, emf or any experimentation on human subjects is conducted and monitored within the law.

The No-HAARP group has also called on the public to demand Congressional investigation into, and public debate of, this emerging new "less-than-lethal" or "nonconventional" weapons technology and its ethical repercussions. The No-HAARP group views HAARP as a clear example of a nonlethal weapons system under development.

Over the last century many nations have signed conventions and treaties in attempts to set rules for the use of increasingly more destructive and terrifying weapons in war. However, *U.S. News* reports that:

...[N]o treaties govern the use of unconventional weapons. And no one knows what will happen to people exposed to them over the long term. Moreover, medical researchers worry that their work on such things as the use of electromagnetic waves to stimulate hearing in the deaf or to halt seizures in epileptics might be used to develop weaponry. In fact, the military routinely has approached the National Institutes of Health for research information.

Above we saw that the Russians have turned medical advances into weapons. The British are also known to be converting medical knowledge into weapons systems. This leads one to ponder how many other nations may be following suit.

The U.S. Air Force expects to have microwave weapons by the year 2015 and other nonlethal weaponry sooner. "When that does happen," warns Steven Metz, Professor of National Security Affairs at the U.S. Army War College, "I think there will be a public uproar. We need an open debate on them now." The controversy over

HAARP is quite possibly an early round in that debate.

Weekend Guardian, of Manchester, England, ran "Field of Nightmares" by Peter Kennard in its 2-3 February, 1991, issue. In it Kennard reported:

In 1982 a US Air Force Review of Biotechnology stated: Radiofrequeny radiation (RFR) fields may pose powerful and revolutionary anti-personnel military threats... RFR experiments and the increasing understanding of the brain as an electrically-mediated organ suggests the serious probability that impressed electromagnetic fields can be disruptive to purposeful behavior and may be capable of directing and or interrogating such behaviour. Further, the passage of approximately 100 milliamperes through the myocardium can lead to cardiac standstill and death, again pointing to speed-of-light weapons effect. A rapidly scanning RFR system could provide an effective stun or kill capability over a large area.

The system, the article said, was developable. Note that this information was taken by the British journalist from an in-house publication of the U.S. Air Force, one of HAARP's operators.

The article further states:

There is little doubt that crowd control devices using Radio Frequency Radiation do exist. The development of such devices would complement sonic and infra-red weapons, which are well known, and were advertised in the British Defense Equipment Catalogue until 1983. These included the Valkyrie, an infra-red device causing night blindness and the Squawk Box or Sound Curdler, developed by the US for use in Viet Nam. The Squawk Box was designed to induce feelings of giddiness and nausea in the victim, and is highly directional, so that as individuals are hit by the invisible effect, distress and confusion is spread amongst a crowd... In 1984 the Ministry of Defense ordered that all advertisements and references to 'frequency weapons,' be cut from the Defense Catalogue.

Other U.S. military documents confirm that radio-frequency antipersonnel weapons programs are underway. One such line of research is being pursued at the Air Force's Armstrong Laboratory at Brooks Air Force Base in Texas. According to budget documents, the lab intends to spend more than $110 million over the next six years "to exploit less-than-lethal biological effects of electromagnetic radiation for Air Force security, peacekeeping, and war-fighting operations."

Particularly cogent to our search for a connection between this line of military research and HAARP is the work by Eldon Byrd. He ran the Marine Corps Nonlethal Electromagnetic Weapons project from 1980 to 1983, and conducted most of his research at the Armed Forces Radiobiology Research Institute in Bethesda, Maryland. "We were looking at electrical activity in the brain and how to influence it," he says. Byrd conducted experiments on animals and humans— including himself—to see if brain waves would "lock on" with waves hitting the brain from outside. His experiments used VLF electromagnetic radiation. He found he could induce the brain to release behavior-regulating chemicals. "We could put animals into a stupor," hitting them with these frequencies, he said. "These fields were extremely weak. They were undetectable," Byrd added. "The effects were nonlethal and reversible. You could disable a person temporarily," Byrd hypothesized. "It [would be] like a stun gun."

U.S. News reported that:

> Byrd never tested any of his hardware in the field, and his program, scheduled for four years, apparently was closed down after two, he says. "The work was really outstanding," he grumbles. "We would have had a weapon in one year." Byrd says he was told his work would be unclassified, "unless it works." Because it worked, he suspects that the program "went black." Other scientists tell similar tales of research on electromagnetic radiation turning top secret once successful results were achieved.

How long before HAARP "goes black"? Bernard Eastlund believes that it will not take long. He said in *U.S. News* :

> The real beauty of HAARP is that nothing you can see on the outside is sensitive. The secret is the beam steering agility and pulsing of the transmissions... When covert operations occur, the science team, the operating funds and the mission will be black.

As previously mentioned, HAARP may have already gone black, at least temporarily, in December 1996 and March and June of '97.

HAARP was mandated by the U.S. Senate to develop "advanced weaponry." Is there any real possibility that at some level HAARP is not a weapon or a research project to develop a directed-energy nonlethal weapon? It is tempting to say 'ah, hah! that's what HAARP is... ' except, it is a great deal more ...

Part Three:
Mind Control

Turning the electrojet into a virtual antenna could put the ability to broadcast in the ELF and/or microwave ranges into the hands of the Conspiracy. In this chapter I want to explore some of the more sinister possibilities associated with this technology, as well as fill in some more of the historical background. The point of this chapter is to establish that there are individuals and government agencies who have a passion to develop mind control technology, and to show that they have the potential to consummate these desires with HAARP.

This line of "scientific" investigation into covertly controlling others really goes back to the previous century. It began, in part, with the work of Sigmund Freud, and especially with that of Wilhelm Wundt, a German physiologist and psychologist. We have all heard of the Austrian doctor and drug addict Sigmund Freud (1856-1939). He developed psychoanalysis as an individualized application of the fledgling (pseudo)science of psychology. At the same time Wilhelm Max Wundt (1832-1920), a professor at the University of Leipzig in Germany, was working up a version for controlling masses of people called, today, Social Psychology. Curiously, Freud and Wundt treated each other with the same destain that Edison and Tesla held for each other.

Wundt founded the world's first experimental psychology laboratory in Leipzig in 1878. Wundt's opinion was that man was just a hunk of meat—that there was no such thing as a "soul." According to Wundt and his successors, the "psyche" (Greek for "soul") that psychology was supposed to be studying ("-ology" for "study of") did not exist (kind of blows their reason for existing, as psyche-ologists anyway, doesn't it?).

Wundt believed that all human actions could be defined in terms of reactions; i.e., you are not aware, you just think you are. He promoted the idea that everything a human being did was a pre-programmed reaction to the environment, and that thought and reason had precious little to do with anything. Wundtian psychology maintains that these reactions are controlled by various factors known only to their "science" (e.g. blood/brain chemistry, educational conditioning, etc.).

Wundt applied these principles to society as a whole, developing techniques for controlling whole populations. A belief that people are merely stimulus-response robots allows you to do just about anything you want to them. Pavlov, the Russian scientist with his famous dogs conditioned to salivate at the ringing of a bell, was working in this same field. The Nazi and Soviet death camp psychological experimenters (of World War II and the "gulags" that followed) and today's industrial psychologists hold this same view of people. Today, the technology for controlling people by conditioning them to respond to certain stimuli is called Behavior Modification, or BehavMod. This field is dominated by B. F. Skinner (1904-1990) and his followers.

There is a very real concern that a conspiracy of persons holding the Wundtian view of people would consider that they have the right, and perhaps even the obligation, to use any technology at their disposal to redesign society. Another possible smoking antenna is that one of the ionospheric heaters in use today (Tromso, Norway) was built by the Max Planck Institute. That Institute was where many of the Nazi death camp psychs received their degrees, and today is a major center for "post-Wundtian" psychological experimentation and education.

Psychopaths, scientists, spies, and the military have attempted, throughout this century, to develop a secret technology that would allow them to control others from a distance. Soviet psychologists and hypnotists used radios to broadcast hypnotic commands to the subjects of their experiments in the 1930s. By the 1950s they were conducting similar experiments with microwave transmissions. By the 1970s they may have graduated to the Woodpecker signal.

The CIA and DOD have jointly pursued virtually the same research as the Communists since the end of World War II. Because this has largely been a clandestine line of research it is difficult to know much about this field with certainty. My research tends to indicate that, while the Russians explored this area in the 1930s, the real developers of this technology were the Nazis, who experimented on hapless victims in the concentration camps. After World War II both the United States and U.S.S.R. grabbed all the Nazi scientists they could. The infamous Operation Paper Clip, for example, brought Werner von Braun and most of his staff to the United States. Born in 1912, von Braun was the Nazi rocket scientist who developed the V-2 rocket which rained death on England. A high ranking SS officer, he was also responsible for the deaths of thousands of slave laborers at the Nazi advanced weapons facility in Peenemunende, Germany. He was saved from the Nuremberg Tribunal by the Office of Strategic Services (OSS—forerunner of the CIA). He was whisked by the OSS to the White Sands, New Mexico, rocketry center in 1946. There he was made a technical advisor to the guided missile group. Later, he headed the Army Ballistic Missile Agency (ABMA). The ABMA became the civilian National Aeronautics and Space Administration (NASA), which von Braun ran until shortly before his death.

Paper Clip and the other operations like it were probably the beginning of the ongoing "mind control" arms race. The U.S. and U.S.S.R were trying to catch up with the Nazis, then with each other. According to recent disclosures and FOIA (Freedom Of Information Act) discoveries, the current primary

American conductors of this mind control research appear to be the CIA, the DOD, the National Security Agency and, curiously enough, the Department of Energy.

A great number of researchers in many countries have looked into ways to control the brain, bypassing the consciousness of the individual. They have used a variety of techniques from pain, drugs and hypnosis, to electric shock and subconscious transmissions of microwave or ELF messages. They have used these techniques singularly (e.g., just using hypnosis) and in combination (e.g., broadcasting hypnotic commands on radio waves).

Not all of these researchers have been "professionals," either. Jefferey Dalhmer, the convicted sex cannibal, had not intended to kill any of his victims. He had been trying to create a zombie-like sex slave but his experiments, mostly involving drilling holes in their heads and pouring in acid, were just a little too crude. Some of the techniques used by the pros, particularly the Nazis, were only slightly more refined.

HYPNOTISM

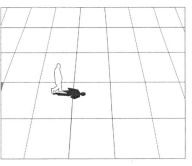

Dr. George H. Estabrooks (1895-1973), speaking as the chairman of the Department of Psychology of Colgate University, said, "I can hypnotize a man without his knowledge or consent into committing treason against the United States." At the time he made that statement Dr. Estabrooks was one of this nation's most authoritative voices in the field of hypnotism. The psychologist told officials in Washington, D.C., that a mere 200 well trained hypnotists could develop an army of mind-controlled fifth columnists in a wartime America.

Knowing full well what hypnotism is capable of, and fearing for the safety of the nation, he laid out a scenario of how an enemy doctor could place thousands of patients under hypnotic mind control, and through them could eventually program key military officers to follow said enemy doctor's instructions. Through such tactics, Dr. Estabrooks claimed, the entire U.S. Army could be taken over. He also suggested that large numbers of saboteurs could just as easily be created and dispatched by an enemy power.

Dr. Estabrooks was then given the opportunity to prove his theory by being allowed to actually conduct experiments on American soldiers. Volunteer soldiers of low rank and little formal education were placed under hypnotism. The tests involved using hypnotism to improve and control the subject's ability to retain complicated verbal information. Subjects demonstrated a surprising ability to retain the information given to them under hypnosis.

Dr. Estabrooks contributed an article called "Hypnosis Comes of Age" to the April, 1971, issue of *Science Digest.* In it he wrote:

One of the most fascinating but dangerous applications of hypnosis is its use in military intelligence. This is a field with which I am familiar through formulating guidelines for the techniques used by the United States in two world wars. Communication in war is always a headache. Codes can be broken. A professional spy may or may not stay bought. Your own man may have unquestionable loyalty but his judgment is always open to question. The "hypnotic courier" on the other hand, provides a unique solution. I was involved in preparing many subjects for this work during World War II. One successful case involved an Army Service Corps Captain whom we'll call George Smith. Captain Smith had undergone months of training. He was an excellent subject but did not realize it. I had removed from him, by post-hypnotic suggestion, all recollection of ever having been hypnotized. First I had the Service Corps call the captain to Washington and tell him they needed a report on the mechanical equipment of Division X headquartered in Tokyo. Smith was ordered to leave by jet next morning, pick up the report and return at once. These orders were given him in the waking state. Consciously, that was all he knew, and it was the story he gave his wife and friends. Then I put him under deep hypnosis, and gave him—orally—a vital message to be delivered directly on his arrival in Japan to a certain colonel—let's say his name was Brown—of military intelligence. Outside of myself, Colonel Brown was the only person who could hypnotize Captain Smith. This is "locking." I performed it by saying to the hypnotized Captain: "Until further orders from me, only Colonel Brown and I can hypnotize you. We will use a signal phrase 'the moon is clear.' Whenever you hear this phrase from Brown or myself you will pass instantly into deep hypnosis." When Captain Smith re-awakened, he had no conscious memory of what happened in trance. All that he was aware of was that he must head for Tokyo to pick up a division report. On arrival there, Smith reported to Brown, who hypnotized him with the signal phrase. Under hypnosis, Smith delivered my message and received one to bring back. Awakened, he was given the division report and returned home by jet. There I hypnotized him once more with the signal phrase, and he spieled off Brown's answer that had been dutifully tucked away in his unconscious mind.

The system is virtually foolproof. As exemplified by this case, the information literally was "locked" in Smith's unconscious for retrieval by the only two people who knew the combination. The subject had no conscious memory of what happened, so couldn't spill the beans. No one else could hypnotize him even if they might know the signal phrase. Not all applications of hypnotism to military intelligence are as tidy as that.

A very frightening aspect of this line of research is the deliberate creation of split-personalities. Remember the films *The Manchurian Candidate* and *Telefon*? Throughout this century spook doctors have looked for ways to create programmed assassins, and the multiple personality type has been an area of keenest interest. Dr. Estabrooks may have been one of those spooks. He wrote:

Perhaps you have read 'The Three Faces of Eve.' The book was based on a case reported in 1905 by Dr. Morton Prince of Massachusetts General Hospital and Harvard. He startled everyone in the field by announcing that he had cured a woman named Beauchamp of a split personality problem. Using post-hypnotic suggestion to submerge an incompatible, childlike facet of the patient, he'd been able to make two other sides of Mrs. Beauchamp compatible, and lump them together in a single cohesive personality. Clinical hypnotists throughout the world jumped on the multiple personality bandwagon as a fascinating frontier. By the 1920's, not only had they learned to apply post-hypnotic suggestion to deal with this weird problem, but also had learned how to split certain complex individuals into multiple personalities like Jeckyll-Hydes. The potential for military intelligence has been nightmarish. During World War II, I worked this technique with a vulnerable Marine lieutenant I'll call Jones. Under the watchful eye of Marine Intelligence, I split his personality into Jones A and Jones B. Jones A, once a "normal" working Marine, became entirely different. He talked communist doctrine and meant it. He was welcomed enthusiastically by communist cells, was deliberately given a dishonorable discharge by the Corps, which was in on the plot, and became a card-carrying party member. The joker was Jones B, the second personality, formerly apparent in the conscious Marine. Under hypnosis, this Jones had been carefully coached by suggestion. Jones B was the deeper personality, knew all the thoughts of Jones A, was a loyal American and was "imprinted" to say nothing during conscious phases. All I had to do was hypnotize the whole man, get in touch with Jones B, the loyal American, and I had a pipeline straight into the Communist camp. It worked beautifully for months with this subject, but the technique backfired. While there was no way for an enemy to expose Jones' dual personality, they suspected it, and played the same trick on us later.

Estabrooks' story is chillingly reminiscent of Lee

Harvey Oswald, President John F. Kennedy's alleged assassin. He had been a Marine, one who became a Communist, moved to Russia, then returned to the United States. FOIA requests revealed that there had been massive correspondence back and forth between J. Edgar Hoover of the Federal Bureau of Investigation (FBI) and Dr. Estabrooks. There were visits of FBI personnel to Estabrooks. Many Military and FBI psychological warfare personnel attended 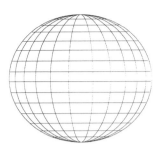 various workshops and symposia held by Estabrooks. Offensive uses of hypnosis in clandestine operations were discussed in the correspondence. From this voluminous evidence, it is possible to conclude that Dr. Estabrooks actually did create split-personality operatives in World War II, or after, and that many people were probably aware of it.

One J.G. Watkins followed in Estabrooks' footsteps in a subsequent series of tests on Army volunteers. He induced soldiers to commit acts which conflicted not only with their moral code, but also the military code drilled into them in basic training. Watkins was trying to see if he could get enlisted men to attack a superior officer, an offense punishable by court martial.

One of the experiments he devised involved placing normal, stable Army privates into deep trances. Once the private was under hypnosis, Watkins would tell the man that the officer sitting across from him was an enemy soldier. Watkins told the entranced private that this officer would attempt to kill him—setting up in the private's mind the belief that he was in a kill or be killed situation. The results were always the same. The hypnotized private would invariably immediately attack the officer. The experiment was repeated several times, and in one case the man who was hypnotized and the man who was attacked were very close friends. In one experiment, the hypnotized subject pulled out a knife and nearly stabbed the officer. As one might expect, Watkins concluded that people could be induced to commit acts contrary to their moral code if their reality were distorted by hypnotism.

Watkins continued with the Army for some time, conducting a number of similar experiments. In one series he used female officers from the Women's Auxiliary Corp (WACs) to explore the possibility of making military personnel divulge military secrets. A related experiment had to be discontinued because a researcher, who had also been one of the subjects, was exposing numerous Top Secret projects to his hypnotist, who did not have the proper security clearance for such information. The information was embarrassingly divulged before an audience of 200 military personnel!

The Army and the FBI were not the only spooks looking at this "technology." In his book *The Search for the Manchurian Candidate*, John Marks described an early attempt by the CIA to create a "programmed assassin." He wrote that Morse Allen, who he described as the CIA's first behavioral research czar, conducted an experiment with two of his secretaries. One secretary, the "victim," Allen put into a deep trance and told her to keep sleeping until he ordered otherwise. The second, the "killer," was hypnotized and told that if she could not wake up her sleeping friend, "her rage would be so great that she would not hesitate to kill." An unloaded pistol was placed nearby. Even though the second secretary had expressed a fear of firearms of any kind, she picked up the gun and "shot" her sleeping friend. After Allen brought the "killer" out of her trance, she had no recollection of the event and denied that she could ever have shot anyone.

MKULTRA

While there is no discernable direct connection between the CIA's experimentation with LSD and other drugs in the '50s and '60s and HAARP today, there is a stunning lesson to be learned in the CIA's use of a new technology (LSD) on unwitting subjects within this country. The potential for similar misuse of technology (HAARP) certainly exists today. I very definitely see a parallel between these two programs. As I relate some of the facts known about MKUltra, please consider: if our government could do that then, what could it do with HAARP now?

Throughout the 1970s the word leaked out that researchers working for the CIA and other spook agencies were engaging in a variety of bizarre, and very illegal, mind control experiments. In 1976, for example, former CIA officials leaked Top Secret documents to journalist James Moore that described mind control methods involving "Radio-Hypnotic Intra-Cerebral Control and Electronic Dissolution of Memory." The lid came off in 1977. MKUltra was a breaking news story, getting national attention. This was due in no small part to the publication of Walter Bowart's classic expose, *Operation Mind Control*. President Carter and the Senate Select Committee on Intelligence called for testimony from then CIA Director Admiral Stansfield Turner. Turner described MKUltra as merely a program of drug experimentation and not one aimed at behavior control. After a FOIA request netted him boxes of CIA records, author John Marks called a press conference. Marks criticized Turner for several "distortions" in his testimony. Marks released a score of CIA documents to reporters that revealed the scope of the behavioral experiments conducted by the CIA. Public outcry soon forced the Senate Subcommittee on Health and Scientific Research, chaired by Senator Ted Kennedy, to hold public hearings.

The Kennedy subcommittee learned the details of the CIA's Operation MKUltra primarily through the testimony of Dr. Sidney Gottlieb (b.

1918), the psychiatrist in charge of the program. He presided over investigations as far ranging as advanced research in amnesia caused by electroshock to leave-no-stone-unturned searches of the jungles of Latin America for toxic leaves and barks. Dr. Gottlieb was a native of the Bronx with a Ph.D. in chemistry from Cal Tech. Gottlieb was the head of a Division of the CIA that was filthy with Ph.D.s called the Technical Services Staff.

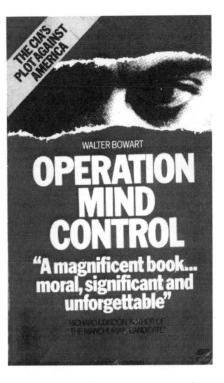

THE CIA'S PLOT AGAINST AMERICA

WALTER BOWART

OPERATION MIND CONTROL

"A magnificent book... moral, significant and unforgettable"

RICHARD CONDON AUTHOR OF "THE MANCHURIAN CANDIDATE"

Gottlieb's boss was Richard Helms, the head of Clandestine Services (officially called the Directorate of Operations, but popularly known within the Agency as the "dirty tricks department"). Helms, who eventually became Director of the CIA, was recruited into the CIA's predecessor, the OSS, by OSS founder General William "Wild Bill" Donovan. Before becoming a spy, Helms had been a young newspaper executive who had gained fame for interviewing Adolf Hitler in 1936 while working for United Press International.

The operational arm of MKUltra was code named MKDelta. The MK in both names is taken from the German spelling of "mind control." MKDelta's purpose, according to Dr. Gottlieb's sworn testimony, was to "investigate whether and how it was possible to modify an individual's behavior by covert means." Claiming the protection of the National Security Act, Dr. Gottlieb refused to tell the Senate subcommittee what had been learned or gained by these experiments.

Dr. Gottlieb stated that the program had been started over concern that the Soviets and other enemies of the U.S. would get ahead of the U.S. in this field. The subcommittee learned that the CIA's experiments had involved slipping LSD to unwitting American citizens in real life situations. Hundreds never recovered from these "trips," and many died.

The idea for the series of experiments that eventually produced MKUltra probably originated back in 1941. In November of that year the OSS invested $5,000 in a "truth drug" program. Early experiments with scopolamine and morphine proved both unfruitful and very dangerous. The program eventually tested scores of drugs, including mescaline, barbiturates, benzedrine, cannabis indica, and many others. Since that time, movies, novels, and the like, have fictionalized, dramatized and sensationalized the use of "truth serums."

Initially, the experiments were done on volunteer U.S. Army and OSS personnel. The testing was also disguised as a remedy for shell shock (or "post traumatic stress disorder" as it is called today). The volunteers became known as "Donovan's Dreamers," so-named after Major General William J. Donovan (1883-1959). "Wild Bill" Donovan was a burly, vigorous Republican millionaire who had started as a White House intelligence advisor prior to the 1941 Japanese attack on Pearl Harbor.

The OSS' experiments were conducted under a "truth drug" committee headed by Dr. Winfred Overholster. They were so hush-hush, that only a few top officials knew about them. President Franklin Roosevelt was one of the few civilians made aware of the experiments. This search for a "truth drug" achieved limited success at that time.

That first round of experimentation was halted after a memo was written: "The drug defies all but the most expert and search analysis, and for all practical purposes can be considered beyond analysis." The OSS, and later the CIA, did not give up on the idea of finding a workable truth serum, however.

The OSS began a new series of field tests in 1943. The most celebrated test was done on New York gangster August Del Grazio, a.k.a. Augie Dallas, a.k.a. Dell, a.k.a. Little Augie. These were conducted by Captain George Hunter White, an OSS agent and ex-law enforcement official. Cigarettes laced with a marijuana derivative were offered to Augie without his knowledge of the content. Augie, who had served time in prison for assault and murder, had been one of the world's most notorious drug dealers and smugglers. He had operated an opium factory in Turkey and was a leader in the Italian underworld on the Lower East Side of New York. The new version of a truth serum must have worked. Under its influence Augie reportedly revealed volumes of information about underworld operations, including the names of high-ranking government officials who took bribes from the mob. Wild Bill Donovan was delighted with the success of the advanced formula. A new memo was issued: "Cigarette experiments indicated that we had a mechanism which offered promise in relaxing prisoners to be interrogated."

The OSS was disbanded after the war, being replaced by the CIA in 1947 when the National Security Act (NSA) took effect. The NSA created the CIA, the National Security Council and much of the intelligence structure we have today. The change from OSS to CIA hardly slowed Captain White and his compatriots. They continued, virtually uninterrupted, in their administering of behavior modifying drugs. White's service record indicates that by 1954 he had become a high-ranking Federal Narcotics Bureau officer who had been loaned to the CIA on a part-time basis. This loaning of agents from one agency to another is common practice. When the Drug Enforcement Agency was formed, for example, about half of its initial personnel were loaned from the FBI and the other half were borrowed from the CIA.

In the early 1950s White reportedly rented an apartment in Greenwich Village, New York, which he equipped with two-way mirrors and other surveillance gadgets. Disguised as a seaman, he drugged people he met in the Greenwich Village scene with LSD and brought them back to his apartment. In 1955, the operation was moved to San Francisco, California. "Safehouses" were established under the code name Operation Midnight Climax in San Francisco and Marin, a fasionable suburb a few minutes north of the city. Improving on White's "Hey, sailor!" ploy, Midnight  Climax hired drug addicted prostitutes who lured men from bars back to the safehouses after their drinks had been spiked with LSD. White filmed the events that followed. The purpose of these "national security brothels" was to enable the CIA to experiment with drug enhanced sexual techniques for extracting information from men. In addition to LSD, Technical Services Staff (TSS) officials gave White even more exotic experimental drugs to test. One TSS source said, "If we were scared enough of a drug not to try it out on ourselves, we sent it to San Francisco." The safehouse experiments continued through 1963.

They were discontinued after CIA Inspector General John Earman criticized Richard Helms, the then outgoing director of the CIA and reputed father of the MKUltra project. Earman charged the new director, John McCone, had not been fully briefed on the MKUltra Project when he took office and that "the concepts involved in manipulating human behavior are found by many people within and outside the Agency to be distasteful and unethical." He stated that "the rights and interest of U.S. citizens are placed in jeopardy."

Earman's criticisms were rebuffed by Helms, who warned, "...positive operation capacity to use drugs is diminishing owing to a lack of realistic testing. Tests were necessary to keep up with the Soviets." However, the lie was revealed in 1964, when Helms testified before the Warren Commission (investigating the assassination of President John Kennedy) that "Soviet research has consistently lagged five years behind Western research."

Upon leaving government service in 1966, Captain White wrote a startling letter to his superior, Dr. Gottlieb. In that letter, Captain White reminisced about his work in the safehouses with LSD. His comments have since been reproduced in scores of books and other publications as a horrifying example of what depths covert operatives can sink to in the name of "science" and "national security." "I was a very minor missionary, actually a heretic," White wrote, "but I toiled wholeheartedly in the vineyards because it was fun, fun, fun. Where else could a red-blooded American boy lie, kill, cheat, steal, rape and pillage with the sanction and blessing of the All-Highest?"

Ten years would pass from the time White penned those words until public outrage forced the Senate to convene hearings into the allegations of Marks, Bowart and others. The CIA was forced to admit that MKUltra existed, that it had been in operation since 1953, and that it consisted of 149 sub-projects involving 44 colleges and universities, 15 research foundations, 12 hospitals and 3 prisons. These "research" locations were not obscure little corners of the world, by any means. These included some of the most prestigious educational and medical organizations in America, and virtually all the principal North American psychiatric and psychological societies. Among those participating were: the American Psychological Association, the Butler Hospital Health Centre (which is part of Harvard), Columbia University, Cornell (one of the principal universities participating in HAARP), Denver, Emory, Florida, George Washington, Harvard, Houston, Illinois, Indiana Universities, Johns Hopkins, University of Minnesota, New Jersey Reformatory, Bordentown in Tennessee, University of Pennsylvania, Penn State, Princeton, Stanford, Wisconsin, the Bureau of Narcotics, McGill University, the National Institute for Health (NIH), the National Institute for Mental Health (NIMH), the National Philosophical Society, and the Worcester Foundation for Experimental Biology.

Eli Lily was the main American supplier of LSD to the CIA. Those of you who can remember the sixties might recall the British rock group, The Animals. One of their songs was: "The Girl Named Sandoz," which referred to the European pharmaceutical giant Sandoz, which discovered LSD in the forties. Sandoz was the original supplier of LSD to the CIA and the military in the 1950s. The CIA wanted a secure American supplier so they contracted with Eli Lily to become their "source," as acid-heads called their pushers in the '60s.

President George Bush was one of the first world leaders to use the phrase New World Order. He was also a former Director of the CIA, and a principal stockholder and former member of the Board of Directors of Eli Lily!

Among the psychs who were identified as LSD pathfinders for the CIA were: Bob Hyde's group at Boston Psychopathic; Harold Abramson at Mt. Sinai Hospital and Columbia University in New York; Harris Isbell of the NIMH-sponsored Addiction Research Center in Lexington, Kentucky; Louis Jolyon "Jolly" West at the University of Oklahoma, and Harold Hodge's group at the University of Rochester. Another major player in MKUltra was the big kahuana of behavior modification, B.F. Skinner himself. Still another player, and one of special note to those of us seeking to understand HAARP, was the Office of Naval Research, one of the two military organizations running HAARP today. Another smoking antenna?

The CIA disguised its involvement by passing the money for MKUltra experiments through three principal conduits: the Human Ecology Foundation (HEF), the Josiah Macey Jr. Foundation, and the Geshickter Fund for Medical Research, a Washington, D.C. family foundation. Dr. Charles Geshickter was one of the MKUltra contractors himself, providing the Agency with a variety of services for more than a decade.

MKUltra was funded by HEF and the others putting out calls for grants, for which people would submit applications. To most it looked like a normal funding foundation. Many participants were unwitting, thinking they were applying for a regular grant. However, other people knew perfectly well there was a front involved. The technical name for this kind of funding is "cutout." HEF, the Josiah Macey Jr. Foundation and the Geshickter Fund were CIA cutouts.

One of the grisliest of the CIA-funded quacks in white coats was Canadian psychiatrist Dr. D. Ewen Cameron. In the 1950s his "research" was funded by the Society for the Investigation of Human Ecology, forerunner of HEF. His procedure consisted of breaking down his patient's behavior patterns, which he called "depatterning," with electro-convulsive therapy (ECT, i.e., electric shocks); with repeated doses of LSD; and in some cases, the paralytic "blowgun" poison, curare. Following these tortures, a tape-recorded message would be repeated for up to 16 hours a day for a week or more. This piece of covert nastiness was summarized in the *U.S. News and World Report*, "U.S. News Investigative Report" of 24 Jan, 1994:

> ...The analogy to brainwashing was obvious to the CIA which provided a $60,000 grant through the Human Ecology Society. Nine of Cameron's former patients, who had sought treatment for depression, alcoholism and other problems at the Allen Memorial Institute at McGill University (Canada), where Cameron was director, filed lawsuit against the CIA in 1979. One patient, Rita Zimmerman, was "depatterned" with 30 electroshock sessions followed by 56 days of drug-induced sleep. It left her incontinent; others suffered permanent brain damage, lost their jobs or otherwise deteriorated. The case, *Orlikow v U.S.* was settled in 1988 for $750,000.

MKUltra was far more than just frying people with LSD. One sub-project was code named MKNaomi, which was a joint venture with the Special Operations Division (SOD) of the Army's biological research center at Fort Detrick, Maryland. Under MKNaomi the SOD men developed a whole arsenal of toxic substances for CIA use. John Marks, author of *The Search for the Manchurian Candidate*, wrote: "If Agency operators needed to kill someone in a few seconds with say, a suicide pill, SOD provided superdeadly shellfish toxins." Agency operatives supplied pills laced with this lethal food poison to its Mafia allies for inclusion into Fidel Castro's milkshake. In other instances, Marks wrote: "If CIA officials wanted an assassination to look like a death from natural causes, they could choose from a long list of diseases that normally occurred in particular countries." SOD also provided the CIA with nonlethal toxins for when they merely wanted to incapacitate someone.

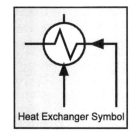

Heat Exchanger Symbol

Just one of the MKUltra projects financed by the Geshickter Fund was the construction of the Gorman Annex at the George Washington University Hospital in Washington, D.C. The CIA funneled MKUltra money to Geshickter, who then funded it out to the contractor. Since this money appeared to be coming from a private foundation, it generated matching funds from another sector of the federal government, and the CIA got to double its budget. The Gorman Annex was built for mind control experimentation on terminal cancer patients. Three career officers, CIA biochemists, were employed at the Gorman Annex under full cover.

The importance of this, in regard to HAARP, is that it proves that some agents of this government do not give a rodent's backside about such niceties as "informed consent" and the Bill of Rights. If they could slip LSD to thousands of unwitting subjects in the name of "national defense" then, they can do equally dastardly deeds today. If HAARP is not strictly under civilian control, it is almost a sure bet that if it can be used against us, it will be.

ELECTROMAGNETISM AND MIND CONTROL

There were three principal North American scientists who pioneered the work of using electromagnetism to control human behavior. Their work began over 30 years ago. These three were: Dr. Jose Delgado (b. 1939), the great guru of American brain tinkerers, and two of his contemporaries. One was the previously mentioned Dr. W. Ross Adey (b. 1922), who did much of his work as a physiologist at the Brain Research Institute at UCLA. The other was Dr. Wilder Penfield (1891-1976), an American whose researches were conducted in Canada.

In 1969 Dr. Delgado, while attached to the Yale University School of Medicine, published his report "Physical Control of the Mind: Toward a Psychocivilized Society." After years of research with electrodes imbedded in the brains of chimps and humans (a technology called electrical stimulation of the brain (ESB)) he stated that it was possible to control human movements, glandular functions, specific mental manifestations, and to produce behavior indistinguishable from spontaneous activity. He wrote: "[T]he individual is defenseless against direct manipulation of the brain because he is deprived of the most intimate mechanisms of biological reactivity."

Later Dr. Delgado told Congress:

We need a program of psychosurgery for political control of our society. The purpose is physical control of the mind. Everyone who deviates from the given norm can be surgically mutilated.

The individual may think that the most important reality is his own existence, but this is only his personal point of view. This lacks historical perspective.

Man does not have the right to develop his own mind. This kind of liberal orientation has great appeal. We must electrically control the brain. Someday armies and generals will be controlled by electric stimulation of the brain.

These remarks of Dr. Jose Delgado appeared in the 24 February, 1974, edition of the Congressional Record, No. 26., Vol. 118. Despite Dr. Delgado's outrageous statements before Congress, his work was financed by grants from the Office of Naval Research (which had participated in MKUltra and who today co-directs HAARP), the Air Force Aero-Medical Research Laboratory, and the Public Health Foundation of Boston.

Amazingly, Dr. Delgado is today regarded as a respected scientist, revered for his pioneering work in developing the technology of electrical stimulation of the brain (ESB). Another example of his work can be found in an article that ran in *The New York Times* on 17 May, 1965, entitled "Matador With a Radio Stops Wild Bull." The piece details Dr. Delgado's experiments at Yale University School of Medicine and his work in the field at Cordova, Spain. *The New York Times* stated:

Afternoon sunlight poured over the high wooden barriers into the ring, as the brave bull bore down on the unarmed matador, a scientist who had never faced a fighting bull. But the charging animal's horn never reached the man behind the heavy red cape. Moments before that could happen, Dr. Delgado pressed a button on a small radio transmitter in his hand and the bull braked to a halt. Then he pressed another button on the transmitter, and the bull obediently turned to the right and trotted away. The bull was obeying commands in his brain that were being called forth by electrical stimulation by the radio signals to certain regions in which fine wires had been painlessly planted the day before.

According to Dr. Delgado, experiments of this type have also been performed on humans. While giving a lecture on the brain in 1965, Dr. Delgado said, "Science has developed a new methodology for the study and control of cerebral function in animals and humans." This section is an examination of the possibility that HAARP is an advance in Dr. Delgado's research, in which we will all become that bull, and without the need of the "painlessly" implanted wires.

Dr. Penfield's experiments consisted of the implantation of electrodes deep into the cortexes of epilepsy patients who were to undergo surgery; he was able to drastically improve the memories of these patients through electrical stimulation. Dr. Adey's work was similar to Dr. Delgado's. He implanted tiny transceivers (radios that could both transmit and receive) into the brains of cats and chimpanzees. These sent signals to a receiver in his lab showing the electrical activity of the brain. These also sent signals back into the brain of the animal, modifying its behavior at the direction of the operator.

The joining of the use of radio transmissions and hypnotism to control a subject is called Radio-Hypnotic Intracerebral Control (RHIC). This technology has been under development since the 1930s, such as in these experiments described by L. L. Vasiliev, professor of physiology at the University of Leningrad:

As a control of the subject's condition, when she was outside the laboratory in another set of experiments, a radio set was used. The results obtained indicate that the method of using radio signals substantially enhances the experimental possibilities. I.F. Tomaschevsky [a Russian physiologist] carried out the first experiments with this subject at a distance of one or two rooms, and under conditions that the participant would not know or suspect that she would be experimented with. In other cases, the sender was not in the same house, and someone else observed the subject's behavior. Subsequent experiments at considerable distances were successful. One such experiment was carried out in a park at a distance. Men-

THE NEW YORK TIMES, MONDAY

RADIO 'MATADOR' STOPS WIRED BULL

Continued From Page 1, Col. 5

our understanding of the mind."

"We are in a precarious race," he said, "between the acquisition of many megatons of destructive power and the development of intelligent human beings who will make intelligent use of the formidible forces at our disposal."

Based on His Experiments

Dr. Delgado's contention that brain research has reached a stage of refinement where it can contribute to the solution of some of these problems is based he said, on many of his own experiments.

These have shown, he explained, that "functions traditionally related to the psyche, such as friendliness, pleasure or verbal expression, can be induced, modified and inhibited by direct electrical stimulation of the brain."

For example, he has been able to "play" monkeys and cats "like little electronic toys" that yawn, hide, fight, play, mate and go to sleep on command.

And with humans under treatment for epilepsy, he has increased word output sixfold in one person, has produced severe anxiety in another, and in several others has induced feelings

STUDYING BEHAVIOR: Dr. José M. R. Delgado in his office at Yale University School of Medicine.

Switzerland used a similar setup to stimulate various cerebral regions in conscious cats. He showed that electrical currents could influence the animal's posture, balance, movement and such basic psychic manifestations as fear and rage.

For some still unexplained reason, those techniques were

those films a of all the an the behavior

This permits tive assessmen social interact: quantification haviorial profi said. This is portant when modifications i of the group p stimulation of sponse in one animals.

For exampl several specifi brain can indu in a monkey,) tive data on t havior, as we others in the more precisel of various, s effects of el tion on individ social behavior

Some of the With such Delgado has ; Monkeys w a button that to the brain member of calms it down animals can b trol one anoth A monkey, tremely aggr will make "int only on compel the colony, friendlier, ones Monkeys a triggered into havior in whicl its mouth, turr

1965 article on Delgado.

tal suggestions to go to sleep were complied with within a minute.

An interesting event of the 1950s that may have indirectly contributed to American efforts to develop RHIC was the invention of the Neurophone by a 14 year-old whiz kid in 1958. The Neurophone converts sound (words, music, whatever) into electrical impulses which can then be transferred through any point on the body directly into the brain. It took over six years to convince the patent office it worked. Finally, the inventor, Patrick Flanagan, went to the patent office with his law-

Mindcontrol researcher Delgado in 1995.

yer and a working model. There, the disbelieving examiner told them if it could make a deaf patent office employee hear, the examiner would grant the patent. The device was tested and to the amazement of the examiner, the deaf employee "heard." The patent was granted on the spot.

In 1962 *Life Magazine* listed Gillis Patrick Flanagan as one of the top scientists in the world—and he was still only a teenager! With the passage of time, the youthful Master Flanagan became Doctor Flanagan, a research scientist at Tufts University. There he worked on a man-to-dolphin speech system for the Navy. That research led to an improved version of the Neurophone. When he attempted to patent his improvements the Defense Intelligence Agency (DIA) slapped it under a secrecy order for four years. Researchers looking into HAARP have noted that the government could well have maintained its interest in Dr. Flanagan's invention. If they could make it work wirelessly, without direct physical contact with the person receiving the messages, they could have one heck of a mind control device.

Many other devices and experiments have been used over the years in attempts to transmit words into the minds of subjects (wittingly or otherwise). Some have been startlingly successful. Some of HAARP's opponents fear that this might be another intended use of that facility. With HAARP as the transmitter, they fear that "words" could be put in the head of anyone anywhere within HAARP's receiving area (which would be, at the least, nearly all of the northern half of the world, and could perhaps be the entire globe).

Another Neurophone-like device was patented by Philip L. Stocklin. He received U.S. patent number 4,858,612 for a modestly designated "Hearing Device." This patent clearly picks up on the idea of beaming sounds directly into a person's brain by means of a microwave carrier. In this device:

[A] microphone is used to transform sound signals into electrical signals which are in turn analyzed and processed to provide controls for generating a plurality of microwave signals at different frequencies. The multifrequency microwaves are then applied to the brain in the region of the auditory cortex. By this method sounds are perceived by the mammal which are representative of the original sound received by the microphone.

The CIA is rumored to have achieved direct communications between the brain and a computer in 1969. In the 1970s the *South China Morning Post* reported that an American university had invented a mind reading machine which could record a person's thoughts. The original purpose of this invention was to help authorities investigate severe auto accidents. It was meant to be used on people who had entered into comas. The CIA was alleged to have learned of it and purchased the patent.

A curious piece of "conformation" is an "affidavit" anonymously posted on the Internet which reads:

In the spring of 1984, I was a lieutenant colonel serving in the National Defense Department of Taiwan. At that time, I read a classified document from the department that I serviced. The document indicated the Military Police Department of Taiwan had purchased the mind (thought) reading machine from the U.S. (In Taiwan, it was called Psychological Language Machine—it means the machine can read minds.). The document was a request to the U.S. for parts to repair malfunctioning machines. Before I left Taiwan, this machine had become the most effective weapon for the security departments of Taiwan, such as the Headquarters of Police Departments, Military Police Department, and the National Security & Investigation Department.

Certainly several researchers have achieved something like this since. For example, in 1994 the Colorado-based company Advanced Neurotechnologies, Inc. announced the development of a device they called Brainlink, a brainwave to computer interface system. Per their released specifications on the device, it amplifies 0.5Hz to 40Hz brainwaves and converts them to digital form. This is just one of several products now, or soon to be, available.

Nexus Magazine, Oct/Nov, 1996, declared:

British scientists are developing a concept for a computer chip which, when implanted into the skull behind the eye, will be able to record a person's every life time thought and sensation.

"This is the end of death," said Dr. Chris Winter of British Telecom's artificial-life team. He predicts that within thirty years it will be possible to relive other people's lives by playing back their experiences on a computer. "By combining this information with a record of a person's genes, we could recreate a person physically, emotionally and spiritually."

Dr. Winter and his team of scientists at BT's Martlesham Heath Laboratories, near Ipswich, call the chip "The Soul Catcher." Dr. Winter said "'an implanted chip would be like an aircraft's black box, and would enhance communications beyond current concepts." For example, police would be able to use it to relive an attack, rape or murder from the victim's viewpoint, to help catch the criminal. "...I could even play back the smells, sounds and sights of my holidays to friends."

Other more frightening applications include downloading an older person's experiences into a newborn baby by transplanting the chip.

Direct human mind/computer interface, via some type of "mind modem," is surely only a few years away from being as common as using fingers on keyboards and eyes on monitors are today. Of course, this will be a two-way street. Some would fear the ability of the machine to extract or enter data directly into one's mind. Other less timid souls no doubt will welcome it. With two people linked together via the computer one could have "virtual" telepathy. Potentially, this could be one of the greatest advancements in human history. That is, if the Conspiracy does not subvert this technology into enslaving us with it, a la Dr. Delgado's belief that "...[M]an does not have the right to develop his own mind."

After Project Pandora explored the bombardment of our embassy in Moscow, the Western intelligence community began to increasingly use microwave, ELF, and other forms of EMR in their clandestine mind control experiments. In 1974 the Army Medical and Information Agency, while responding to a FOIA request, produced a document entitled "Biological Effects of Electromagnetic Radiation" which discussed the research of Dr. Allen Frey and others. It revealed that scientists, at least ones working for the military, knew full well that the biological effects of microwave radiation had potential for application as offensive weapons.

Among the research paths taken by the scientists included in the Army report were: research into internal sound perception for disorienting or disrupting behavior patterns or for use in interrogations; electronic alteration of the blood-brain barrier permitting neurotoxins in the blood to reach the brain, resulting in severe neuropathological symptoms; and induction of voices inside the brain by use of signal modulation at very low power densities.

Dr. Frey's work was over a decade old at the time that report was made available. He published an article, "Human Auditory System Response to Modulated Electromagnetic Energy," in the July, 1962, issue of the *Journal of Applied Physiology*. In that article Frey discusses that even deaf people can pick up transmitted radio frequency (RF) sound patterns and speech, as the brain is a receiver. Dr. Frey elaborated on one experiment in which he used pulsed microwaves to stop the heart of a frog. He also discovered that microwaves directed at the hypothalamus had a profound effect on the emotions.

In research reminiscent of Philip Stocklin's "Hearing Device," Dr. Frey discovered that microwaves of 300 to 3,000 MHz could be "heard" by people, even if they were deaf, if pulsed at a certain rate. To his subjects the sounds seemed to be originating just in back of their heads. The sounds boomed, clicked, hissed or buzzed, depending upon the frequency. The real importance of this line of research was that this sound was being transmitted to the recipient without wires, and without the need of being in direct physical contact with the subject, unlike Dr. Flanagan's Neurophone.

A clicking identical to that heard by Dr. Frey's subjects, was heard nearly three decades later, in March of 1978, when the city of Eugene, Oregon, was doused in microwave radiation. *The Oregon Journal* broke the story under the headline: "Mysterious Radio Signals Causing Concern." The Federal Communications Commission (FCC) concluded that the signals came from a Navy transmitter, one located hundreds of miles away in California. The FCC's report of the affair concluded: "[M]icrowaves were the likely cause of several sudden illnesses among faculty researchers at Oregon State University." Many Oregonians complained of headaches, fatigue, inability to sleep, reddening of the skin, "clicks in the head" and a buzz that harmonized with a high pitched wail.

A similar situation developed later that year in Timmons, Ontario, Canada. Dr. Robert Beck issued a report on ELF fields and EEG (electroencephalogram) entrainment in which he reported finding alarming mood alterations in Canadians. Similarly, in the early 1980s another researcher, William Bise, discovered dangerous changes in the brain wave patterns of people in the Pacific Northwest. Both Dr. Beck and Mr. Bise, like many other observers, believed these changes were caused by the Soviet Woodpecker transmissions.

Putting voices in people's heads (or at least trying to) has been a popular pastime in military/intelligence circles for decades. Another FOIA request in 1974 resulted in The Joint Publications Research Service in Arlington, Virginia, making available a monograph entitled "Psychotronics in Engineering" by J.F. Schapitz, which proved to be another important discovery. Dr. Schapitz wrote that the spoken words of a hypnotist could be conveyed directly into the subconscious portion of the brain by means of modulated electromagnetic energy. He believed that he could use this method to program the subconscious without employing any technical devices for receiving or transcoding the messages and without the person exposed having any chance to control the information input. This technology, he said, could be used to induce hypnotic states in subjects at a distance; and by using words modulated on the microwave carrier frequencies, human subjects could be conditioned to perform various acts. He further proposed a research program to develop this technology. He also suggested recording the brain wave patterns induced by various drugs, then beaming these patterns via microwave at test subjects in an attempt to cause mental disruption in the subject appropriate to the prerecorded drug. His research project was later funded by the U.S. DOD, the same folks funding HAARP. Despite FOIA requests, the results of his work have never been revealed. Could HAARP be used someday to send a target population on an LSD-like trip? The answer seems to be "yes." This could be used to do more than merely disrupt soldiers in battle. Imagine the chaos, death and destruction that could be induced if they were to beam a "prerecorded drug" at a population center that made the people go wild with, say, sexual desire, or uncontrolled rage. LSD might seem mild compared to what they could do with "ecstasy," "crack," or "ice."

Dr. Schapitz' inspiration may have been an experiment done the preceding year at Walter Reed Hospital. There, in 1973, Dr. Joseph C. Sharp, while in a soundproof chamber, heard words spoken to him from outside the room. They had used a pulsed microwave audiogram (computer simulation of a voice) broadcasting from 300 MHz to 3 GHz. The words reached Dr. Sharp's brain in such a way that he was able to understand the words that were spoken.

That experiment prompted the following comment in *The Body Electric: Electromagnetism and the Foundation of Life,* by Robert O. Becker, M.D., and Gary Selden (Wm. Morrow & Company, 1985): "Such a device has obvious applications in covert operations designed to drive a target crazy with 'voices' or deliver undetected instructions to a programmed assassin." Daily the news blares wild tales of people who have committed terrible crimes after having been instructed by voices in their heads. One such was former mental patient Mark Chapman, killer of John Lennon of The Beatles. As he walked up to Lennon that morning in New York City a voice in his head kept repeating "do it, do it, do it…"

What percentage of these folks are actually crazy and what percentage are the victims of an out-of-control government agency "testing" new toys? There are literally hundreds of cases of people who not only believe that they are the victims of such harassment, but have filed lawsuits against several governments, including the United States, Sweden, Great Britain and

Canada.

This reprehensible research into controlling the minds of others apparently continues unchecked to this day. Incredibly, the results from research projects of this type are often published in publicly available scientific and technical journals and by mainstream publishing houses. Interested readers might consult, for example, James C. Lin's *Electromagnetic Interaction With Biological Systems* (Plenum Press, 1989). Professor Lin, then with the Department of Bioengineering, University of Illinois, Chicago, was the chap who designed the above-referenced experiment at Walter Reed and has published a number of books and articles on this subject.

The experiment was but part of a long series of tests that began in 1965 after the Advanced Research Projects Agency (ARPA) set up a lab at Walter Reed. In time this lab's research confirmed that microwaves cause central nervous system effects and can influence behavior.

Not every scientist has cooperated with the CIA and the military, thankfully. One scientist with the courage of his convictions was Dr. John C. Lilly, who pioneered man-dolphin research, as well as the use of psychedelic (mind altering) drugs to explore and understand human consciousness. In the mid-1950s he was conducting experimental studies on monkeys at the National Institute of Health (NIH). In studies similar to Delgado's, he discovered a method of inserting electrodes into the brain to stimulate precise centers of pleasure, pain, fear, anxiety and anger. An unexpected result of his work was that, as Lilly refined his brain "maps," officials of the CIA and other agencies descended upon him with requests for briefings. Dr. Lilly insisted that all briefings remain unclassified and completely open to the public. One can imagine that this did not set well with "security"-minded officials. Lilly became concerned that his research might result in CIA agents roaming the globe on deadly missions with remote controlling electrodes strategically implanted in their brains. It quickly became apparent to him that the NIH was a front for people he did not want to deal with. Realizing that it would be impossible for him to work at NIH without compromising his principles, he resigned in 1958.

In 1970 the RAND Corporation (an offshoot of the Air Force), published two companion reports. The first, "A Brief Survey of Literature Relating to Influence of Low Intensity Microwaves on Nervous Function," found that the U.S. microwave guidelines in effect for the public provided for nonthermal levels of microwaves which could be demonstrated to produce behavioral disturbances in humans. These disturbances include: irritability, loss of memory, fatigue, headache, tremors, hallucinations, autonomic nervous system disorders and disturbed sensory functioning. The report covered several possible mechanisms which could account for these effects.

The companion report, "A Direct Mechanism for the Direct Influence of Microwave Radiation on Neuroelectric Function," was produced for RAND by R. J. MacGregor. In it he reported that specific power levels can produce auditory hallucinations in a field that would still be averaged as low intensity and nonthermal. Keep in mind that the safety standards set by the U.S. government for microwave exposure are based on the presumption that if it doesn't heat, it doesn't harm. He concluded that neuroelectric effects should exhibit a maximum effect in the microwave range.

After the success of the pulsed-microwave audiograms at Walter Reed, plans were drawn up by researchers under the umbrellas of several agencies, mostly the CIA's MKUltra, to develop mind control techniques through experiments on human volunteers. Using Lin's and Frey's techniques and expanding on Dr. Schapitz' theories, they intended to try transmitting hypnotic commands directly into the subconscious portion of the mind. It is still unclear if they attempted these experiments, as the relevant documentation has been destroyed.

One CIA research program in the field of electromagnetic behavior modification that followed on the successes of Dr. Delgado's work was code named Sleeping Beauty. Dr. Ivor Browning was put in charge of a laboratory in New Mexico. His work centered around working with the hypothalamus or "sweet spot" of the brain. Here he found that direct stimulation of this so-called "pleasure center" of the brain could produce intense euphoria in recipients of the stimulation.

Dr. Browning wired a radio receiver into the pleasure center of a donkey, with which he could create intense happiness in the animal. Using the wash of pleasure as an "electronic carrot," Browning sent the unwitting creature up a 2,000 foot New Mexico mountain and returned it to its point of origin. As long as the donkey stayed on the path proceeding toward its destination, it was rewarded with a continuous flow of pleasure; if it strayed from its intended path, the signal stopped. Dr. Browning said: "You've never seen a donkey so eager to keep on course in your whole life!"

FOIA released documents have revealed that the CIA utilized that same electronic carrot technique on pigeons. Equipped with miniature microphone-transmitters, the pigeons were induced to land on the ledge of a KGB safehouse where the devices could monitor conversations within.

Electromagnetic radiation has been used extensively by both the CIA and the KGB. One example of Soviet use is seen in a 1989 report of the KGB subjecting people undergoing interrogation to electromagnetic fields. These fields, otherwise undetected by the subject, were reported to produce a panic reaction, thereby bringing them closer to breaking down under questioning. The subjects, of course, were not told that they were being placed under the influence of these beams. This seemed to validate the revelations of a bizarre device revealed a few years earlier by Dr. W. Ross Adey. He had released photographs and a fact sheet concerning what he called the Russian Lida machine. This device supposedly consisted of a small transmitter emitting 10-Hertz waves, which was said to make the subject susceptible to hypnotic suggestion. The device utilized a now long-outmoded vacuum-tube design. Substantiating this report, former American POWs returned from Korea said that they had seen similar devices used during interrogation sessions in POW camps there.

Robert O. Becker, M.D., wrote in *Crosscurrents*:

> Since the mid-1970s, [Dr. Jose] Delgado has been director of the premier Spanish neurophysiological laboratory, Centro Ramon y Cajal. His interest has shifted from direct electrical stimulation of the brain to the broader area of the biological effects of electromagnetic fields. He has studied the influence of specific frequencies of magnetic fields on the behavior and emotions of monkeys, without using any implanted electrodes or radio receivers. While Delgado did not publish any of this work in the scientific journals, its existence leaked out.

Hundreds of researchers have charted the brain's electromagnetic output in the last few decades. There is now general agreement in this field that they have found four basic clusters of brain wave frequencies, each with an associated mental state. The generalized frequencies are: Beta(13-30Hz); Alpha(8-13Hz); Theta(4-7Hz); Delta(0.5-4Hz).

The first cluster, called "beta waves" is associated with a "normal" level of awareness, when one's attention is directed outward toward everyday actions. At the top end of the beta waves, up around 30 plus cycles per second, researches have discovered agitated states, such as anger or fear or the effects of stress, any of which can impair thinking and reasoning skills. The second cluster of brain waves is called "alpha waves," associated with relaxed states of mind. These seem to be the ideal states for learning and focused mental functioning. Numerous electronic meditation and bio-feedback machines are on the market that claim to aid one in achieving alpha state and/or the state below it, called theta state. "Theta waves" have been linked to mental imagery, access to deep-rooted memories and internal mental focus, such as in meditation. This state is often seen in children and is commonly used in behavior modification and in lucid dreaming ex-

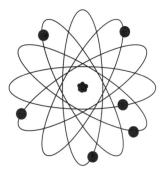

periments. The fourth and lowest range of the human brain is in the ultra slow (.5-4 hertz) "delta waves" which are found in deep sleep.

One long-term goal of the CIA has been to find out whether or not mind control could be achieved through the use of a precise, external, electromagnetic means. Researchers, both Western and Soviet, now know that the human brain operates within this narrow band at the very bottom of the electromagnetic scale. ELF waves carry no ionizing radiation (the kind of radiation that

comes from atomic bombs) and produce very low heat, therefore they do not manifest gross, observable physical effects on living organisms.

Only after decades of study is evidence of the health risks associated with ELF becoming generally known. However, their very indetectablity makes ELF signals ideal for covert use. Once the government's pet psychs had that piece of information, a whole new wave of research started up, homing in on using EMR in the ELF range as a handle on mind control. A very serious problem with HAARP is that this very frequency range is targeted for extensive experiments using the HAARP array.

In previous chapters I mentioned that the Soviets had made considerable progress in determining useful and dangerous ELF frequencies. For example, published Soviet experiments with ELF showed that there was a marked increase in psychiatric and central nervous system disorders and symptoms of stress for sailors working close to ELF generators. Western science has not lagged in making similar discoveries, even if the media has failed to report these discoveries to the general public.

For example, in California, Dr. Adey demonstrated that animal brain waves could be altered directly by ELF fields. He showed that monkey brains would fall in phase (or be "entrained") with ELF waves. These waves can easily pass through the skull, which normally protects the central nervous system from outside influence. As mentioned above, there are hundreds of "brain boost" and "bio-feedback" machines on the market purporting to aid one in achieving a desired mental state, such as "alpha" or "delta" states for increased thinking or deep meditation. These devices, when directly attached to the head, as in Dr. Delgado's early work, send the brain a weak ELF signal in the same range as the desired state. The brain, receiving the incoming "message" goes into sympathetic resonance with it, i.e. "locks on." If HAARP is allowed to broadcast we could all be locking on to its "message."

Another researcher in this field in the 1970s was Dr. Elizabeth Rauscher, Director of Technic Research Laboratory, in San Leandro, California. In the mid-1990s she was very successful at predicting earthquakes by monitoring background ELF. She has been studying the effects of ELF on people for decades. In one series of experiments in ELF effects on human subjects, she discovered that ELF at one frequency produced nausea for more than an hour. Another frequency, one she called "the marijuana frequency," gets people laughing. "Give me the money and three months," she said, "and I'll be able to affect the behavior of eighty percent of the people in this town without their knowing it."

ABUSE OF POWER

The Government's past record of abuses in the area of civil rights is well documented. Within the past 30 years alone, we have witnessed the effects of operations with names like: MKUltra, MHChaos and COINTELPRO. Public outcry over the revealed crimes of these programs led to the issuance of many Executive Orders (EOs) and the implementation of regulations. These prohibited the military and the intelligence community (IC), and particularly the CIA, from engaging in assassination, conducting domestic intelligence gathering operations, experimenting on involuntary human subjects, and a host of other clearly criminal activities. These laws and EOs, of course, would not have been necessary if these instruments of state power shared our belief in the principles of a constitutional republic.

Numerous researchers and citizen alert groups have generated mountains of evidence that oversight committees oversee little and restrictions on intelligence operations are met with open hostility or cunning subterfuge. As we all know, where there are laws, there are loopholes, and individuals and institutions who deliberately capitalize upon the existence of said loopholes. The still officially denied Iran-Contra/Contra-cocaine connection is one of the more blatant examples.

An indisputable case of abuse was reported by the President's Intelligence Oversight Board (IOB) in 1996. The IOB is a special panel appointed by President Clinton to investigate allegations of unlawful activity in the IC. It issued a 28 June, 1996, report on U.S. ties to Guatemala's repressive armed forces. IC-watchers have known for years that the CIA station in Guatemala has assisted that country's brutal security forces for decades. The IOB's unusually critical report, calling the CIA to task for its relationship with Guatemalan military personnel guilty of severe human rights abuses, came to these spook watchers as a welcome breath of fresh air.

President Clinton ordered the IOB review in March 1995, after allegations surfaced that the CIA had financed "assets" in the Guatemalan military who were responsible, at least in part, for the abduction, torture and murder of U.S. citizens in Guatemala. In one high profile case, a team of Guatemalan military personnel (among them CIA assets) were said to have tortured and executed Efrain Bamaca Velasquez, a rebel leader married to American lawyer Jennifer Harbury. The allegations generated substantial press coverage, compelling Clinton to order the investigation.

Among the board's most significant conclusions are the following:

We found... two areas in which CIA's performance was unacceptable. First, until late 1994, insufficient attention was given to allegations of serious human rights abuse made against several station assets or liaison contacts. Second, the CIA failed to provide enough information on this subject to policy-makers and the Congress to permit proper policy and Congressional oversight.

In the course of our review, we found that several CIA assets were credibly alleged to have ordered, planned, or participated in serious human rights violations such as assassination, extrajudicial execution, torture, or kidnapping while they were assets—and that the CIA's Directorate of Operations (DO) headquarters was aware at the time of the allegations.

...a number of the station's liaison contacts—Guatemalan officials with whom the station worked in an official capacity—were also alleged to have been involved in human rights abuses or in covering them up.

The IOB's findings have confirmed what many activists and critics of U.S. policy toward Guatemala have long alleged: that the CIA put some of the world's most notorious human rights abusers on the payroll. A spokesman for the human rights advocacy group Amnesty International said the IOB report "clearly points to a systemic problem of neglect to the human rights dimension of intelligence operations." Of course, I am making this point because I believe that if the CIA can do that in Guatemala they can do it anywhere; if they get ahold of HAARP how safe will our human—and civil rights be?

Laws, EO, and Oversight Boards notwithstanding, today Big Brother is watching like never before. Police TV cameras are going up on street corners across America, and around the world. Private industry and businesses likewise have gone monitor-crazy, with cameras watching both employees and customers equally. In 1996 the President signed into law a Telecommunications Bill which requires all new telephone equipment to be pre-equipped with a device to allow the government to tap in at any time. Several other recent bills, such as the Anti-Terrorism Bill, have asked for unprecedented, and clearly unconstitutional, expansion of police and federal wiretap and surveillance powers. A recent newsbite reported that under the Clinton administration wiretaps have gone up by 40% over the period that George Bush was in office.

One appalling example of Big Brotherism is the Financial Crimes Enforcement Network (FinCEN). The Justice Department created the FinCEN after several cabinet level agencies signed a Memorandum of Cooperation in 1995. FinCEN now monitors databases from the IRS, FBI, Drug Enforcement Administration, Secret Service, Customs Service, Postal Service, Census Bureau, CIA, National Security Agency (which intercepts data on international wire transfers), Defense Intelligence Agency, Bureau of Alcohol, Tobacco, and Firearms, the Immigration and Naturalization Service, National Se-curity Council, the Federal Deposit Insurance Corporation, the Comptroller of the Currency, the Federal Reserve, and the State Department's Bureau of Intelligence and Research.

FinCEN also accesses state records of real estate ownership, property tax payments, motor vehicles, drivers' licenses, etc. It also accesses commercial databases that assist it in obtaining credit records, telephone records, magazine subscription lists and even supermarket purchase data—every purchase you make with one of those cool new discount shopper cards goes straight to FinCEN. FinCEN has access to all of this information and all of these databases without need of a warrant.

FinCEN uses this data to create dossiers on every person its artifically intelligent computer system suspects of possibly engaging in a financially traceable crime. These dossiers are then transmitted to any and all federal agencies which might feel compelled to investigate these suspected crimes. If the CIA truly is "prevented" from engaging in domestic surveillance, then they are about the only agency that is!

Another way around laws and directives against spying on Americans and engaging in other domestic intelligence operations is found in the ruse of hiding behind a "national security" smokescreen. The military/industrial/intelligence community has used the "national security" dodge for decades. In the absence of clear definitions of such terms as "national security" and "national security risk" they have discovered a catch-all cover.

Another tactic used by federal and military agencies to circumvent the wishes of "We the People" and our elected representatives has been resorting to black budgets—funding themselves with income not derived from Congress and the national budget. The illegal resupply of the Contras by Ollie North, et al, is an example of a black budget operation. Still another way around oversight has been the use of uninformed contractors. EOs and regulations which limit intelligence activities do not extend to non-intelligence government agencies or to their contractors. Executive Order 12333 specifies that government contractors do not need to know that their services support U.S.

Intelligence objectives. This is probably the situation with HAARP. Many universities participate in the HAARP project. Some of them have strict policies prohibiting them from engaging in secret projects. HAARP's apparent openness allows them to participate with "clear conscience." EO 12333 allows the CIA/DOD to contract out a project, like HAARP, without the participants having a clue as to the real objective of the project.

In its report of 8 July, 1992, the Senate Subcommittee on Oversight of Government Management addressed the problem of tracking funds granted to government-contracted research and development (R&D) centers. The report notes that the problem is compounded by DOD's penchant for creating hard-to-monitor "shell" contractors as disbursement centers for funding programs. Neither the contractors nor their subcontractors are directly accountable to Congress. Being beyond Congressional oversight, they have the license to operate as government surrogates in intelligence operations about which "officially" they know nothing.

The Army's Research and Technology Program sponsors 42 laboratories and R&D centers, employing approximately 10,000 scientists and engineers. The annual budget of $1.3 billion is only a small part of overall DOD research spending. Weapons research, which includes the development and testing of "nonlethal" weapons, is not governed by laws restricting the activities of intelligence agencies, though it may be presumed that these agencies contribute to and benefit from such research.

We have seen that radio waves (especially in the microwave band) can be used to put words into people's heads. We have also seen that those words can be used to drive a person crazy or to hypnotize them. We have seen that the intelligence community and the military have an ongoing desire to "win the battle for the minds of men," and do not seem to care if they have to turn "men" into "zombies" in order to accomplish this aim.

How many more Watkins and Delgados are there out there, waiting for a chance to tinker with people's heads? Who might have an interest in using the information that such researchers unearth to further their schemes for a Brave New World? HAARP, tellingly, is owned and managed (if not operated on a day by day basis) by the very people who have been at the forefront of this covert war for decades. Can we really believe their saintly expressions of altruistic good intentions now, after they have burned, drugged and electrocuted the brains of our fellow Americans for at least three generations?

Unfortunately, this chapter barely touches on this cesspool of nastiness in the name of National Security, much less the globalist implications. For a far more detailed and penetrating analysis of the Conspiracy's use of mind control, read Jim Keith's 1997 Adventures Unlimited book, *Mind Control, World Control*.

To sum up what we know about U.S. government-sponsored research into the bioeffects of exposure to microwave, ELF and other forms of electromagnetic radiation, we can say that: it is expensive, extensive and continuing; the U.S. government has a record of having engaged in mindcontrol experimentation using this technology; various agencies of the government have a record of circumventing legal restrictions placed upon their activities; neither Congress nor the courts appear willing to look closely into black intelligence and weapons procurement programs; a number of U.S. government agencies might have interest in testing directed-energy technologies on U.S. citizens under non-clinical/non-controlled (real life) circumstances. For example: the DOD, might want to test ranges and degrees of "non-lethality"; the DOE could want to explore "safety" limits; the CIA would surely want to test behaviour modification capabilities; and the NSA would be interested in such testing for technological refinement purposes.

Part Four:
Environmental Modification

Mankind has always had a keen interest in the weather. Throughout human history we have seen the effects of weather on crops, and the loss of life and property through the violence of storms. In ancient times people made sacrifice to the gods in a crude attempt at influencing the weather. In many parts of the world people still conduct elaborate rituals for rain and fertility. Today science has joined in the war against unruly nature and unpredictable or unwanted weather.

"Environmental modification" is the term used to describe human intervention, intentional or unintentional, in the atmospheric processes and events that produce the world's weather. Environmental modification, or ENMOD, also includes other environmental modification, such as altering ocean currents, depletion of the ozone layer or production of greenhouse gases. ENMOD covers both local, regional and global effects.

Deliberate scientific modification of the environment, and of the weather in particular, has taken place since the middle of this century, beginning in 1946 in the U.S. with efforts at cloud seeding. A variety of cloud seeding technologies are employed commercially in this country, and around the world, in attempts to:
 •clear fog from airports,
 •augment snowpacks in mountain regions,
 •increase rain from summer
 •reduce destruction from hail, and even to
 •put out forest fires.
Unintentional modification has taken place since ancient times. The transformation of ancient Mesopotamia (Sumeria and Babylon) from a rich agricultural region (the Fertile Crescent) into a desert through over-farming is but one example. Weather can be modified inadvertently by cities and powerplants

(causing such phenomena as smog and acid rain), and through agricultural activities such as irrigation and deforestation.

In the 1950s weather modification was the stuff of science fiction and popular "frontiers of science" stories; but by the late 1970s it had become not only science fact, but the subject of national and international law. For example the U.S. became a signatory to the United Nations' Convention on the Prohibition of Military or Any Other Hostile Use of Environmental Modification Techniques (ENMOD Convention). The ENMOD Convention prohibits the use of techniques that would have widespread, long-lasting or severe effects through deliberate manipulation of natural processes and cause such phenomena as earthquakes, tidal waves and changes in climate and weather patterns.

Several researchers have commented that the United Nations would not have bothered to create a law against environmental modification unless someone actually had the technology to do it (or at least thought they would have such technology in the not-too-distant future). Note that the deliberate causation of earthquakes is one of the prohibited uses. Can the military, and/or their scientists, call up an earthquake on demand? In a moment I will show that there is a growing body of evidence that they can—and that HAARP may be a part of this technology.

U.S. involvement in and support for weather control research, at a federal level, goes back to the very beginning of scientific weather modification. No readily available accounting of federal funding for those purposes, however, exists prior to fiscal year (FY) 1959. At that time Congress directed the National Science Foundation "to initiate and support a program of study, research, and evaluation in the field of weather modification" and "to report annually to the President and the Congress thereon." Beginning with about $3 million in FY 1959, direct federal funding for research into deliberate and inadvertent weather modification rose to more than $20 million by FY 1980 and by then had come to involve as many as seven federal agencies.

In addition to the National Science Foundation, principal participants have been the Departments of Commerce, Defense, and Interior. Other lesser players have included the Department of Agriculture's Forest Service, the Departments of Energy and Transportation, and NASA. These funds supported research and experimentation in precipitation enhancement (so-called rain making), fog and cloud modification, hail and lightning suppression, hurricane modification, and studies of unintentional weather modification.

In 1958 Captain Howard T. Orville, White House advisor on weather modification, described for the press a very Tesla-like study by the Department of Defense. The DOD, he said, was studying "ways to manipulate the charges of the earth and sky and so affect the weather" by using electronic modification of the atmosphere to ionize or de-ionize selected regions of the sky over targeted areas. Decades of bizarre experiments, strange weather and weather-related disasters have followed that statement. Many Americans, my father for one, blamed the weird weather on atmospheric nuclear testing; but few knew about the many other attempts at manipulation and control of the atmosphere. The government has continued to do strange things in, and to, the sky since.

In the 1960s a number of significant upper-atmospheric experiments took place. In one, copper needles were dumped into the ionosphere as a "telecommunications shield." The government claimed they were trying to create an artificial ionosphere so as to maintain radio communications without interruption. The natural ionosphere is regularly affected by a number of factors, particularly sun spot activity, which can adversely affect radio reception. They attempted to put 3.5 billion copper needles, each 2 to 4 cm long, into orbit at an altitude of a little under 2,000 miles up. These were supposed to form an artificial uniform ionosphere about 6 miles thick and 25 miles wide. The United States planned to add to the number of needles if the experiment was successful. This plan was strongly opposed by the International Union of Astronomers.

A bizarre variety of chemicals were also dumped into the upper atmosphere, such as barium powder, with even less plausible explanations. Israeli scientists even proposed using deadly e-coli bacteria as cloud seeding material. This suggestion was made on the grounds that the "standard" seed, silver iodide, only worked on cold clouds and the bacteria would work in warm weather. It is unclear at this time if their suggestion was ever acted on.

It should be noted that the Navy has been involved in weather modification for some time. It was the Navy that developed the pyrotechnic seeding devices that became a standard of the industry for many cloud seeders.

Scientific research into weather modification really took off in the 1970s. In part this was due to increasingly successful use of cloud seeding technology. The evolution of a scientific infrastructure was perhaps of even grater importance. Ever more powerful computers and sophisticated statistical approaches became available. Also, increasing scientific manpower kept pace with growing research budgets. This allowed for investigation and research into atmospheric dynamics of sufficient scope to pay off in meaningful scientific results. The weather balloons and sounding rockets of the fifties gave way to the geosynchronous satellites and ionospheric heaters of the seventies.

If anything, the pace of discovery in this field has only continued to accelerate. That is why some researchers dismiss the official claims that HAARP is intended to make basic discoveries, i.e., "characterize" the ionosphere. These scoffers believe that weather researchers left the "age of discovery" long ago— the metaphorical days of the weather Columbuses and Magellans are long past. Now is the age of application.

Possible proof of that may be seen in a wire story from 1997. The Associated Press (AP) reported that an unnamed state-owned Russian company offered to use man-made "cyclones" to clear the smoke-hazed skies of Malaysia. " AP said, "Skies from Thailand to Australia have been choked with thick haze for four months, endangering the health of millions. ...Indonesian forest fires—some set intentionally to clear land—were blamed for much of the smog." In a classic "come-on" the Russians offered to demonstrate their technology for free—the first time. According to AP, *The Star* and other Malaysian newspapers on 13 November, 1997, reported that Environment Minister Law Hieng Ding said: "Since it does not cost us anything, there is no harm in allowing them to demonstrate to us." *The Sun*, another Malaysian paper, quoted Minister Law as saying, "The new technology uses satellites and not rockets, gigantic fans, airplanes or chemicals. I cannot tell you in detail now about the whole mechanism involved except that it is strong enough to change weather systems." AP said that if the test proved successful the Malaysian government was prepared to spend millions to clear the air. It is uncertain if the Russian test was successful. The fires burned out and the air eventually cleared without human intervention.

NUCLEAR ENMOD

More than 300 megatons yield worth of nuclear bombs were exploded in the atmosphere in the 1950s and '60s. This released a vast quantity of charged and radioactive particles, as well as over 40,000 electromagnetic pulses (EMPs).

Early HAARP literature discussed the possibility of using HAARP to create artificial EMPs. This was suggested as a way to determine the success of "hardening" electronic devices against the effects of the EMP without having to use nuclear devices. This of course would save millions of dollars as well as remove the threat of nuclear contamination of the environment. However, if HAARP could be used to create artificial EMPs, that would give it tremendous potential in times of war—from knocking out incoming missiles to wiping out enemy computers.

An important breakthrough in understanding the upper atmosphere occurred in 1958 when Dr. James Van Allen proved the existence of zones of charged particles trapped in the earth's magnetic field, the magnetosphere, thousands of miles up, well above the highest levels of the gaseous envelope of the atmosphere.

Later that same year, Project Argus, as part of the International Geophysical Year (1958-59), detonated three nuclear devices in the Van Allen Radiation Belts between August and September of 1958. This was done despite heavy protest by leading world scientists. These detonations have since cost the taxpayers of the world trillions of dollars. How? Prior to Project Argus the Van Allen belts were quite weak. These explosions of nuclear devices in them "beefed" them up by hundreds of times. Now, whenever a space vehicle is launched, it must pass as rapidly as possible through these belts. This is to reduce the amount of time the craft's occupants, payload and delicate electronics are exposed to their damaging radiation. If Project Argus, and the other nuclear detonations that followed, had not gone forward, many scientists believe that we could have used shallower, less fuel-intensive trajectories to launch space missions into orbit and beyond.

Not only did the Project Argus explosions augment the existing belts, they also created several new inner radiation belts, generating world-wide effects. Other upper atmospheric nuclear blasts since have created even more new radiation belts as well as severely reshaping and destablizing the naturally existing ones. Some scientists have estimated that it may take centuries for the belts to restablize to their natural shape, altitudes and intensities. Project Argus is another sterling example of the bull-headed, "who gives a damn, we'll do what we want" attitude of DOD scientists. Do we really want these types of people mucking about with the ionosphere? Dr. Van Allen enthusiastically supported Project Argus and today supports HAARP.

Project Argus is hardly the only time scientists have acted with insufferable arrogance. One such event was the very one that ushered in the Atomic Age. Just prior to the detonation of the first atom bomb by the Manhattan Project, a few dozen of Manhattan's scientists became alarmed that the bomb might set off a chain reaction in the atmosphere. Their concern was that the heat of the blast might be sufficient to cause the oxygen in the air to burn. If the bomb had set the atmosphere on fire it would have wiped out all life on this planet, leaving the earth a scorched cinder. The burning sky in the films *Voyage To the Bottom of the Sea* and *Damnation Alley* reflect this fear. A sizable minority of Manhattan Project physicists officially begged for the cancellation of the bomb shot, designated "Trinity Test." The Department of War (now Defense) ignored their pleas and, risking the possible total destruction of this world, went ahead with the "war effort," detonating the first atomic device in the early morning hours of 16 July, 1945.

With the very real dangers posed by HAARP, and the official non-consideration of same (perhaps as part of yet another "war effort"), it would seem that nothing has changed. We were "lucky" with the bomb. The air did not burst into flame, however, recently released studies from the National Cancer Institute shows that children's cancer rates have climbed every year since Trinity, due to radioactive fallout. Will we be as "lucky" with HAARP?

Evidence against the use of nukes has been mounting since the Trinity shot. One example was the Baby Tooth Survey, the findings of which were released in 1962. The Committee for Nuclear Information (CNI) had collected over 80,000 baby teeth and from them determined that the level of strontium-90 in baby teeth had increased 14-fold between 1949 and 1957. Strontium-90 is a deadly radioactive substance released in nuclear explosions. The Baby Tooth Survey helped to stimulate the public outrage that led to the signing of the Limited Test Ban Treaty (LTBT).

The LTBT was concluded between the U.S. and the U.S.S.R. in 1963. Since then over 100 nations have signed on to this pact banning nuclear weapons testing underwater, in the atmosphere, or in outer space. It does not stop nuclear testing, only limiting nuke shots to underground tests in an effort to reduce the environmental damage of nuclear testing. France and China have not signed the LTBT.

The year before the LTBT went into effect the U.S. set off a nuclear detonation in the upper atmosphere that was a thousand times larger than the Project Argus explosions. That was the Starfish burst of 9 July, 1962. It was part of a series of atmospheric tests to see what effects nuclear devices would have on the ionosphere. Starfish exceeded all predictions. The magnetic storm it created destroyed three satellites and blacked out Hawaii!

Not to be outdone, the U.S.S.R. undertook similar nuke shots in the upper atmosphere later in that same year. These detonations created three more new radiation belts between 4,300 and 8,000 miles above the earth.

In the 1990s the National Cancer Institute (NCI), a U.S. government agency, investigated fallout from aboveground atom bomb shots staged inside the U.S. in the 1950s and '60s. These were mostly conducted at the Nevada Test Site, located in the desert a few dozen miles north of Las Vegas. The NCI's August, 1997, report makes it clear that these nuclear bomb tests sent clouds of fallout over virtually all of the continental U.S. The focus of the NCI's study was an isotope known as iodine-131 (I-131), which, like strontium-90, is among the harmful substances spewed out by atomic explosions and carried by the wind and deposited by rain. These radioactive particles, I-131, accumulate in the thyroid gland, and are a "suspected" cause of cancer.

According to an NCI fact sheet, the institute found that the fallout was so pervasive that "everyone living in the contiguous 48 states was exposed to I-131 at some level." They estimated that 10,000 to 75,000 cases of thyroid cancer may have resulted from these tests. "For most people," the NCI reports, "the greatest I-131 exposure came from drinking contaminated milk." Cows (and goats, whose milk concentrates iodine-131 more than cows) ate grass tainted with fallout, which was in turn concentrated in their milk and was then drunk by unsuspecting Americans. Rural children received higher levels of exposure than their urban counterparts. This was because farmers often kept a cow for home consumption, so farm children drank fresh milk laced with fresh fallout, whereas city kids received milk that could have taken up to a week to make the trip from dairy to distributor to store to home or school. In that week much of the radioactive I-131, which has a half-life of 8 days, would have decayed back into non-radioactive iodine.

Downwinders (http://www.downwinders.org), an organization of civilian and military victims of nuclear tests, issued a statement calling the NCI report too little, too late. The group is challenging the government to investigate and report on the full range of radioactive poisons spewed out by nuclear tests. In a prepared statement they asked:

Absent from the study are such isotopes as Strontium 90, Cesium 137, Zirconium, and on and on. These all have half-lives much longer than those of Iodine 131, with many still in existence today. Many of these, like Strontium 90, seek out tissues of the body and there become lodged and remain for the lifetime of the persons exposed... Such exposures can lead to leukemia and other cancers. The worst case is that if the Iodine 131 resulted in 10,000 to 75,000 cases of thyroid cancer alone, how many cases did the other isotopes produce, and of those hundreds of thousands of cases that they would induce, how many innocent, unwitting, and unsuspecting Americans died?

Other public health specialists and victims of the tests have voiced agreement that the information in the NCI's report should have been made available decades ago. Senator Tom Harkin of Iowa, a state with surprisingly high exposure rates, has begun hearings on the matter. Harkin, who lost a brother to thyroid cancer in June 1997, and who has himself had extensive thyroid problems, has pledged to find out what the government knew, when it knew it, and why such alarming information was kept from the public.

It is important to remember that until Energy Secretary Hazel O'Leary began the make the truth known in 1994, the government had been reassuring the public for decades that there were no health risks associated with these aboveground nuclear tests—just as they try to reassure us today about HAARP. Did they know the danger back in the '50s and '60s and cover it up from the "get go" because they considered that a "few" deaths from cancer were the "price of freedom"? Or were they truly ignorant of the dangers of the testing, and only later covered it up as typical bureaucratic CYA ("cover your ass")? Will we find out that HAARP is deadly dangerous only decades after the victims have been buried?

Apparently hundreds of different radiation experiments were conducted on unwitting human subjects after the development of the atomic bomb—such as intentionally serving plutonium to test children in their Quaker Oat Meal. These atrocities were kept secret for decades. They only became public knowledge after Energy Secretary O'Leary declassified documents that revealed and verified the federal government's involvement. Today evidence is coming forward of similar covert testing of electromagnetic and radio-frequency weapons involving non-consenting human subjects. Is HAARP going to be just one more? What shocking revelations of dirty deeds done with HAARP do future generations have to look forward to?

ENMOD LEGISLATION

In 1976 U.S. Senator Claiborne Pell (D-Rhode Island) said:

The U.S. and other world Powers should sign a treaty to outlaw the tampering with weather as an instrument of war. It may seem farfetched to think of using weather as a weapon—but I am convinced that the U.S. did in fact use rainmaking techniques as a weapon of war in Southeast Asia. We need a treaty now to prevent such actions—before military leaders of the world start directing storms, manipulating climates and inducing earthquakes against their enemies. It may seem a great leap of imagination to move from an apparent effort by the U.S. to muddy the Ho Chi Minh trail in Laos by weather modification to such science fiction ideas as unleashing earthquakes, melting the polar ice cap, changing the course of warm ocean currents, or modifying the weather of an adversary's farm belt. But in military technology, today's science fiction is tomorrow's strategic reality.

As Bernard Eastlund put it: "The boundary between science fiction and science comes with can you actually make the thing that you're proposing." HAARP seems to have crossed that boundary.
In 1966 Dr. Gordon J. F. MacDonald (born 1929) wrote:

The key to geophysical warfare is the identification of environmental instabilities to which the addition of a small amount of energy would release vastly greater amounts of energy.

This was in *Geophysical Warfare: How to Wreck the Environment* a chapter he contributed to Nigel Calder's book, "Unless Peace Comes: A Scientific Forecast of New Weapons" (Viking Penguin, 1968). Dr. MacDonald was no off-the-deep-end loony; he was one of this nation's top, internationally recognized scientists. At the time he penned those words he was Associate Director of the Institute of Geophysics and Planetary Physics at the UCLA. He was also a member of the President's Science Advisory Committee, and was later made a member of the President's Council on Environmental Quality.

He published numerous papers and articles on future weapons technology (with which Senator Pell was apparently familiar). These suggested such coming "advances" as manipulation or control over the weather and climate, including ocean waves and melting or destabilizing of the polar ice caps; intentional ozone depletion; triggering earthquakes; and control of the human brain by utilizing the earth's energy fields. In 1969 Dr. MacDonald wrote:

Our understanding of basic environmental science and technology is primitive, but still more primitive are our notions of the proper political forms and procedures to deal with the consequences of modification.

It would appear that the gap between our understanding of environmental science and technology, and our ability to grapple with this knowledge as a body politic, has changed little in the intervening decades. We need to find ways to prevent science from creating ever more and bigger monsters to come out of Pandora's Box. This requires you, the reader, the citizen, to take action. Your assistance is needed to create the necessary "forms and procedures to deal with the consequences of modification."

Professor MacDonald's recipe of "little in/big out" is one of the basic principles that HAARP works under. HAARP clearly is designed to exploit environmental weaknesses, just as Dr. MacDonald suggested. It is very difficult to read his material and look at HAARP and not see a weapons system such as he described.

In the HAARP literature scientists repeatedly refer to "nonlinear" processes—what are they? Research scientist Al Zielinski explains by giving the following example of nonlinear "little in/big out" effects:

Experiment #1
Imagine we had an unlimited amount of dominoes and we lined them up from here to, let's say, Paris. Then we could tip the first domino with 10 grams; it will fall down and cause the second domino to tumble, too, etc. The first action of 10 grams will cause all the dominoes to tumble including the last domino in Paris.

From this experiment we should understand that it is not the 10 gram action that causes all the dominoes to tumble, but the 10 gram action just creates an imbalance of the first domino. It is the gravity, however, that causes the dominoes to fall. In other words: only a 10 gram action is required to trigger a gravitational activity of all our dominoes from here to Paris.

Experiment #2
Imagine we had an unlimited amount of special dominoes of which only the first one we line up here is of normal size, and all the subsequent dominoes we line up again from here to Paris are of continuously increased size. By the time we reached Paris, the last domino block would be 1000 meters high and weigh millions of tons. Again we tip the first domino here with 10 grams, which will fall down causing all the subsequent dominoes to tumble. By the time the gravitational action reaches Paris, the last domino in Paris will smash the Eiffel Tower.

From this experiment we should understand that it is not the 10 gram action here that will smash the Eiffel Tower in Paris, but it is the gravitational energy that is picked up on the way to Paris that smashes the Eiffel Tower.

In other words: only a 10 gram action is required to trigger a nonlinear gravitational activity which will cause the destruction of the Eiffel Tower.

Perhaps the U.S.' first steps in international weather accords were taken by the 90th Congress, which in 1968 passed Concurrent Resolution 67. That Resolution declared that U.S. policy was to cooperate with other nations in the weather modification field.

A formal agreement on weather modification information exchange was signed with Canada in March of 1975. That agreement was inked after emotional concern surfaced over a U.S. proposal to engage in commercial cloud seeding in northern Washington state, near the Canadian border. In that agreement, the U.S. and Canada promised to provide advance notification and consultation with respect to activities conducted within 200 miles of the international boundary, or whenever either party believed the effects of weather modification activities would be significant to the other party. Similarly, the U.S. initiated negotiations with Mexico in 1978 toward the possibility of a joint experimental program on hurricanes in the Eastern Pacific. Technical discussions with a number of countries have taken place over the years since.

The 1978 Convention on the Prohibition of Military or Any Other Hostile Use of Environmental Modification Techniques (ENMOD Convention) prohibits the use of deliberate manipulation of natural processes (causing such phenomena as earthquakes, tidal waves and changes in climate and weather patterns) the effects of which would be:

(1) widespread (defined as encompassing an area on the scale of several hundred kilometers),

(2) long-lasting (defined as lasting for a period of months, or approximately a season), or

(3) severe (defined as involving serious or significant disruption or harm to human life, natural and economic resources, or other assets).

This treaty was proposed in no small part as a response to the U.S.' using cloud seeding techniques during the Vietnam War. A pilot program known as Project Popeye was conducted in 1966 in an attempt to extend the monsoon season in Southeast Asia. The purpose was to slow traffic on the Ho Chi Minh Trail by seeding clouds above it in hopes of producing impassable mud. Silver iodide was dispersed from C-130, F4 and A-1E aircraft into clouds over portions of the trail winding from North Vietnam through Loas and Cambodia into South Vietnam. Positive results from the initial test led to continued operations from 1967 to 1972. Some scientists believe that it did hamper North Vietnamese operations, even though the effectiveness of this program is still in dispute. The Russians thought

the program worked, and perhaps not unnaturally, objected.

The existence of Project Popeye first came to light when Dr. Daniel Ellsberg released the so-called *Pentagon Papers* in 1970. It hit public consciousness when syndicated columnist Jack Anderson revealed it, under the code name "Intermediary-Compatriot," in his *Washington Post* column of 18 March, 1971. Senator Claiborne Pell became a leading advocate for the ENMOD Convention after conducting hearings (in 1972 and again in 1974) into the DOD's use of weather modification as a weapon of war. A subcommittee chaired by Minnesota Congressman Donald Fraser did the same in the House of Representatives in 1974 and 1975.

Lowell Ponte was another influential voice calling for limits on the military's ability to wreck the environment. He had worked as a DOD consultant on environmental and bizarre weapons for the International Research & Technology Corporation of Washington, D.C. and, later, became editor of *Skeptic Magazine*. In his book, *The Cooling* (Prentice-Hall, Inc., 1976), he described those Congressional subcommittee hearings thusly: "What emerged was an awesome picture of far-ranging research and experimentation by the Department of Defense into ways environmental tampering could be used as a weapon."

Senator Pell wrote:

> Apart from the sheer horror of the prospect of unbridled environmental warfare, there is, I believe, another compelling reason to ban such action. We know, or should know, by now, that no nation can maintain for long a monopoly on new warfare technology. If we can develop weather warfare techniques, so can and will other major powers. Experience has taught us that the weapons that make us feel secure today, will make us feel very insecure indeed when our adversaries possess the same capabilities.

Senator Pell, with Representatives Gilbert Gude, of Maryland, and the above mentioned Congressman, Donald Fraser, were the three leading legislative critics of American military research into weather and climate modification research. Together, they sent a letter to President Gerald Ford urging increased government support for the peaceful uses of such modification. They also urged that all such research and operations, military and non-military, be overseen by a civilian agency answerable to Congress and the President. Their recommendations were ignored.

In *The Cooling* Lowell Ponte describes the events that led to the ENMOD Convention:

> During a summit meeting between President Nixon and Soviet Premier Leonid Brezhnev on July 3, 1974, the nations agreed to conduct discussions toward a ban on environmental warfare. Before the first of

these discussions, set for Moscow in November, got underway, the Soviet Union introduced a resolution before the United Nations General Assembly to ban environmental warfare. When revised, the resolution was passed by the body 102 votes to none. the U.S. and half a dozen other nations abstained from the vote. Senator Pell suspected that the president felt miffed by the surprise Soviet action, a move that made it appear that the Soviet Union and not the U.S. had taken the lead in trying to ban environmental modification. In fact, the Soviet resolution was similar to one passed by the North Atlantic Assembly in November 1972 and to another authored by Senator Pell and passed by an 82 to 10 vote by the U.S. Senate in July 1973.

Discussion between U.S. and Soviet negotiators resumed in Washington, D.C., on February 24, 1975. On August 21, 1975, the two nations presented their jointly produced draft treaty banning environmental modification as a weapon of war to the thirty-one-nation Geneva Disarmament Conference.

The ENMOD Convention was later passed by the United Nations General Assembly and opened for signature in 1977. It came into effect 5 October, 1978, when it was certified by the required total of 20 nations. It is a treaty without teeth, however, as nothing in it provides for international inspection or monitoring. Without such provisions violations of this treaty are difficult, if not impossible, to detect or determine.

After the DOD's efforts at cloud seeding in Vietnam produced mixed results, the DOD declared that "weather modification has little utility as a weapon of war." Many have remarked on what obvious malarkey that statement was. Clearly, weather control could have a marked effect on the outcome of military operations. The problem of course was not whether weather control should be effected, but how could it be done. Many researchers believe that the DOD never truly gave up trying to find out how. HAARP could potentially be that long-sought weather weapon—and a potential violation of the ENMOD Convention.

On the domestic side of the question, The National Weather Modification Policy Act was passed in 1976. It directed the Secretary of Commerce to conduct a comprehensive study of the status of weather modification science and technology and to submit to the President and the Congress a report on the findings, conclusions, and recommendations of the study. To conduct that study the Secretary of Commerce created the Weather Modification Advisory Board. That Board gave its findings, via the Secretary of Commerce, in The National Weather Modification Policies and Programs report of 1979, which was submitted to Congress in November of that year.

The Secretary of Commerce was given this task because one of the agencies of his Department, the National Oceanic and Atmospheric Administration (NOAA), was the major player in weather modification at the time. NOAA got a lot of good press in the '60s and '70s for its many research projects. For example, NOAA has pursued an experimental program since 1967 to study the potential for augmenting rainfall from subtropical cumulus clouds, the results of which have important implications for developing countries in the tropics, where clouds of this type account for most of the rainfall.

Another NOAA operation was Project Stormfury. Per a posting on the Internet, Stormfury was:

> ...an ambitious experimental program of research on hurricane modification carried out between 1962 and 1983. The proposed modification technique involved artificial stimulation of convection outside the eyewall through seeding with silver iodide. The invigorated convection, it was argued, would compete with the original eyewall, lead to reformation of the eyewall at larger radius, and thus, through partial conservation of angular momentum, produce a decrease in the strongest winds.

> Since a hurricane's destructive potential increases rapidly as its strongest winds become stronger, a reduction as small as 10% would have been worthwhile. Modification was attempted in four hurricanes on eight different days. On four of these days, the winds decreased by between 10 and 30%. The lack of response on the other days was interpreted to be the result of faulty execution of the seeding or of poorly selected subjects. These promising results came into question in the mid 1980s because observations in unmodified hurricanes indicated: that cloud seeding had little prospect of success because hurricanes contained too much natural ice and too little supercooled water, and that the positive results inferred from the seeding experiments in the 1960s stemmed from inability to discriminate between the expected results of human intervention and the natural behavior of hurricanes.

The Weather Modification Advisory Board (WMAB) proposed the establishment of a comprehensive, and well funded, continuing research program by the federal government into weather modification. It also proposed multilateral research and development agreements and comprehensive international accords, such as the ENMOD Convention. The WMAB concluded, "The prime requirement of a national weather modification policy is to learn more about the atmosphere itself." HAARP's promoters would have us believe that HAARP is an expression of that recommendation.

At the time of its 1979 report, the WMAB indicated that, "NOAA regards itself and is regarded by Congress, as the focal Agency for matters having to do with the atmosphere and the oceans." At that time NOAA had several research laboratories under its domain, including:

The National Severe Storms Laboratory in Norman, Oklahoma

The National Hurricane and Experimental Meteorology Laboratory in Miami, Florida

The Research Facilities Center in Miami, Florida

The Atmospheric Physics and Chemistry Laboratory in Boulder, Colorado

The Wave Propagation Laboratory in Boulder, Colorado

The Geophysical Fluid Dynamics Laboratory in Princeton, New Jersey

The Air Resources Laboratories which were located at several sites around the country.

NOAA was also responsible for the federal government's civilian atmospheric services, including: The National Weather Service, The National Environmental Satellite Service and The Environmental Data and Information Service.

WMAB said of NOAA in its report: "It is thus the primary source within the Federal government of the talents, observations, data, and information essential to weather modification field programs and evaluations."

I always found it amusing that the name of the agency given the task of understanding rain and oceans was pronounced "Noah." One would think from the above description of NOAA's purview that NOAA would be intimately involved with HAARP, as, if nothing else, HAARP is supposed to be upper-atmospheric research. And yet, neither NOAA nor any of its laboratories or sub-agencies have any participation whatsoever in HAARP. This I take as a tacit admission that HAARP really has nothing to do with atmospheric research. If HAARP truly is what it claims to be, it should be under the Department of Commerce, not Defense. Of course, since NOAA is involved in weather modification, putting HAARP under NOAA could be construed as an admission of its uses in that regard.

For those of you who want to be politically correct (PC), *The National Journal* reported on 20 May, 1978, that NOAA no longer uses such terms as "rain making," "weather modification" or even "climate control." The appropriate PC buzz-phrase is "weather resource management."

IONOSPHERIC ENMOD

As we have seen, some of the fundamentals of radio and electromagnetics were explored and patented by Nickola Tesla at the turn of the century. He, of course, was not alone in this. After Marconi demonstrated the workability of radio, thousands of scientists and amateur enthusiasts explored its possibilities. One important discovery relating to HAARP was the confirmation, in 1924, that radio waves bounce off the ionosphere, explaining over-the-horizon radio communications. "Ionospherics" has been a developing science since.

Perhaps the most important inadvertent discovery in ionospherics was the "Luxembourg Effect." In the early 1930s a high power radio station was built in the tiny European country of Luxembourg. In 1933, a researcher named Tellegen reported that the broadcast from the Luxembourg station could be heard in the background of a program transmitted from a much weaker radio station in Beromunster, Switzerland. Soon after, in 1934, researchers Bailey and Martyn suggested that the effect was caused by the powerful Luxembourg transmitter modifying the radio propagation characteristics of the ionosphere through which the signals traveled. When the Beromunster signal passed through this region its propagation was affected by the modified iono- spheric conditions, and in this way amplitude modulation from the Luxembourg signal was transferred to the Beromunster signal. The Luxembourg Effect became known as "cross-modulation." This set scientists to thinking of ways to use the Luxembourg Effect to "characterize" the ionosphere using high power radio waves in controlled experiments.

In early modification experiments researchers beamed high power radio waves into the sky, producing small changes in ionospheric properties. Low power waves were then used to see how the ionosphere's ability to propagate radio transmissions had been changed. From these experiments developed ionospheric heating, where the high power radio waves were employed to produce large scale electron temperature "enhancements."

This led to the birth of HAARP's grandparents in the 1970s. In 1972 Showen found elevated electron temperatures in measurements taken from the Arecibo, Puerto Rico, incoherent scatter radar. He used a high power 40 MHz wave to modify the ionosphere. This was the same sort of ionospheric heating that HAARP will be used to generate. By the mid-70s HF (High Frequency) experiments in heating the ionosphere were being conducted at Plattesville, Colorado and Armidale, New South Wales, Australia as well as at Arecibo. By the end of the decade the previously mentioned Max Planck Institute of West Germany had built a 100-megawatt heater near Tromso, Norway. That facility, called the European Incoherent Scatter Radar site (EISCAT) is currently run by a five-country consortium.

HAARP's joint operators have released numerous "fact" sheets about HAARP. One, in a "Question and Answer" format, gave a great deal of general info on the project, such as this fluff:

What is the Value of Ionospheric Research?
The ionosphere begins approximately 35 miles above the earth's surface and extends out beyond 500 miles. In contrast to the dense atmosphere close to the earth which is composed almost entirely of neutral gas, the thin ionosphere contains both neutral gas and charged particles

known as ions and electrons. This ionized medium can distort, reflect and absorb radio signals, and thus can affect numerous civilian and military communications, navigation, surveillance and remote sensing systems in many varied ways. For example, the performance of a satellite-to-ground communication link is affected by the ionosphere through which the signals pass. AM broadcast programs, which in the daytime can be heard only within a few tens of miles from the station, at night sometimes can be heard hundreds of miles away, due to the change from poor daytime to good nighttime reflection from the ionosphere ...

Since the sun's radiation creates and maintains the ionosphere, sudden variations in this radiation such as those caused by solar flares can affect the performance of radio systems. Sometimes the changes are sufficient to induce large transient currents in electric power transmission grids, causing widespread power outages. Lightning is known to cause substantial heating and ionization density enhancement in the lower ionosphere, and there are indications that ground-based HF transmitters, including radars and strong radio stations, also modify the ionosphere and influence the performance of systems whose paths traverse the modified region. Perhaps the most famous example of the latter is the "Luxembourg" effect ...

The proliferation of space-based civilian and military systems whose performance depends on transionospheric paths encourages not only good characterization and monitoring of the ionospheric state, but also an examination of what controlled local modification of the ionosphere, using ground HF transmitters, could do for and to these systems. Thus, while the HAARP facility is expected to provide significant advancement in understanding ionospheric science by stimulating and controlling plasma processes in a tiny localized region within the ionosphere, it also has the potential for significantly affecting the planning and economics of space-based systems.

At some level, HAARP may actually be just more investigation into the nature and character of the upper atmosphere. Then again, HAARP may be the bridge between the identification of forces stage and the manipulation of forces stage. Per HAARP official documents, HAARP is intended to create events in the ionosphere so that scientists can observe the interaction and dynamics of the various layers and regions of the upper atmosphere. These experiments are quite apart from the earth penetrating tomography tests and most do not directly involve manipulating the electrojet.

From another HAARP fact sheet, dated 4 November, 1993:

The proposed research will be undertaken using high power radio transmitters to probe the overhead ionosphere, combined with a complement of modern scientific diagnostic instruments to investigate the re-sults of the interactions. HAARP will be constructed at auroral latitudes in Alaska. A unique feature of the research facility would be a high power high-frequency radio transmitter with the capability of rapidly steering a narrow beam of energy toward a designated region of the sky. Similar, though less capable, research facilities exist today at many locations throughout the world and are operated routinely for the purpose of scientific investigation of the ionosphere. In the U.S. such systems are located in Arecibo, Puerto Rico and Fairbanks, Alaska. Other installa-tions are at Tromso, Norway; Moscow, Nizhny Novgorod and Apatity, Russia; Kharkov, Ukraine, and Dushanbe, Tadzhikistan. None of these existing systems, however, have the combination of frequency capabil-ity and beam steering agility required to perform the experiments planned for HAARP.

Investigations to be conducted at the HAARP facility are expected to provide significant scientific advancements in understanding the iono-sphere. The research facility would be used to understand, stimulate and control ionospheric processes that might alter the performance of communication and surveillance systems. This research would enhance present civilian capabilities because it would facilitate the development of techniques to control ionospheric processes…

…The beam would be several degrees wide, depending on frequency, and thus would influence a region several miles in diameter in the lower ionosphere, expanding to several tens of miles in the upper ionosphere.

Chemical "detonations" in the ionosphere covering 40-100 km were used in some of these heater experiments elsewhere around the world. Sugges-tions for similar experiments over HAARP are discussed in the scientific lit-erature for the project. Chemicals released over these other heaters have in-cluded: titanium, boron, barium, strontium, lithium, europium, and calcium. Some Alaskans, and Canadian "downwinders," are less than enthusiastic at the prospect at having such chemicals dumped into the air over their heads.

The heart of HAARP, its antenna array called the ionospheric research in-strument (IRI), has been described as an "ionospheric heater" because its pow-erful radio waves cause the ionosphere to vibrate. This excitation of the iono-sphere should cause it to be warmed by a few degrees. While that may sound like a small change, in so delicate a natural system its potential effect is huge.

From "Frequently Asked Questions About HAARP":

Is HAARP capable of affecting the weather?
The ionosphere is created and continuously replenished as the sun's radiation interacts with the upper levels of the Earth's atmosphere. There is no evidence, however, that ionospheric variations can affect the at-

mosphere below, even at the extraordinarily high levels that the sun can produce during a geomagnetic storm. If the electromagnetic disturbances caused by the sun itself don't affect the weather, there is no chance that HAARP can do so either.

HAARP's promoters insist that HAARP cannot and will not affect the environment on the ground nor the weather immediately above it. They have arrived at this belief by ignoring evidence that fails to suit their purposes. The above statement that there is "no evidence" is an outright lie. Scientifically verified connections between the uppermost levels of the atmosphere and the lowest have yet to become "universally accepted by the large majority of the research community." However, that does not mean that such a connection does not exist, or that there is "no evidence" in the matter.

In 1975 Stanford professor Robert Helliwell reported that VLF emissions from power lines were altering the ionosphere. This shows that events on the ground can affect portions of the sky, scores of miles up. Conversely, Gary Lockhart demonstrated that the reverse, the ionosphere affecting the ground, was also true. In his book, *The Weather Companion,* (Wiley & Sons, Inc.) Lockhart wrote: "We can artificially influence the earth's aurora with a relatively small amount of energy, and we know that outbursts of the northern lights do change weather patterns."

Similarly, atmospheric researcher Charles A. Yost wrote: "If the ionosphere is greatly disturbed, the atmosphere below is subsequently disturbed." There is indeed mounting evidence that upper atmospheric events do affect lower atmospheric weather, and vice versa. However, in the staid, conservative world of mainstream science, that evidence is not yet "conclusive." As long as this subject remains controversial HAARP scientists feel safe in discounting it— and apparently feel equally safe in lying about its existence.

Previously I mentioned PACE (Planetary Association for Clean Energy). In their newsletter (Vol.3, No. 1, June, 1981) they reported that Dr. Ralph Markson of MIT, discovered research results which…

> …suggests that if atmospheric variations do affect the weather, the appropriate use of Extremely Low (ELF) and Very Low (VLF) Frequency radio waves might do the same trick.
>
> It is known that VLF radio waves, such as those generated by lightning, can cause trapped particles to be dumped into the atmosphere by destabilizing plasma in the magnetosphere. Experiments to cause such triggered particle precipitation have been conducted from the space shuttle.

Several respected scientists have commented that events in the atmosphere cannot be localized, that anything that happens anywhere in the atmosphere affects the balance of the entire system, i.e., all weather is global weather. HAARP documents repeatedly state that the affected area would be directly over the HAARP site, but that too is a lie. The IRI has the "beam steering" capacity of some 30 degrees, allowing them to affect regions many miles away from the IRI, even over the horizon.

We get more of the same from the HAARP document "What Are the Effects of HAARP on the Ionosphere?" Under the heading of "Overview of Active Ionospheric Research," it says:

> In the field of geophysics, the use of high power transmitters such as the HAARP Ionospheric Research Instrument (IRI) is called "active ionospheric research." The HAARP IRI will be used to introduce a small, known amount of energy into a specific ionospheric layer for the purpose of studying the complex physical processes that occur in these naturally occurring plasma regions that are created each day by the sun.

The mixing of references to HAARP and other ionospheric heaters in the same statement, seen above and in many other HAARP documents, is called "positioning" in advertising. Its intention is to get the viewer or reader to associate the two items positioned together (such as a bar of bath soap and a fresh smelling day) as being equivalent. You are supposed to think that the soap will make you smell fresh, and you are supposed to think, in HAARP's case, that all ionospheric heaters are the same. None of the other ionospheric heaters in use, however, are anything like the HAARP array. They have neither the broadcast strength nor the Eastlund patented focusing and "beam steering" capacity. To compare HAARP to the other minuscule "active ionospheric research" facilities around the world is like comparing a Bengal tiger to a common house cat.

Eastlund clearly saw his apparatus as capable of weather modification. He wrote of this feature in his patents and has spoken with writers, such as in the *Omni* interview, at length about it. The official HAARP literature discusses how heating the ionosphere will cause it to expand. Those documents then go off into mind-numbing technical babble about electrons per cubic centimeter and so on, carefully ignoring the implications, and connection to Eastlund's work.

One example of this is in HAARP's ability to use this heating to tilt or raise a portion of the ionosphere. The ionosphere acts as a radio mirror, making it possible to hear shortwave radio broadcasts thousands of miles from their point of origin by bouncing the radio waves off of it. By altering the position of a portion of the ionosphere, HAARP could radically alter the radio reflective properties of the ionosphere, which could be used to misdirect radio communications, jam-

ming, in effect, world-wide radio messages. In wartime this could be a powerful weapon. Also, knowing precisely where the ionosphere was being "perturbed" the side using such a weapon could jam the enemy's transmissions while keeping their own broadcast channels open.

HAARP may serve to create bounce spots of precisely known locations and characteristics, called artificial ionospheric mirrors (AIMs). HAARP-generated AIMs could enhance radio transmissions by providing a stable artificial ionosphere. These AIMs could also give the DOD over-the-horizon radar capability, allowing HAARP's operators to detect incoming cruise missiles, low-flying aircraft and other stealthy aerial objects. Curiously, while some official HAARP documents openly discuss using HAARP to create AIMs, other, equally official documents deny that HAARP would be used for this purpose. Who's zooming who?

One internal document states that HAARP's research would "be focused towards identifying and exploiting techniques to greatly enhance C3 capabilities." C3 is military jargon for Communication, Command and Control. That same document further states that one function of HAARP would be the "generation of ionospheric lenses to focus large amounts of HF energy at high altitudes in the ionosphere, thus providing a means for triggering ionospheric processes that potentially could be exploited for DOD purposes." What "purposes" might those be?

Convection, which causes weather in the troposphere, cannot occur in the stratosphere because the air there gets warmer as altitude increases. However, convection can occur in much of the ionosphere. In the lower regions of the ionosphere the temperature falls off with height, just like in the troposphere. If a portion of the ionosphere in that region were heated it would rise, causing plumes of lower level ionospheric material to invade the middle levels. Once into the thermosphere, the top of the ionosphere, the reverse occurs and the air again gets hotter with height. This convection in the lower ionosphere is just one way that AIMs could be created.

Paul A. Kossey, et al., covered the subject in depth in a paper entitled: "Artificial Ionospheric Mirrors (AIM) A. Concept and Issues" in "Ionospheric Modification and its Potential to Enhance or Degrade the Performance of Military Systems" prepared for AGARD Conference Proceedings 485, October 1990. In it, he and his co-authors discuss how AIMs could enhance, as well as degrade, communications. The up side of AIMs is that they could be used to create many more communications channels. A ground based "radiator" might generate a series of AIMs, each of which would be tailored to reflect a selected transmission frequency. Such an arrangement would greatly expand the available bandwiths and also eliminate the problem of interference and crosstalk (cross modulation as in the Luxembourg Effect). They also make it clear that using AIMs to disrupt communications could be done covertly, as the interference they create would be indistinguishable from that occurring naturally.

Eastlund saw the plumes of rising ionospheric material used to create AIMs as being artificial lenses, capable of focusing solar energy to specific regions of the atmosphere, or even onto the ground. Have you ever played with a magnifying glass on a sunny day? Many children have used this bit of applied science to fry ants. Imagine being able to do this to a battlefield. We know that the DOD attempted to use cloud seeding to create impassable mud during the Vietnam War. How much do you think the DOD would like to be able to put its hands on a weapon that could fry enemy tanks on their way to the front?

As the *Omni* article expressed it:

As he did his computations, Eastlund realized that the amount of energy he was dealing with was enormous. He calculated that once the radio waves reached the ionosphere, they would interact powerfully with the charged particles trapped there. The result would be a magnetic phenomena known as the mirror force. Essentially what would happen is that a huge section of the charged atmosphere would be pushed upward and outward from earth by this electromagnetic force.

"You can," says Eastlund, "virtually lift part of the upper atmosphere." Eastlund also says: "[Y]ou could construct plumes of atmospheric particles to act as a lens or focusing device for sunlight. By being able to intensify and control light, one could heat a specific part of the earth and learn to manipulate local wind patterns."

What this means is that by controlling local weather patterns, one could, say, bring rain to Ethiopia or alter the summer storm pattern in the Caribbean.

The *Omni* article went on to quote Richard Williams, a physicist at Princeton, who stated that he thought Eastlund's device "...might become a serious threat to the earth's atmosphere" and "could cause irreversible damage ...Effects in the atmosphere cannot be localized ...The language of the patent indicates that it is clearly intended to provide effects on a global scale." And yet HAARP literature insists that the effects of HAARP will be "localized" to a "tiny region" of the sky.

As for weather modification, in peacetime this could be a wonderful boon for mankind. The jet stream could be carefully rerouted to bring needed rainfall to drought-stricken areas or to send overburdened clouds away to prevent flooding. Hurricanes could be stopped in their tracks or moved out to sea. In war, however, this could be a devastating weapon: low-lying countries could be blanketed in floods of Biblical proportions, or the enemy's ability to feed its people could be destroyed by denying crops rainfall. These uses would clearly be violations of the United Nations Environmental Modification Treaty.

Could this be why the current HAARP literature makes every effort not to mention HAARP's ability to affect other regions of the sky or the earthly environment? If they were to openly discuss this aspect of their research their "tiny" Bengal tiger would be out of the bag.

EARTHQUAKES ON DEMAND?

American scientists have discovered that earthquakes cause changes in the ionosphere and magnetosphere. There is some reason for concern (albeit small) that the reverse, causing changes in the ionosphere and/or magnetosphere, could trigger earthquakes. Others believe that radio transmissions through the earth, using "Tesla technology," could cause earthquakes and atmospheric disturbances in locales far from the transmitter. Is it possible that HAARP, or the Woodpecker, could cause earthquakes, intentionally or otherwise, by mimicking natural forces, or exploiting weaknesses in nature, as Dr. MacDonald suggested? The creation of man-made earthquakes would certainly be a very Tesla-like application of environmental modification technology.

At first blush one is tempted to dismiss the concept of "earthquakes on demand" as simple lunacy. However, Tesla nearly flattened New York City with an artificially created earthquake. It was caused by a device he constructed in his lab to demonstrate the principle of harmonic resonance. He drove a steel pile deep into the earth beneath the building, then had a steam-driven piston tap it at a precise frequency. Nothing happened for many minutes. Tesla almost abandoned the experiment, then suddenly he realized that the building was indeed going into harmonic resonance. In a few minutes the whole building was shaking violently. It was then that he realized that the neighboring buildings were shaking too. Expanding out from his lab was an ever-widening circle of quaking structures. He nearly could not get the steam hammer stopped and had to take a sledge to the rig. By the time he had the experiment shut down, thousands of windows were broken and many thousands of citizens were angry and frightened.

Over 40 years later, the *New York American* ran an article on 11 July, 1935, entitled: "Tesla's Controlled Earthquakes." It stated that Tesla's "experiments in transmitting mechanical vibrations through the earth—called by him 'the art of telegeodynamics'—were roughly described by the scientist as a sort of 'controlled earthquake.'" The article quoted Tesla as saying:

> The rhythmical vibrations pass through the earth with almost no loss of energy ...[I]t becomes possible to convey mechanical effects to the greatest terrestrial distances and produce all kinds of unique effects ...The invention could be used with destructive effect in war...

In an interview in *The World Today,* February, 1912, Tesla said that it would be possible to split the planet by combining vibrations with the correct resonance of the earth itself. He said: "Within a few weeks, I could set the earth's crust into such a state of vibrations that it would rise and fall hundreds of feet, throwing rivers out of their beds, wrecking buildings and practically destroying civilization."

Earlier we discussed the Russian Woodpecker and some of its effects. An even more radical take on the Russian Woodpecker program was offered in the January 1978 issue of *Specula* magazine. In describing the Woodpecker signals, they said:

An electromagnetic signal of certain frequencies can be transmitted through the earth which, when introduced into the earth at certain multiples of 30 degrees, will form standing waves in the earth itself …In certain incidence angle cases, the standing waves also induce a strange phenomenon: coherence to the standing wave is formed in the molten core of the earth itself, and a tiny fraction of the vast, surging electromagnetic currents of the liquid core begin to feed into and augment the induced standing wave.

At this point, one has established a sort of giant triode: the inducing signal one is putting into the earth is the grid signal, and the vast energy in the molten core of the earth is the cathode and power supply. The established coherence serves as an amplification factor for the grid signal, and much more energy is now present in the standing wave than the minuscule amount being fed in from the earth's surface. By interferometer type techniques, multiple "giant resonance" waves of this type can be combined so that a "beam" or focused effect of very great energy now exists inside the earth.

Depending upon the frequency, focusing, wave shape, etc., one can …induce a variety of effects such as earthquakes, induced at a distant aiming point, severe disturbances in the middle and upper atmosphere over the target area …and anomalous weather effects.

Those "atmospheric disturbances" are known as the Tesla Effect. Tesla's attempts at broadcast power at the turn of the century caused incredible lightning storms that started hundreds of forest fires, and lightning strikes knocked out the power grids in Colorado and Utah. Tesla himself claimed to be able to "split the earth like an apple" with his equipment. Tesla demonstrated the potential for causing earthquakes through either creation of artificial standing waves, or through inducing sympathetic resonance.

On June 13th, 1975, Leonid Brezhnev, then Premier of the Soviet Union, declared: "We have new kinds of weapons more terrible than anything the world has known." Supporting that contention, the January 1977 issue of *Newsweek Magazine* reported that Maj. Gen. George J. Keegan, Chief of Intelligence, USAF (Ret.) said:

> The Soviets are working on dramatically exotic new weapons, twenty years ahead of anything ever conceived in the U.S.—so awesome as to lead the Soviets to believe that in the coming decade they would be capable of total neutralization of our ballistic and submarine missiles.

Is HAARP an attempt to close this EMR/ELF weather/mindcontrol weapons gap?

Andrija Puharich, M.D., LL.D. in January 1978, issued a detailed research paper titled, "Global Magnetic Warfare—A Layman's View of Certain Artificially Induced Unusual Effects on the Planet Earth during 1976 and 1977." He was primarily looking into the Soviet experiments with Tesla Magnifying Transmitters (TMT). Controlled earthquakes, he believed, were part and parcel of that work. Of them he wrote: "Of the many great earthquakes of 1976, there is one that demands special attention—the July 28, 1976 Tangshan, China earthquake." That earthquake destroyed the city and killed an estimated 650,000 people. Nearly a year after the quake *The New York Times* reported, on 5 June, 1977, that:

> ...[J]ust before the first tremor at 3:42 AM, the sky lit up "like daylight." The multi-hued lights, mainly white and red, were seen up to 200 miles away. Leafs [sic] on many trees were burned to a crisp and growing vegetables were scorched on one side, as if by a fireball.

Numerous researchers have since become convinced that a TMT was used to effect that quake. In January 1981, *The Washington Post* reported: "The world sustained 71 significant earthquakes during 1980, up from 56 the previous year, and the world death toll climbed to 7,140, five times the 1979 figure, the U.S. Geological Survey said." Perhaps it is just coincidence, but as the Russian Woodpecker signal increased in strength, the number of earthquakes increased also.

Another leading U.S. Tesla researcher and nuclear engineer, Lt. Col. Thomas Bearden, lecturing at a Symposium of the U.S. Psychotronics Association (USPA) in 1981 stated:

> Tesla found that he could set up standing waves ...in the earth (the molten core of the earth, or, just set it up through the rocks—the telluric activity in the rocks

would furnish activity into these waves and one would get more potential energy in those waves than he put in. He called the concept—the magnifying transmitter.

Bearden described the workings of TMTs:

They will go through anything. What you do is that you set up a standing wave through the earth and the molten core of the earth begins to feed that wave (we are talking Tesla now). When you have that standing wave, you have set up a triode. What you've done is that the molten core of the earth is feeding the energy and it's like your signal—that you are putting in—is gating the grid of a triode ...Then what you do is that you change the frequency. If you change the frequency one way (start to dephase it), you dump the energy up in the atmosphere beyond the point on the other side of the earth that you focused upon. You start ionizing the air, you can change the weather flow patterns (jet streams, etc.)—you can change all of that—if you dump it gradually, real gradually—you influence the heck out of the weather. Its a great weather machine. If you dump it sharply, you don't get little ionization like that. You will get flashes and fireballs (plasma) that will come down on the surfaces of the earth ...you can cause enormous weather changes over entire regions by playing that thing back and forth.

Elsewhere Bearden wrote:

As a consequence of the Soviet breakthrough and decades of feverish development, monstrous strategic weapons undreamed of in the West are already in Soviet hands... A noose is slowly and steadily being tightened about our throats, and it is already the 11th hour.

If HAARP is a TMT, and these researchers correctly understand Tesla's work, we could be in a lot of trouble. It is quite possible that the scientists working on HAARP do not know what they are playing with. Scientists are seldom familiar with the details of research beyond their own discipline. It is quite reasonable to expect that the atmospheric scientists working on HAARP would know little or nothing of "scalar" technology, Tesla effects and the like.

Beyond that, their ignorance may be compounded if HAARP is indeed a military project. The military has devised a way of keeping secrets called "compartmentalization." In a compartmentalized operation each unit knows only what it needs to know and is often unaware of the existence of any other units. Only the control group really knows what is going on.

The scientists working on HAARP seem to genuinely believe that they are working on a purely civilian research project. To my eyes this makes HAARP look like a typicaly military compartmentalized project. The civilian scientists on the ground are probably working completely unaware of the military's (or the Conspiracy's) real intentions. If there is a control group familiar with TMTs directing the actions of scientists and technicians unschooled in Tesla technology, those lower level operatives could be directed to wreak  havoc with created weather or manufactured earthquakes, and never have a clue that they were doing it.

Even if the HAARP program is exactly what it says it is, "just" more atmospheric science, pure science could result in pure disaster through pure ignorance. What if the DOD, or the Conspiracy, however, is fully aware of HAARP's potential? Could induced earthquakes be used as "bargaining chips" in global power negotiations? Some believe that they already have.

In 1984, at another USPA Symposium, Thomas Bearden delivered a lecture entitled "Soviet Weather Warfare Over North America." In it he identified new and unusual cloud formations that have occurred at many places in America. These he believes are the signature of TMTs in use. One of these weird cloud patterns was described by him as a "giant radial" with long thin lines running out from the center of a ring. These types of cloud radials, he said, "strongly resemble the old Japanese 'Rising Sun' war flag." These also strongly resemble the underground antenna formations of the Ground Wave Emergency Network (GWEN) system.

A number of disturbing effects have been detected in the vicinity of GWEN antenna arrays. For example, they have been demonstrated as being capable of disrupting or altering the earth's magnetic field within a 200 to 250 mile radius of the installation. Although denied in official HAARP literature, credible scientific evidence documents that alterations of the earth's magnetic field can influence precipitation, i.e., cause rainfall. The GWEN sites were dead center of the areas of the Midwest that were flooded in the great flood of 1993.

In that 1984 lecture Bearden went on to talk of the Soviet's use of non-Hertzian scalar waves (electro-magnetic-gravitational waves of pure potential) which he and others say is the basis of the Woodpecker signal:

> By interfering two beams of such scalar waves at a distance, a scalar interferometer is produced. By slow rotation of the transmitter, the entire distant interference zones—and the highs and lows—can be moved along. This scheme then allows the capturing and movement of high

cloud masses, direct manipulation of high and low pressure areas, diversion of jet streams, and extensive Soviet control over the weather patterns of North America.

Numerous reports in the mainstream press seem to support Colonel Bearden's assertions. For example, *The Washington Post* reported, August 9, 1983, statements from A. James Wagner, meteorologist with the prediction branch of the Weather Service's Climate Analysis Center in Washington, D.C., in which he described a weather system that had caused a disastrous drought and heat waves. With an understanding of TMTs in mind one can see the "fingerprint" of the Woodpecker at work, creating a standing wave over America, in his comments: "Within this vast formation, air is moving vertically between the earth and the atmosphere, without much lateral movement." Wagner was further reported as stating that this giant high pressure blockage milled around "from week to week."

A similarly weird phenomenon was reported in *The Chicago Tribune,* 11 December, 1986. The report said that "giant whirlpools, some nearly 60 miles wide, have been detected moving along Norway's coasts at speeds of up to four knots, posing serious threats to mariners …[T]hese giant whirlpools have no obvious center and are difficult to spot." The article stated that these mammoth whirlpools were unheard of before 1980. Just a coincidence that they began to appear only after the U.S. and U.S.S.R. began experimenting with generating and broadcasting ELF waves?

Aviation Week & Space Technology Magazine ran a remarkably similar story in its 16 March, 1987, issue. Claiming to have received copies of transmissions from the Soviet space station MIR that were intercepted by Western Intelligence sources, they said that "The MIR crew reported seeing an unexpected ocean phenomenon: 'Powerful concentric waves going out in the midst of a serene sea.' The cosmonauts did not report where they saw the wave, but said the circular features were many miles across."

ELF AND EARTHQUAKES

ELF waves may be a natural component of earthquake phenomena. *The Washington Times* reported 29 March, 1992, on the incidence of ELF signals being associated with earthquakes, thusly:

> Satellites and ground sensors detected mysterious radio waves or related electrical magnetic activity before major earthquakes in Southern California during 1986-87, Armenia in 1988, and Japan and Northern California in 1989.

An Athens University physicist has also reported observing electromagnetic signals in six out of seven quakes in Greece over a several year period.

A very remarkable piece of the mystery is revealed in a condition known as "Charlotte's Syndrome." The bizarre case of Charlotte King, who "hears" the Earth, yields valuable insights into perception, physics, and the geo-sciences. Charlotte King was taped by the *Good Evening* crew (KGW-TV, Portland), giving warning before the 22 April, Joshua Tree magnitude (M) 6.3 shaker; then, she predicted the Cape Mendocino earthquakes of Saturday and Sunday, April 25th (M7.1) and 26th (M6.6; M6.7). On Monday she warned that, "It's not over yet," for Southern California. The tape aired on Monday, April 27, 1992.

When a volcanic eruption started nearly anywhere in the world, Charlotte King felt abdominal pain. When Washington State's Mt. Saint Helens reawakened, the strong pains doubled her over. When the mountain erupted on 18 May, 1980, she suffered a minor stroke. This was reported in her 1981 appearance on the TV show, *That's Incredible!* One scientific research team spent fourteen years investigating "Charlotte's Syndrome." They concluded that she was sensitive to fluctuations in the earth's electromagnetic field.

Piezoelectricity (from the Greek "piez" meaning "to press" and "electricity") is a little understood phenomena. Scientists have demonstrated that under certain conditions crystals can be forced to give off a flow of electricity if subjected to high pressure. The earthquake precursor signals Charlotte King feels could be the result of tectonically induced piezoelectricity. That is, pressure in the earth's crust could squeeze some types of rocks so hard that they discharge electricity. The electrical flow would have electromagnetic effects, perhaps including a "broadcast" in the ELF range being picked up by Charlotte's brain.

Several researchers in the UFO field have discovered that some UFOs might actually be "earthquake lights" caused by this same piezoelectric phenomena. Lights leaping away from mountain peaks have been seen and recorded since ancient times, and could be a similar type of discharge.

Dr. Elizabeth Rauscher, Ph.D. (whom I quoted earlier) and Mr. William L. Van Bise, an Electrical Engineer, attended an International Workshop held at Lake Arrowhead, California, 14-17 June, 1992. That workshop's title was: "Low Frequency Electrical Precursors: Fact or Fiction?" Dr. Rauscher, a particle physicist and former science advisor to the United Nations, and Van Bise presented a paper on measurement of ELF signals. Dr. Rauscher announced that a magnitude 7 or greater earthquake would strike "in the region of the conference, very soon." On June 28th the Landers quake, (M7.5), struck 44 miles east of the conference site; several hours later Big Bear Lake, only 20 miles east, was hit by a M6.6 temblor. They were able to focus on the area, timing, and strength because of extensive contacts with Charlotte King. They used an antenna array, located near Reno, Nevada, to pick up signals at 3.8 cycles per second. More details were presented by them a year later at a similar conference in Tokyo, in September 1993.

On 8 January, 1994, Dr. Rauscher called the earthquake prediction registry at the Library of Congress to report impending events likely to occur within 30 days. Unique signals from the earth indicated that one or more quakes would occur in or near the Los Angeles area. The Northridge quake struck on January 17th. Unusual surges of signals from 3.8 to 4.0 Hz were recorded beginning two weeks before the quake.

Another pair of researchers, R. J. Mueller and M. J. S. Johnston, reported in *Physics of the Earth and Planetary Interiors,* Vol. 57, 1989, that they had detected a large-scale magnetic field disturbance coming from the 18 May, 1980, eruption of Mount St. Helens. They wrote, "A traveling magnetic field disturbance was detected on an 800-km linear array of recording magnetometers installed along the San Andreas fault system in California, from San Francisco to the Salton Sea."

Begich and Manning, in *Angels Don't Play This HAARP,* shared a quote from private correspondence that they had had with Leigh Richmond Donahue, a researcher with the Centric Foundation of Maggie Valley, North Carolina. In writing about Ms. Donahue they said:

> [She] tracked events during the postwar years and through 1977 alongside a physics genius, her late husband Walter Richmond. She writes, "…when the military sent up a band of tiny copper wires into the ionosphere to orbit the planet so as to 'reflect radio waves and make reception clearer' we had the 8.5 Alaska earthquake, and Chile lost a good deal of its coast. That band of copper wires interfered with the planetary magnetic field."

Will HAARP similarly interfere with the earth's magnetic field? If so, how could we tell?

AIR FORCE 2025: OWNING THE WEATHER

"Weather as a Force Multiplier: Owning the Weather in 2025" was a research paper prepared by Col. Tamzy J. House, Lt. Col. James B. Near, Jr., LTC William B. Shields (USA), Maj. Ronald J. Celentano, Maj. David M. Husband, Maj. Ann E. Mercer, and Maj. James E. Pugh. They presented it on 17 June, 1996, to Air Force 2025. This paper was described as:

> [A] study designed to comply with a directive from the chief of staff of the Air Force to examine the concepts, capabilities, and technologies the U.S. will require to remain the dominant air and space force in the

future ...

They wrote that the views expressed in that report were strictly those of the authors and did not reflect the official policy or position of the U.S. Air Force, Department of Defense, or the U.S. government. However, they also stated that the weather modification capabilities described in that report were consistent with the "operating environments and missions" of the Air Forces' long- range planning office. I believe that HAARP is definitely a part of these long-range plans. "Air Force 2025" is probably a clear indicator of where the military plans to go with weather modification technology in the years ahead. The Executive Summary of 2025 begins:

In 2025, US aerospace forces can "own the weather" by capitalizing on emerging technologies and focusing development of those technologies to war-fighting applications. Such a capability offers the war fighter tools to shape the battlespace in ways never before possible. It provides opportunities to impact operations across the full spectrum of conflict and is pertinent to all possible futures.

A high-risk, high-reward endeavor, weather-modification offers a dilemma not unlike the splitting of the atom. While some segments of society will always be reluctant to examine controversial issues such as weather-modification, the tremendous military capabilities that could result from this field are ignored at our own peril. From enhancing friendly operations or disrupting those of the enemy via small-scale tailoring of natural weather patterns to complete dominance of global communications and counter-space control, weather-modification offers the war fighter a wide-range of possible options to defeat or coerce an adversary. Some of the potential capabilities a weather-modification system could provide to a war-fighting commander in chief (CINC) are listed in table 1.

Technology advancements in five major areas are necessary for an integrated weather-modification capability: (1) advanced nonlinear modeling techniques, (2) computational capability, (3) information gathering and transmission, (4) a global sensor array, and (5) weather intervention techniques. Some intervention tools exist today and others may be developed and refined in the future.

Table 1—Operational Capabilities Matrix
DEGRADE ENEMY FORCES   ENHANCE FRIENDLY FORCES
Precipitation Enhancement   Precipitation Avoidance
—Flood Lines of Communication - Maintain/Improve LOC
—Reduce PGM/Recce Effectiveness - Maintain Visibility

—Decrease Comfort Level/Morale - Maintain Comfort Level
Morale Storm Enhancement
 Storm Modification—Deny Operations- Choose Battlespace Environment
Precipitation Denial
Space Weather—Deny Fresh Water   - Improve Communication Reliability
—Induce Drought   - Intercept Enemy Transmissions
Space Weather   - Revitalize Space Assets
—Disrupt Communications/Radar   - Fog and Cloud Generation
—Disable/Destroy Space Assets   - Increase Concealment
Fog and Cloud Removal   - Fog and Cloud Removal
—Deny Concealment   - Maintain Airfield Operations
—Increase Vulnerability to PGM/Recce - Enhance PGM Effectiveness
Detect Hostile Weather Activities - Defend against Enemy Capabilities.

Current technologies that will mature over the next 30 years will offer anyone who has the necessary resources the ability to modify weather patterns and their corresponding effects, at least on the local scale. Current demographic, economic, and environmental trends will create global stresses that provide the impetus necessary for many countries or groups to turn this weather-modification ability into a capability.

[A]ppropriate application of weather-modification can provide battlespace dominance to a degree never before imagined. In the future, such operations will enhance air and space superiority and provide new options for battlespace shaping and battlespace awareness. "The technology is there, waiting for us to pull it all together;" in 2025 we can "Own the Weather."

"Chapter 4: Concept of Operations" gets to the heart of the matter. Here are some particularly juicy paragraphs pulled from the text:

The essential ingredient of the weather-modification system is the set of intervention techniques used to modify the weather. The number of specific intervention methodologies is limited only by the imagination, but with few exceptions they involve infusing either energy or chemicals into the meteorological process in the right way, at the right place and time. The intervention could be designed to modify the weather in a number of ways, such as influencing clouds and precipitation, storm intensity, climate, space, or fog.

[I]nternational agreements have prevented the US from investigating weather-modification operations that could have widespread, long-lasting, or severe effects. However, possibilities do exist (within the boundaries of established treaties) for using localized precipitation modification over the short term, with limited and potentially positive results.

These possibilities date back to our own previous experimentation with precipitation modification. As stated in an article appearing in the *Journal of Applied Meteorology*,

> [N]early all the weather-modification efforts over the last quarter century have been aimed at producing changes on the cloud scale through exploitation of the saturated vapor pressure difference between ice and water. This is not to be criticized but it is time we also consider the feasibility of weather-modification on other time-space scales and with other physical hypotheses.

The desirability to modify storms to support military objectives is the most aggressive and controversial type of weather-modification. The damage caused by storms is indeed horrendous. For instance, a tropical storm has an energy equal to 10,000 one-megaton hydrogen bombs, and in 1992 Hurricane Andrew totally destroyed Homestead AFB, Florida, caused the evacuation of most military aircraft in the southeastern US, and resulted in $15.5 billion of damage.

Modification of the near-space environment is crucial to battlespace dominance. General Charles Horner, former commander in chief, U.S. space command, described his worst nightmare as "seeing an entire Marine battalion wiped out on some foreign landing zone because he was unable to deny the enemy intelligence and imagery generated from space." Active modification could provide a "technological fix" to jam the enemy's active and passive surveillance and reconnaissance systems. In short, an operational capability to modify the near-space environment would ensure space superiority in 2025; this capability would allow us to shape and control the battlespace via enhanced communication, sensing, navigation, and precision engagement systems.

Modification of the ionosphere to enhance or disrupt communications has recently become the subject of active research. According to Lewis M. Duncan, and Robert L. Showen, the Former Soviet Union (FSU) conducted theoretical and experimental research in this area at a level considerably greater than comparable programs in the West.

A number of methods have been explored or proposed to modify the ionosphere, including injection of chemical vapors and heating or charging via electromagnetic radiation or particle beams (such as ions, neutral particles, x-rays, MeV particles, and energetic electrons). It is important to note that many techniques to modify the upper atmosphere have been successfully demonstrated experimentally. Ground-based modification techniques employed by the FSU include vertical HF heating, oblique HF heating, microwave heating, and magnetospheric modification. Significant military applications of such operations include low frequency (LF) communication production, HF ducted communications, and creation of an artificial ionosphere. Moreover, developing countries also recognize the benefit of ionospheric modification: "in the early 1980's, Brazil conducted an experiment to modify the ionosphere by chemical injection."

...[M]odification of the ionosphere is an area rich with potential applications and there are also likely spin-off applications that have yet to be envisioned.

...The major disadvantage in depending on the ionosphere to reflect radio waves is its variability, which is due to normal space weather and events such as solar flares and geomagnetic storms. The ionosphere has been described as a crinkled sheet of wax paper whose relative position rises and sinks depending on weather conditions. The surface topography of the crinkled paper also constantly changes, leading to variability in its reflective, refractive, and transmissive properties.

...An artificial ionospheric mirror (AIM) would serve as a precise mirror for electromagnetic radiation of a selected frequency or a range of frequencies. It would thereby be useful for both pinpoint control of friendly communications and interception of enemy transmissions.

The ionosphere could potentially be artificially charged or injected with radiation at a certain point so that it becomes inhospitable to satellites or other space structures. The result could range from temporarily disabling the target to its complete destruction via an induced explosion. Of course, effectively employing such a capability depends on the ability to apply it selectively to chosen regions in space.

In contrast to the injurious capability described above, regions of the ionosphere could potentially be modified or used as-is to revitalize space assets, for instance by charging their power systems. The natural charge of the ionosphere may serve to provide most or all of the energy input to the satellite. There have been a number of papers in the last decade on electrical charging of space vehicles; however, according to one author, "in spite of the significant effort made in the field both theoretically and experimentally, the vehicle charging problem is far from being completely understood." While the technical challenge is considerable, the potential to harness electrostatic energy to fuel the satellite's power cells would have a high payoff, enabling service life extension of space assets at a relatively low cost. Additionally, exploiting the capability of powerful HF radio waves to accelerate electrons to relatively high energies may also facilitate the degradation of enemy space assets through directed bombardment with the HF-induced electron beams. As with artificial HF communication disruptions... the degradation of enemy spacecraft with such techniques would be effectively indistinguishable from natural environment effects. The investigation and optimization of HF acceleration mechanisms for both friendly and hostile purposes is an important area for future research efforts.

"Chapter 5: Investigation Recommendations. How Do We Get There From Here?" concludes with:

Even today's most technologically advanced militaries would usually prefer to fight in clear weather and blue skies. But as war-fighting technologies proliferate, the side with the technological advantage will prefer to fight in weather that gives them an edge. The US Army has already alluded to this approach in their concept of "owning the weather." ["Weather a Force Multiplier," *Military Review,* November/ December 1995] Accordingly, storm modification will become more valuable over time. The importance of precipitation modification is also likely to increase as usable water sources become more scarce in volatile parts of the world.

As more countries pursue, develop, and exploit increasing types and degrees of weather-modification technologies, we must be able to detect their efforts and counter their activities when necessary. As depicted, the technologies and capabilities associated with such a counter weather role will become increasingly important.

The world's finite resources and continued needs will drive the desire to protect people and property and more efficiently use our crop lands, forests, and range lands. The ability to modify the weather may be desirable both for economic and defense reasons.

The lessons of history indicate a real weather-modification capability will eventually exist despite the risk. The drive exists. People have always wanted to control the weather and their desire will compel them to collectively and continuously pursue their goal. The motivation exists. The potential benefits and power are extremely lucrative and alluring for those who have the resources to develop it. This combination of drive, motivation, and resources will eventually produce the technology. History also teaches that we cannot afford to be without a weather-modification capability once the technology is developed and used by others. Even if we have no intention of using it, others will. To call upon the atomic weapon analogy again, we need to be able to deter or counter their capability with our own. Therefore, the weather and intelligence communities must keep abreast of the actions of others.

[W]eather-modification is a force multiplier with tremendous power that could be exploited across the full spectrum of war-fighting environments. From enhancing friendly operations or disrupting those of the enemy via small-scale tailoring of natural weather patterns to complete dominance of global communications and counter-space control, weather-modification offers the war fighter a wide-range of possible options to defeat or coerce an adversary. ...But, while offensive weather-modification efforts would certainly be undertaken by US forces with great caution and trepidation, it is clear that we cannot afford to allow an adversary to obtain an exclusive weather-modification capability.

Is HAARP a part of such a futuristic scenario? Remember those DOD "purposes" that HAARP research is supposed to further? I think by now it should be obvious what they are—weather modification, creation of AIMs and artificial ionospheres, destruction of enemy space "structures" (MIR space station?), identification of enemy underground targets, etc. The authors of 2025 insist that we cannot allow potentially hostile governments to develop this technology and not do like-wise. Perhaps they are right. Clearly this is, or should be, a significant national debate. The military, by lying about HAARP, is attempting to prevent that debate and win it by default.

What about the wilder stuff? Can HAARP set off earthquakes? To be honest, I do not know if it can—but I suspect that you would not want to find out the hard way. I doubt if the guys in the field working on HAARP have any clue that HAARP could do this (unless they have read this book, or the earlier one by Begich and Manning). I also doubt if any of them take such a possibility seriously.

So, we have examined several sides to this coin of whether HAARP is science out of control or a secret weapons system. It seems pretty obvious to me that it is both. HAARP's real purpose may lie beyond amoral science or immoral weapons development, however. Some researchers believe that HAARP embodies a hidden agenda of the Conspiracy, one whose true goals are even more outrageous than anything I have covered yet. The next two chapters will examine those possibilities.

The HAARP Antenna Array

e simplest antenna systems consist of a single antenna element, often in the form of a *dipole* or a *loop* . These simple antenna types nerally have a broad radiation pattern such that radio signals are transmitted (or received) over a very large number of directions. is broad coverage may be desirable for some applications. Cellular telephones, for example, must be able to send and receive the nversation toward the nearest cellular tower no matter where the user may be located and without the user having to point the ndset. As a result, the antenna used in this application (a form of dipole) has a very broad area of coverage.

r other applications, it may be possible to determine where the radio signal should be transmitted. For example, antennas used on mmercial and DoD satellite systems are designed to transmit (and to receive) their radio signals toward the surface the Earth since at is where the users are. These satellites, often located at geostationary altitudes, use antennas with fairly narrow radiation patterns maximize the power reaching the Earth and to minimize the power that is wasted by being transmitted in other directions.

e HF antenna system to be used for Active Ionospheric Research at the HAARP site will assist other facility instruments in the idy the overhead ionosphere. As a result, it too has been designed to optimize or restrict the transmission pattern to lie within a irrow overhead region. To achieve this desirable antenna pattern, the HAARP system uses an "*array*" of individual antenna ements. The HAARP antenna array is similar or identical to many other types of directive antenna types in use for both military and vilian applications including air traffic control radar systems, long range surveillance systems, steerable communication systems and ivigation systems.

rray Basics

/henever two or more simple antenna structures (such as the individual dipoles used at HAARP) are brought together and driven om a source of power (a transmitter) at the same frequency, the resulting antenna pattern becomes more complex due to *interference* etween the signals transmitted separately from each of the individual elements. At some points, this interference may be *constructive* iusing the transmitted signal to be increased. At other points, the interference may be *destructive* causing a decrease or even a incellation of transmitted energy in that direction.

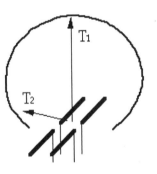

Figure 1. An array of two dipole antennas.

In Figure 1 to the left, two dipole antennas are placed close to each other and excited with a transmitter. The transmitter's power is split evenly between the two elements so that the *excitations* applied to each dipole are equal in amplitude and phase. The resulting antenna pattern is narrower or sharper in the *broadside* direction than it would have been for either dipole alone. Moreover, the strength of the transmitted signal in the broadside direction (T1 in the figure), is stronger than the transmitted signal would have been for one dipole antenna with the same total transmitter power. The ratio of the strength of the signal **at the pattern maximum** (i.e. at T1) to the signal for a single antenna element is called the *pattern gain* . Pattern gain is accomplished at the expense of power transmitted in other directions. The strength of the signal off-broadside (T2 in the figure) would be weaker for the case of two dipoles (as shown) than it would have been for a single dipole.

he purpose of an antenna array is to achieve directivity, the ability to send the transmitted signal in a preferred direction. If a large umber of array elements can be used, it is possible to greatly enhance the strength of the signal transmitted in a given direction while uppressing or even eliminating the signal transmitted in other directions.

From the HAARP home page.

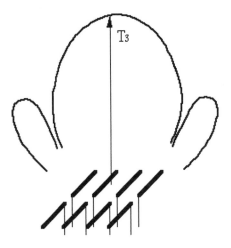

By adding additional antenna elements, the pattern can be further narrowed. Figure 2, to the left, shows four dipole antennas placed near each other and excited from a single transmitter whose power has been equally split four ways such that the signals arriving at the dipoles are of equal magnitude and all of the same phase. The pattern in this case is narrower than the previous example for two dipoles. Additionally, the strength of the signal in the broadside direction is stronger than the strength of the signal in the two dipole case (T3 > T1). Again this is accomplished by the removal of power that had been radiated in unwanted directions into the main, broadside direction or *main lobe* .

Figure 2 also shows the appearance of lower level maxima or *sidelobes* in the total antenna pattern. Sidelobes are a characteristic feature of most complex antenna arrays. Sidelobes are generally undesirable characteristics of an antenna system and numerous techniques have been developed over the years to suppress them.

Figure 2. An array of four dipole antennas. The pattern is sharper and sidelobes may be present.

It is theoretically possible to suppress sidelobes completely in an array of antenna elements if the excitation of each element is controllable. The process of shaping the antenna pattern so as to eliminate sidelobes is called *tapering* . Eliminating sidelobes results in less total gain at the pattern maximum, however, and it yields a broader main lobe.

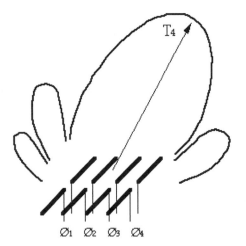

While the shape of the antenna pattern can be tailored by careful choice of the *amplitude* of the individual element excitations, the angle at which the pattern maximum occurs can be changed by adjusting the *phase* of the excitations of each of the antenna elements. If the elements are all driven *in-phase* , the pattern maximum will occur broadside to the array. If the phases of the excitations to each element are chosen correctly, however, the peak of the main lobe can be shifted (or steered) to a new angle relative to broadside. In general, the maximum signal strength at the new pointing angle (T4 in Figure 3 to the left) is close to but less than the broadside case.

When the pattern is steered to a new direction, the shape and direction of any sidelobes that may have originally been present changes. If the pattern is steered too far relative to the element spacing, a new lobe (called a grating lobe) will appear with a peak in its pattern nearly equal to the main lobe. The point where this occurs is the maximum useful steering angle.

Figure 3. An array of four dipoles in which the individual elements are driven at a predetermined relative phase.

From the HAARP home page.

Chapter Five:
Secret Science of the Conspiracy

So far we have looked at what HAARP is, and what it can do, from a fairly conventional perspective. We are about to boldly go where only supermarket tabloids usually venture. So far we have seen that it is difficult to accept the government's word about HAARP's true purpose. They claim that it is just another piece of civilian "big science." Many researchers, including establishment scientists, question that assertion. We have also seen that, even if HAARP were exactly what it says it is, it might still be extremely dangerous. There is little evidence that the scientists working on HAARP really have a clue of what they are fooling with. We have also seen that it could well be the proof-of-concept stage for a new weapons technology. As an electromagnetic "brain bomb" the military may have a machine that leaves the enemy unable to think or act coherently, without causing any damage to equipment and "minimal" injury to people. HAARP's ability to broadcast in the ELF range might also be the ultimate development in mind control technology. If HAARP can put words into the minds of all people within its broadcast area, it could well be an expression of the century-old goal of behavior modification psychology to totally control and change society to their idea of what mankind should be.

Or it could be something even wilder. As I suggested in the introduction, there are other possible interpretations of who might really be behind HAARP and what secret agenda they might be pursuing. In this and the following chapter I will offer a few of these other interpolations. I want to begin this line of investigation by presenting a theory espoused by Richard Hoagland, a NASA consultant, former science advisor to Walter Cronkite, and an Angstrom Science Award winner. Mr. Hoagland has spent the last several years promoting a manned mission to the planet Mars to investigate several remarkable features photographed by one of NASA's orbital probes to that world.

On the planet Mars, in an area called the Cydonia Region there appears to be a face looking up and out into space. This face, if it is one, is a mile and a half across, three or four miles long, and over a thousand feet in height from the level plain on which it rests to the tip of its nose. In that same vicinity there are several other features that appear to be other than the work of nature, including a few pyramids. NASA insists the "face" is just a trick of light, but many experts disagree. *The Case for the Face: Scientists Examine the Evidence for Alien Artifacts on Mars* is a 1998 AUP publication. It is a compilation of the work of 20 scientists, in various fields whose research indicates that the face and other features are artificial. The includes an article by Vince DiPietro, a NASA scientist who is credited with the first detailed anaysis of the face and other features.

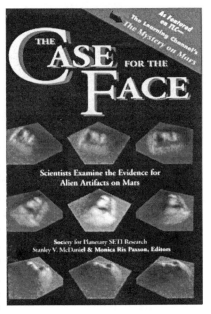

Hoagland believes that it truly is a face, carved there by some ancient race of beings. He also believes that there is a direct connection between it and the Great Pyramid at Giza. Hoagland suspects both "monuments" of being the handiwork of one or more previous high technology civilizations that flourished here, on this earth, thousands of years ago. If these cultures in fact existed, they must have been destroyed by cataclysmic events—disasters so devastating that the very memory of them has been all but wiped from human memory.

The idea of previous high-tech civilizations on this planet is quite possibly more than just wild speculation on Hoagland's part. Cultures around the globe have preserved oral traditions of previous advanced civilizations. The archeological record also bears mute witness to lost cultures that may have rivaled our own. While mainstream science has yet to acknowledge the truth of this, many "rogue" scientists, researchers and authors have espoused this cause and have presented evidence to support this theory throughout this century.

According to author David Hatcher Childress in his books such as *Vimana Aircrarft of Ancient India and Atlantis* and *Lost Cities of China, Central Asia & India* (both Adventures Unlimited Press, Kempton, Illinois), the Mahabharata, one of India's sacred texts, tells the story of the fall of the Rama culture. The Rama culture, per the Ramayana, a part of the Mahabharata, existed about twenty thousand years ago. It had flying machines and weapons of mass destruction. It had visited the stars. It was destroyed by engaging in a world-wide war with another high tech civilization on the other side of the earth from it. The apocalyptic "World War III" might already have happened twenty thousand years ago! Some of the island people of the South Pacific trace the cause of their taking to boats and venturing into the empty sea to the fall of Rama, and their becoming refugees from that catastrophe. Some people believe that the last Ice Age was the result of the "nuclear winter" that followed that war.

From the oral traditions of the native peoples of North America to the ancient cuneiform clay tables of Sumeria, many people around this world have preserved stories of former human greatness and/or contact with star-going beings who educated mankind. These might well have resulted from terrestrial humans from advanced cultures making contact with far more primitive ones. Along with the spotty written and oral records, there are also puzzling physical artifacts. The non-rusting iron tower in India that predates all known cycles of habitation, or the mysterious Sphinx, which may be ten thousand years older than previously guessed, are but two of the thousands of strange artifacts scattered about this planet.

From Erich Von Daniken's *Chariots of the Gods?* to T. Lobsang Rampa's *Cave of the Ancients,* from Churchward's *Lost Continent of Mu* books to Edgar Cayce's dream memories of past lives, from Zacharia Sitchin's reexaminations of ancient Sumerian texts to L. Ron Hubbard's past life regression technology, many authors and researchers have attempted to pierce the veil of humanity's amnesia. Richard Hoagland is one such researcher. He has also made a connection between these seeming relics from previous "epic civilizations," as he calls them, and HAARP.

What might the so-called "Face on Mars" and the Great Pyramid at Giza have in common with HAARP? HAARP received funding from the U.S. Senate in no small part because of its possible ability to see deep into the earth via earth penetrating tomography. Richard Hoagland believes that the secret manipulators of mankind, who, for simplicity's sake, I have called the Conspiracy, want to use this technology to search for repositories of wisdom and artifacts from these previous epic civilizations. The key to recognizing HAARP's part in this, for Hoagland, lies in James Clerk Maxwell's "hyperdimensional" physics and NASA's bungled "tethered satellite" experiment of March 1996.

MAXWELL'S "HYPERDIMENSIONAL" PHYSICS

James Clerk Maxwell (1831-1879), a Scotsman, was one of the greatest mathematicians of all time. He produced revolutionary theories on electricity and magnetism, and on the kinetic theory of gases. As an experimental physicist he also did some of the basic work in understanding color perception and color blindness. He is most famous for his equations linking electricity and magnetism. His groundbreaking work led to the development of quantum physics in the early 1900s and to Einstein's theory of relativity. The publishers of Cowles Encyclopedia (1964 edition) listed him as one of the "one hundred greatest men and women in history." The unit of magnetic flux, the maxwell, is named for him.

Maxwell's first major contribution to science was a study of the planet Saturn's rings, which won him the Adams Prize at Cambridge. Maxwell showed that stability could be achieved only if the rings consisted of numerous small solid particles, an explanation confirmed 100 years later by the Voyager 1 spacecraft.

Maxwell's most important achievement was his extension and mathematical formulation of Michael Faraday's theories of electricity and magnetic lines of force. Magnetic field lines were introduced by Michael Faraday (1791-1867) who named them "lines of force." Faraday was one of the great discoverers in electricity and magnetism, responsible for the principles by which electric generators and transformers work, as well as for the foundations of electrochemistry.

In one of the most elegant theories of all time, Maxwell wrote down the equations that described electromagnetism and the propagation of electromagnetic waves. These four partial differential equations, now known as Maxwell's Equations, first appeared in fully developed form in *Electricity and Magnetism* in 1873. They are one of the great achievements of 19th Century mathematics, and are now the cornerstone of electromagnetic theory.

One of the first things Maxwell did with his equations was to calculate the velocity of the propagation of an electromagnetic wave. When he did so, he found that the velocity was almost identical to the measured velocity for light. Based on this, he was the first to propose that light was actually an electromagnetic wave. Maxwell wrote: "We can scarcely avoid the conclusion that light consists in the transverse undulations of the same medium which is the cause of electric and magnetic phenomena." Maxwell used the later-abandoned concept of "the ether" to explain that electromagnetic radiation did not involve action at a distance. He proposed that electromagnetic-radiation waves were carried by the ether and that magnetic lines of force were disturbances of the ether.

Maxwell's younger colleague, the German Heinrich Hertz, for whom the basic unit of measuring frequency (the hertz) was named, calculated in 1886 that waves of this type would be broadcast by a rapidly alternating current in a short antenna. He then obtained such a current from an electric spark (which does produce a fast back-and-forth oscillation of electric charge) and demonstrated his "Hertzian waves" experimentally. His work was continued by scientists all over the world, such as Alexander Stepanovich Popov who around 1895 detected radio waves from lightning (a natural spark), and Tesla and Marconi.

The waves that carry radio and television, microwaves, infrared, visible light, ultraviolet, x-rays and gamma rays are all variations of the same basic concept envisioned by Maxwell, namely, they all belong to the family of electromagnetic waves. This family is known today as the electromagnetic spectrum.

Richard Hoagland is one of several scientists who believe that Maxwell's equations point to a universe composed of more than the conventionally accepted dimensions of height, breadth, width and time. Experiments in hyperdimensional physics have been conducted throughout this century but so far have yet to produce conclusive results. Some mathematicians think they have proven hyperdimensionality, others dismiss such claims as "junk science."

Some writers, like Abbot in his brilliant satire *Flatland,* argue that our minds are too limited to grasp the fact of higher dimensions. New Agers have tried to make contact with these higher dimensions and their inhabitants throughout this century, as did "spiritualists" in the preceding century. Some UFO researchers believe that UFOs and their occupants do not come from other worlds but from other dimensions of this one.

THE TETHERED SATELLITE EXPERIMENT AND THE CONSPIRACY

As well as believing in hyperdimensional physics, Richard Hoagland believes that there is a conspiracy within NASA, a secret group subverting the space agency to accomplish its own ends. As he expressed it to Art Bell on "Coast To Coast A.M." on 7 March, 1996:

We're finding that what we have is a NASA within a NASA. We have most of the system that doesn't understand what's been going on and a tiny cadre of people inside who have been manipulating data, manipulating communications, manipulating people to get them to do things that they are not even aware that they're doing. Those who they're doing it for, who they have implicit trust in, …are not leveling with them about all the implications.

Jim Keith, in two books from IlumiNet Press: *Casebook On Alternative 3: UFOs, Secret Societies, and World Control* (1994) and *Saucers of the Illuminati* (1993), came to a similar conclusion: that there is a secret space program operated by the Conspiracy. Author Bruce Cathie, working with the same hyperdimensional material as Hoagland, came to a similar conclusion. Cathie believes that the Conspiracy was exploring the hyperdimensional grid that surrounds this planet by detonating nuclear devices at key latitudes and longitudes on the world grid to "tweak" the hyperspacial envelope of earth.

Hoagland maintains that the HAARP project's earth penetrating tomography function is the real reason for the project's construction, but not for military purposes, or even, as Dr. Begich suggested, for oil exploration. Hoagland believes that the ultimate insiders who pull the military and NASA's strings are seeking the repositories left by previous civilizations. He further believes that these insiders, the Conspiracy, are aware of hyperdimensional physics and are attempting to use this 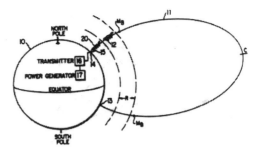 knowledge to further their interests. The fact that the tethered satellite experiment got away from them, he believes, proves that they do not fully understand what they are dealing with.

There is a very high degree of probability that HAARP is, at the least, a military project masquerading as a civilian one. Hoagland believes that the tethered satellite experiment of March 1996, similarly was a secret project hiding behind a civilian facade. The tethered satellite experiment was built by the Italian Space Agency. It was claimed that the purpose of the experiment was to see if electricity could be generated by dragging a wire through the "F" layer of the ionosphere, a region of electrically charged particles. This was an attempt to demonstrate the concept of using the ionosphere to refuel spacecraft, as discussed in the previous chapter. In the experiment the space shuttle was to release a satellite that was "tethered" to the shuttle by a 13 mile-long cable. The satellite was supposed to collect energy from the ionosphere for a period of time, then be reeled back into the shuttle bay. The experiment "failed" when the tether was severed, as I will detail in a moment.

Hoagland told Art Bell that he realized the HAARP connection when researcher Bruce dePalma showed him some calculations he had made on the tethered satellite experiment. DePalma had come to the conclusion that the experiment as designed would be a terribly inefficient way to generate power, but that it would make an excellent antenna for rebroadcasting in the ELF range.

As previously discussed, the HAARP transmitter array is a high frequency transmitter, broadcasting in the range of 2.8 to 10 MHz. However, that broadcast is modulated by ELF signals so even without affecting the ionosphere, magnetosphere or the electrojet, it has some ELF broadcasting potential. This, Hoagland and dePalma reasoned, would allow the HAARP array to use the "unintended" antenna of the "untethered" satellite just as HAARP has been designed to use the aurora. It is to be noted that HAARP's designers have clearly spelled out in the HAARP literature that they intend to use satellites as part of the HAARP series of experiments, such as they later did with the NASA WIND satellite in August 1997. Hoagland firmly believes that this was one of those long-planned-for events.

Once the tethered satellite became untethered when its mooring cable melted, that satellite became a "balloon" dragging a 13 miles-long metal "string." That "string" could then act as a resonating antenna, one rebroadcasting with thousands of times the original signal strength of any properly tuned energy reaching it. The ground based transmission would have to be at a frequency that matched the impedance and the size of the antenna, which was calculated to be roughly 13 to 14 KHz—perfect for earth penetrating tomography! Further, Hoagland believed that because of the trapping, ducting, and wave guide properties of the ionosphere, electromagnetic energy directed at the untethered satellite could be transmitted from virtually any place on earth.

If HAARP were to broadcast the required ELF radio waves, Hoagland said, they would literally bounce their way around the curvature of the earth until they reached this "antenna" hanging two hundred miles above the earth. It, in turn, would resonate with those waves and reradiate them in a spherical pattern, straight down, at whatever it happened to be passing over at that moment in its orbit around the earth. The ELF beam from this antenna could be used to communicate with, or probe, any area or object the satellite passed over. As Hoagland put it: "The more I looked into the HAARP literature, and what Bruce had come up with in terms of his speculations, the more I realized that this thing really seemed to have a double duty."

Hoagland dismisses the claims of the tethered satellite being an experiment in electrical generation. He points out that the satellite, which officially was supposed to conduct only four experiments, weighed 1,100 pounds. This he considers proof that it was really supposed to do something else, as we have sent probes to Jupiter and Saturn whose instrumentation weighed only 10 or 15 pounds. NASA reported that the satellite's batteries were dead once the shuttle had lifted the object into space. This, Hoagland believes, is further evidence that intent to generate electricity was a fraud. Why, he wondered, would they not have a way to store the electricity generated so as to charge those batteries? In fact, Hoagland insisted that nowhere on the satellite or the shuttle was there any device of any kind to collect and use the electricity this satellite was supposed to be generating. Why? For Hoagland the answer was obvious; that was not what it was for.

This is where the orbit of the accidentally untethered satellite became very interesting to him. During the two weeks that it circled the globe, completing one orbit every ninety minutes, it passed over some places he found very interesting, especially, the Giza plateau. Hoagland maintains that the location of HAARP in Alaska, at 62 degrees north latitude (62 deg 23.5' N) and 145 degrees west longitude (145 deg 8.8' W), is perfect for using Maxwell's hyperdimensional physics to probe the Giza plateau.

Hoagland maintains that what happened to the astronauts on the tethered satellite shuttle flight was not supposed to happen. For the two weeks it remained in orbit the tether glowed with tremendous brightness and was seen from all over the earth. Hoagland says that they inadvertently created a visible symbol of their playing around with forces bigger than all of us by not realizing that the tether would create what amounted to a 13 mile-long direct short circuit between two layers of the ionosphere. Hoagland adds that that miscalculation was compounded by their failure to understand Maxwell's hyperdimensional physics. Hoagland believes that a significant portion of the energy in the earth's electro-dynamic circuit is generated by this planet driving a hyper-dimensional generator. Hoagland explains the tether's glowing as the result of this hyperdimensionally produced power sending incredible current, both in terms of voltage and amperage, down that wire.

Further, he speculated that this current may or may not have interfered with their real purpose, which, he claims, was to do some clandestine experiments. The scenario he proposed was that the Conspiracy had planned all along for the tethered satellite to be cut loose, and that was when they had planned to conduct their real experiments. He speculated that their plan had been to go through with the bogus electrical generation experiments. They would attempt to generate power and so on. But, when they were finished and attempted to reel the tethered satellite back into the cargo bay the astronauts would have announced that, "Oh! Whoops! We have a problem Houston, we can't reel it back in."

Then Houston could have conveniently instructed the astronauts to jettison the tethered satellite, so they could close the doors and go home. Then they could go forward with some clandestine experiments with everyone on the ground thinking that the tethered satellite was just more space junk. With the astronauts safely on their way home nobody, he says, would ever have even noticed or questioned that the then untethered satellite was providing its own power, and the conspiracy would be able to begin performing a series of experiments without anybody noticing.

But something went wrong: serendipity, as Hoagland expressed it, stepped in. That Friday night, 1 March, at 7:30 pm Central Standard Time, as the shuttle, with the still tethered satellite, was about to cross the equator at the terminator (the line between day and night), somebody at the computer opened the circuit for four minutes. This allowed an enormous voltage, perhaps as much as 300,000 volts, to build up in this 13 mile-long wire. Then it zapped over to the ground at the shuttle, frying the tether and melting it in space. It pulled apart like taffy, which can be seen on the close-up TV footage released by NASA.

Hoagland said:

What I think happened is, that a little 'bomb' went off in that payload bay at the top of that tower. An electromagnetic bomb, because you basically had a direct short. It leaped across from the tether to the shuttle, and in space, with no air, you know, just the "F" layer of the atmosphere which is very, very thin up there, it had to have been hundreds of thousands of volts to jump that couple, three, four feet. At which point, all hell, literally, broke loose in that shuttle. That's why they sounded so panicked.

HAARP AND THE TETHERED SATELLITE

Dr. Nick Begich has reported that a round of full power tests of the earth penetrating tomography application of HAARP was being conducted at the same time as the tethered satellite experiment. Officially, the HAARP literature says no such experiments took place. These tests, Dr. Begich claimed, occurred between March 16th and 22nd. During that time the satellite repeatedly overflew Giza until it was destroyed on reentry into the earth's atmosphere on March 20th. It is interesting to note that the FCC was warning pilots not to depend on satellite locator beacons during this period.

All the important numbers in the HAARP program, such as the number of antennas in the first stage array (48 towers, 72 feet tall) and the broadcast power of the array (360 million watts), Hoagland claims are hyperdimensional numbers. Hoagland considered this additional proof of a conspiratorial connection to HAARP. This indicates a possibility that the Conspiracy caused HAARP to be constructed as part of their "secret science," as discussed in Jim Keith's books.

If these numbers sound familiar to you (multiples of 12 and 60) they should. The mathematics system we use in the West to measure time and degrees of arc within a circle comes from the math of ancient Sumeria. Sumeria (or Sumer) is the oldest human civilization admitted to by mainstream science. Sumeria existed about 7,600 years ago in what is now southern Iraq near the current city of Basra. •If key pieces of our math—telling time and dividing a circle—have survived from Sumeria, how much of Sumeria's math and technology might have survived from a previous, now forgotten, "epic" civilization? The little we know of Sumarian mathematics suggests that they were familiar with hyperdimensional physics. How much of that science might have survived to this day, hidden in secret societies that kept the knowledge alive, generation after generation, father to son or teacher to initiate, for millennia?

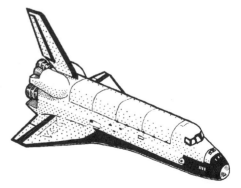

One such secret society is the Freemasons, who trace their origin back to Sumeria. As I shall show shortly, Free-masonry has very close ties to the Conspiracy. It is not beyond the realm of possibility that they, or some other similar group with connections to the Conspiracy, going back hundreds, evens thousands of years, may be in possession of technology (or bits of half remembered technology) from thousands, even tens of thousands of years ago.

Earlier I mentioned the Vedas and the Mahabharata of ancient India. The Vedas and the Mahabharata, including thefamous Ramayana, were epic poems, memorized and passed down as oral tradition, for literally thousands of years. In the Vedas there are over 30,000 lines of poetry describing aircraft which they called "Vimanas": everything from guidance control to proper diets for pilots! If such data has survived in the open, in the Vedas, what might have been preserved in secret?

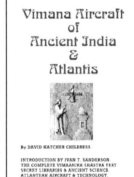

Vimana Aircraft of Ancient India & Atlantis

By DAVID HATCHER CHILDRESS

INTRODUCTION BY IVAN T. SANDERSON.
THE COMPLETE VIMAANIKA SHASTRA TEXT
SECRET LIBRARIES & ANCIENT SCIENCE
ATLANTEAN AIRCRAFT & TECHNOLOGY.
SANSKRIT SCHOLARS & VIMANA TEXTS.

Hoagland, like so many others, believes that HAARP is hardly for pure science. He thinks we are far beyond such raw science activities as probing and characterizing the ionosphere. We have been sounding the upper atmosphere with balloons, satellites, orbiting geophysical observatories, radar, etc. for all of the second half of this century. He finds it ludicrous for the Air Force to expect the public to buy a need to characterize the ionosphere in the '90s, when they have been beaming high frequency radio energy into the ionosphere for decades. Hoagland told Art Bell:

> The point is, we're down to the level of technical application and the question is, what is it really being used for? And that's why the numbers are important. The acronym is important. And its siting is important, relevant to the hyperdimensional grid on this planet.

Hoagland does not believe that HAARP's intent is anything as small as finding oil, or even the concerns of the "Cold War." He believes that HAARP's having a multinational makeup, exemplified by the presence of the former Soviet scientist Academician Roald Zinurovich Sagdeev on an early advisory panel, is evidence that what HAARP is all about is something far larger than mere profit or national rivalries.

Speaking with Art Bell and Dr. Nick Begich on Art Bell's *Coast To Coast A.M.* on 7 March, 1996, Richard Hoagland said:

> [I]t is becoming more and more probable that we are not the first. That, Art and Nick, we are heir to a legacy of preceding previous cycles of high technological civilization on this planet that, for whatever rea-

son, have disappeared leaving only traces—both physical traces and legendary, historical, textual, or artifact traces. In that model, if there is a precipitant catastrophe which overwhelms the human species on a periodic, or quasi-periodic basis... it looks as if, maybe, there is an effort to save some people when these times approach where whatever happens is going to happen... So, one of the models has been that when the previous civilizations realized their number was up, a group, an elite, tried to preserve themselves through availing themselves of various options, up to and including digging big holes in the ground, and hiding, and hoping it would go away. Or hoping they could come out after it had gone away.

This is remarkably similar to the Alternative 3 "hoax" scenario aired on the BBC in the 1970s and examined at length in Jim Keith's book *Casebook on Alternative 3: UFOs, Secret Societies and World Control.* The three "alternatives" involved ways the Conspiracy could avoid the end of the world (an end caused by overpopulation, pollution, etc.). The first alternative was to use nuclear devices detonated in the atmosphere to blow holes in the upper atmosphere to release pent up heat and pollution. It could be argued that that alternative has already been tried and failed.

The second alternative was to go underground, digging underground cities for the elite to escape in. COG (Continuancy Of Government), currently managed by FEMA (the Federal Emergency Management Agency) is a program that has spent billions of dollars since the 1950s building a hundred or more underground facilities. These were constructed as shelters for government officials in case of nuclear war. Some, like the Mt. Weather facility, are whole cities underground with populations in the thousands.

The third alternative was to evacuate the elite from earth. This necessitated creating a secret space program to establish colonies on the moon and Mars. Jim Keith became convinced that though the tale told on the BBC show was fiction, it was awfully close to actual secret projects and programs. Projects such as what Hoagland suspects HAARP of being are not out of the question.

It is his belief that it is the military, manipulated by this "NASA within a NASA," i.e., the Conspiracy, who would have the resources and the ability to "lie on a global scale" to carry out such a program. During the interview with Nick Begich on *Dreamland*, Hoagland further offered two reasons why the military would be using HAARP to look for ancient repositories. One would be to hide in them if it became necessary, and the other, which he thought was more likely, was:

...[S]uppose we're not the first... suppose someone has put caches of... electronics and libraries, and storehouses of information, and other material buried deep, deep, deep, with a technology that we can't even hope to match. Wouldn't our guys like to find that stuff? Wouldn't it be like Christmas? All that neat stuff they could turn into new weapons—and that's where the military comes back into its own.

Later on that same show Richard Hoagland continues, speaking to Nick Begich:

> Where our two investigations cross here is that between… me looking at ancient civilizations and remnants, either on-planet or off-planet, and you wondering why HAARP is sited where it is, and why it appears to be much more powerful than it needs to be, and why there are layers of deception and confusion and cover… What I have found is, in looking for these underground cavities, read 'bases, tunnels, stores of something,' the siting of HAARP is very specifically situated to probe the Giza plateau.

Hoagland went on to explain that he believed that the series of nuclear tests in the South Pacific conducted by the French in the few weeks prior to that interview were attempts to use the hyperdimensional grid surrounding the earth to also probe the Giza plateau. Hoagland said:

> In fact, if you look at the atoll in the South Pacific, where the French were detonating the nuclear weapons, it is precisely one hundred and eighty degrees on the opposite side of the world from the Giza plateau. If the Giza plateau… represents the marker of the last high epic of civilizations, circa twelve thousand years ago, then it stands to reason that somewhere under that plateau there's an awful lot of neat stuff. The current folks that are sitting on that neat stuff are the Egyptians. Well, maybe our guys want access to what their guys already suspect or have brought up, and suspect that it's much deeper than the Egyptians, with their own technology, could get to.

Richard Hoagland insisted that the French tests and the HAARP tests were a concerted effort by the Conspiracy, using the resources of many nations, to probe Giza with the most sophisticated technology that they had at their disposal. Richard Hoagland saw a direct connection between HAARP and the French nuclear test, because, as he said:

…[T]he way you tweak the spider

web of hyperdimensional physics is, you pluck the web with nuclear weapons placed at certain strategic latitudes and longitudes.

Bruce Cathie was the first to recognize this, although he thought you could only detonate a nuclear weapon at those latitudes and longitudes. In fact, I think they were using the weapons over the last thirty years to probe this hyperdimensional grid. And again, we're not talking about most of the military-industrial complex. We're talking about a tiny group within that uses the resources of nations, and corporations, and institutions to fulfill their own ends, while ostensibly in service to other objectives.

Is Richard Hoagland's perspective on HAARP accurate, or just wild speculation? Unless some HAARP or NASA insider comes forward with proof, we will probably never know. We do know that the Giza Plateau has been heavily studied for underground structures for decades and many amazing discoveries, such as numerous rooms beneath the Sphinx, continue to be found. Has HAARP been surreptitiously drafted to aid in this research?

Or might Richard Hoagland be only partly right? In that interview with Art Bell and Nick Begich, he suggested that there were two big reasons for subverting the military and scientific establishment in this fashion: one, as presented above, is to search for repositories; the other that he speculated on, then dismissed, was alien contact. Dr. Eastlund, who conceived of the original sky buster that became HAARP, saw his apparatus as capable of creating a "full planetary shield," exactly as Ronald Reagan had envisioned his SDI to be. What if that shield were not intended to stop Soviet, Red Chinese, or even Iraqi missiles but something, or someone, far more deadly?

ALIEN CONTACT

At the beginning of this book I mentioned MJ-12. According to the tales, MJ-12 was a super high-echelon, ultra top secret group of military and government insiders created after the crash and recovery of a UFO near Roswell, New Mexico in 1947. According to the likes of John Lear and Bill Cooper, the MJ-12 group has since become the dominant force in world politics, controlling governments, cutting deals with the aliens and so on. Ufologists of their sort have maintained that MJ-12, and the presence of aliens among us, is The Conspiracy. What if they are right? What if there really is an ultimate conspiracy between extraterrestrials (E.T.s) and, say, the Trilateral Commission?

It does make sense that if an alien culture wanted to make official contact with the Peoples of the Earth, they might want us to have a single voice (i.e., a single world government) to speak for all of mankind. Is the current push to create a one-world government a movement to bring us into some larger galactic order? Is MJ-12 the real savior of earth? Will a United Federation of Earth soon be building real spaceports? Are we about to find the earth in a trade imbalance with the Pleiades star cluster?

Most of the UFO whistleblowers on this plot, however, insist that the aliens are not here for our benefit. In most of their stories they say that the E.T.s consider us to be a stupid, inferior lifeform, regarding us in much the same way as we regard cattle. They are said to consider us useful only as DNA suppliers, and, perhaps, as lunchmeat. Is the earth about to become a planetwide genetics factory or fast food restaurant, one with humanburgers as the principal entree? Or is that what the conspiracy just wants us to think?

This dark side of paranoia, often fostered in fact by "ex" military intelligence operatives, or those fed by them, claiming that there is a central contact group, such as the alleged MJ-12, being used by the aliens to create a single earth government which would ultimately become the sheep with the bell for the rest of us to follow (into the slaughterhouse or shearing pen, as they elect)?

There have been a lot of movies and TV shows in recent years about contact with intelligences from beyond the earth. Some, like *Close Encounters Of The Third Kind, E.T.* and the TV show *Alf,* have depicted the aliens as good guys who are here to help us, or at least to be our friends. Other films and shows, like *Independence Day* and *Third Rock From The Sun* show the aliens as invaders, here to steal our world from us. Some people have suggested that, since the Conspiracy owns the media, these shows are actually psychological programming, intended to soften up the public into accepting the official line when the aliens are revealed. Others think that, yes, these shows are meant to condition the public, but that there are no aliens; they are just a hoax perpetrated by the Conspiracy to foist off their New World Order (NWO).

HAARP, or a device like HAARP, could play a role in either real or imaginary "the aliens are coming!" scenarios. If HAARP is *Star Wars* technology coming on-line, it might be used, not to fight the Russians or the Chinese, but invading aliens. The concept behind using a HAARP-like apparatus to create a "full, global shield" is fairly simple, if difficult to achieve. Eastlund believed his device could create "relativistic particles," which are charged particles, such as electrons, moving at the speed of light. It is believed that these particles could destroy any space vehicle they encounter. They could, at least in theory, prevent any nation on earth from getting its ICBMs through the HAARP-generated relativistic particle cloud to destroy any other nation. Using this capability HAARP might also be able to prevent alien spacecraft from entering the earth's atmosphere. In Eastlund's patent he laid out how to use his apparatus to create relativistic particles. In HAARP's current plans, the completed FIRI would

probably not be able to produce them, but, as we have discussed, there is nothing but time, money and public opinion preventing them from expanding HAARP to full Eastlund/Star Wars capacity.

Contrariwise, if there were no aliens but the people of the earth could be made to believe that there were, nation would be forced to band with nation to fight the common enemy. Currently there are several devices being tested by the military for putting holograms into the air. On 31 January, 1996, for example, CNN Worldwide News reported that the Secretary of the Air Force had announced the development of a "next generation" of military defense weapons which included the projection of holographic images into the sky to terrify or disorient the enemy. Some researchers insist that HAARP could be used in this way. With HAARP as a planetary movie projector (or at least providing the audio track by beaming words into our heads), and the Conspiracy writing the script, what might they do? What amazing nonsense might they be able to convince the world of?

This hoaxing of the populace, if it could be pulled off, could be just the ticket for creating the NWO. Some researchers believe that the military and/or the CIA-intelligence community (such as the National Reconnaissance Organization, which manages our spy satellites) have secretly placed other bits of Star Wars type weaponry in orbit, such as nuclear lasers. Some of these researchers have speculated that by firing these weapons at targets on earth, in combination with visual and audio illusions created by HAARP (and similar devices), the Conspiracy could create the ultimate "Invaders From Mars" movie, played out in the sky above our heads.

Chapter Six:
Just What is the Conspiracy?

Let us return to an examination of the Conspiracy. There have been tens of thousands of books written in the last two centuries blowing the whistle on the existence, and the personnel, of a number of Conspiracies—some real, some imagined. The majority of books written in the last few decades have been written by authors with considerably right-of-center viewpoints. During the Cold War these writers mainly viewed them in terms of the so-called Worldwide Communist Conspiracy; or, like Rush Limbaugh or John Stormer, saw a conspiracy of the (poorly understood and ill-defined) "left" using Communism and Socialism as pawns in their game. A few conspiracy books, like Gary Allen's *None Dare Call It Conspiracy*, (Concord Press, 1971), have come from shocked liberal journalists, slam dunked into tight right tail-spins by their discoveries.

Recently, since the (prematurely announced) "death of Communism" and the appearance of the phrase "New World Order" on the tongues of the world's leading politicians, a number of writers from the far right and the far left, and from a remarkable amount of country in between, have denounced an astonishing variety of conspiracies, including:

• The clearly criminal activities of some government officials, such as the theft by Ed Meese's Justice Department of the Promus software from Inslaw and their subsequent driving of that company into bankruptcy in an attempt to hide the crime, all the while selling it illegally to police departments around the world;

• To outrage over treasonous dirty tricks like "October Surprise" (the alleged deal between the Reagan-Bush campaign and the Iranians to keep the American Embassy hostages captive in Iran until after the election to prevent Jimmy Carter from pulling off an "October Surprise" of getting them released before the November election and in so doing win re-election);

• The high-handed contraventions of Congressional wishes such as Ollie North's Iran/Contra gun running scheme, not to mention the CIA's alleged

use of the returning planes by filling them with cocaine to raise "black budget" fund;

• To mounting frustration with federal regulatory agencies staffed by men from the industries they are supposed to regulate, stifling competition and worse (such as the FDA, largely manned by individuals who, after serving their "time" at the FDA, go on to jobs with 5 and 6 figure incomes in the very drug companies they were supposed to have been watchdogging);

•The actions of seemingly out-of-control federal agencies, like the Bureau of Alcohol, Tobacco and Firearms (BATF) and its botched raids on the Weavers (Ruby Ridge, Idaho) and the Branch Davidians (Waco, Texas);

•To more "traditional" concerns over our mounting national debt, federal deficit spending, and abuses of the IRS;

•The suspicions that international bankers and currency speculators may be controlling the American economy through the privately owned banks of the Federal Reserve System and manipulation of interest and currencies at home and abroad; and

•The power of the ruling elite and their organizations for societal control, particularly the philanthropic trusts, the Council on Foreign Relations and the Trilateral Commission.

All the way to off-the-deep-end stories of the government cutting deals with aliens from outer space; Unfortunately, I do not have the space here to document the existence of any particular conspiracy, nor to prove this or that individual's participation in it. All I can do here is give a brief overview of a few basic Conspiracy Theories, so as to give an insight into who might want to use a HAARP-like device to affect changes in society—or even the salvation or eradication of life on earth.

THE NEW WORLD ORDER

At the top, big business and big banking are really one vast interlocked system—one controlled by a few score men (and a handful of women) at the very apex of society. This has been accomplished by virtue of their sitting on each other's Boards of Directors, owning each other's stock, marrying into each other's families, having institutional interconnections into government and other sectors of society (like academia, labor unions and charitable organizations), etc. This interwoven web of relationships, possibly dominated by the international bankers, such as the Rockefellers and the Rothchilds, could be The Conspiracy.

The international bankers, to some degree, run both the governments of the world and the major national and multinational banks and corporations from their position in the heart of this web of financial, familial, and political connections. They are among the oldest of the "old money" ruling elites. Many of them are royalty with connections going back centuries. They finance governments as well businesses, gaining a say in the operations of both. They also own or have control of (via director interlocks, voting blocks of stock, etc.) the media (newspapers, movies, radio and television) around the world, indirectly controlling the information that reaches us.

TOP SECRET

The super rich have also played a role in the creation of "think tanks" (like The Centre for the Study of Democratic Institutions and The Brookings Institution in the U.S., or the Royal Institute for Foreign Affairs and the Tavistock Institute of England) and "citizens" advisory and cooperation groups (like Cecil Rhodes' Round Table in England; Groupe Bilderberg and The Club of Rome under NATO; The Council on Foreign Relations here or the "world-wide" Trilateral Commission). These organizations are where the opinions of government and business are formulated before being promulgated by their lackeys in the media. In the U.S. these organizations also draft "model" legislation for introduction to Congress. Throughout this century such bills have regularly been rubber-stamped into law.

Long ago members of the power elite recognized that change was inevitable. They could see that their only wise course was to become the agents of change, controlling the direction of history into avenues that would be least damaging/most profitable to their economic empires. They have had the time and resources to set up mechanisms among themselves to arrive at a consensus of what they want to do, as well as the wealth and will to carry out the plans these organizations have developed.

Their large endowments to colleges and universities have seldom been motivated by simple civic pride. These have been used to create special schools (like the Model School at Columbia) and other academic organizations (like The Center for Advanced Studies at Stanford). These institutions have aided in the internal deliberations among the wealthy by supplying experts and generations of student intellectual manpower. Additionally, these schools were used to train both the elite and their hand-picked employees in the skills needed to implement their desires (through such programs as the Rhodes Scholarships).

Further, the elite have been instrumental in the creation of governmental agencies (The Atomic Energy Commission, the Food and Drug Administration, etc.) and special boards, panels and committees to infiltrate the government with themselves and their employees to ensure that their plans are carried out. Daily Congress relies on the "expert testimony" of these minions of the conspiracy. This is not something new, they have been doing this for well over a century.

Beyond that, they have even created movements, causes and perhaps even a "New Age" religion or two to control the hearts and minds of the people. In America this started with the Settlement House movement of the 1880s. In

Europe this goes back even farther. Karl Marx was a hireling of the English Fabian Socialists, a cadre of rich and politically powerful men. Communism and Socialism were either created by the elite, or subverted by them early on. Today Communism and Socialism are sociological "Trojan Horses," meant to create authoritarian governments which would then fall under the sway of the multination-  als. Movements not created by them have been taken over; like the environmental movement which has been used to convert "conservationism" into a new "green" form of Communism.

As an environmentalist I am appalled by the potential for ecological disaster posed by the HAARP project. Environmental disasters, actual and potential, seem to be part of the Conspiracy's plans. On 12 September, 1989, *The Washington Post* reported that Barber Conable, World Bank President and member of the Trilateral Commission, made a speech in Tokyo, Japan, at a conference on "Global Environment." In it he revealed what appears to be one of the long-range goals of the international banking crowd. He was reported as having said that "...[W]hile higher temperatures may cause 'a number of disasters,' they might also 'warm cold and unproductive lands in the north into productivity.'" Several think tanks with ties to the Conspiracy have since produced reports that suggest that global warming is really a good thing after all.

The Conspiracy has certainly made a great deal of "hay" off of global warming. They certainly seem to be using it as a vehicle to create a demand for international regulation and monitoring, which would lead ultimately to a One World Government. Some researchers speculate that if HAARP can alter weather patterns, it could secretly be used to create more adverse weather conditions that would make the peoples of the world beg for more global controls, i.e., the NWO. As has been reported in the press, many people already believe that HAARP has been used in this way.

Power mad despots have attempted to subjugate their fellow man since ancient times. Could global "crisis management" be playing into the hands of madmen, giving them a pretext to create a world-wide policestate that would make the Nazis look like pikers? It is certainly not inconceivable. Napoleon and Hitler tried to rule the world. Once upon a time Alexander the Great nearly accomplished it. Some view this push for an global ecological authority as mankind's last great hope. Others see it as a treasonous, criminal conspiracy to destroy the world's legal governments and replace them with a single totalitarian regime—both may be right.

If the above is more or less true, then it would give the international bankers and their symbiotes (i.e. the New World Order) enormous potential not only for unimaginable wealth, but immense power to control whole societies. This, in capsule form, is one telling of the Conspiracy, one told primarily from what the Conspiracy-owned media calls the "paranoid ultra-right."

The mainstream press, for obvious reasons, ignores the NWO or insists that it is the figment of the imaginations of demented, gun-toting loonies. While there may be some truth to that, how do you explain "The Declaration of Interdependence," which was signed on 30 January, 1976, in Washington, D.C., by 32 Senators and 92 Representatives? It contains this most revealing line: "Two centuries ago our forefathers brought forth a new nation: now we must join with others to bring forth a new world order." Many who denounce conspiracy theories and conspiracy theorists insist that the New World Order was just the coalition of allied nations formed to throw the Iraqis out of Kuwait. Yet, this Declaration of Interdependence, signed by top American politicians, called for the creation of "a new world order" a decade and a half before the Gulf War!

Some believe that the NWO is a Freemasonic plot. Take a one dollar bill out of your pocket. On the back side of the bill are the obverse and reverse faces of the Great Seal of the United States of America. Notice the eye in the triangle at the top of the unfinished pyramid? Those are important symbols within Freemasonry. The eye may represent a number of things, not the least of which is the "All Seeing Eye" of the Supreme God of the Freemasons, GAOTU or Great Architect of the Universe. The unfinished pyramid also represents a number of things including the idea that God's plan for this world is not yet complete. The pyramid is also a classic depiction of an aristocratic social order with the ruling few at the top and the powerless many at the base: a social order such as what the great architects of the NWO desire.

Beneath the pyramid is a scroll that reads: "NOVUS ORDO SECLORUM." This translates from the Latin as: NOVUS: new; ORDO: order; SECLORUM: the secular world: a.k.a.: New World Order. For the last 200 plus years the phrase "New World Order" has been something of a campaign slogan for the Conspiracy. Conspiracy researchers around the globe were therefore terribly startled when George Bush began using that phrase in public. This was the equivalent of the Conspiracy waving a red flag before the conspiracy research community's eyes.

For a more succinct definition of the New World Order, I offer the following transcript of author Lindsey Williams speaking on *The Jim French Show* on KIRO radio, Seattle, Washington, on 10 February, 1991:

> Lindsey Williams: There's a new expression that's very common now, heard quite often [from] our President, entitled "New World Order," and no one ever seems to know the definition to it.

TOP SECRET

Jim French: Do you have a definition of it? Is there an official definition of it? When George Bush says "New World Order" what does he mean?

Lindsey Williams: Well... there was [sic] some very close friends of President Bush who met in Germany recently at what was dubbed as the Brandt Commission; it was also called the Fifth Socialist International. A very prestigious group of people and at their meeting they formally adopted a definition of the expression "New World Order." Ah, just a few individuals who were there... Former World Bank President, Robert McNamara was there, who by the way is a personal friend of President Bush; former Secretary of Commerce, Peter Peterson was present; none other than *Newsweek* magazine's owner and editor, Katherine Graham, was there... just to name a few of the very prestigious individuals who were there.

Jim French: This is the "Brandt Commission?"

Lindsey Williams: "Brandt Commission." I don't know why they called it the "Fifth Socialist International," or why they called it "Brandt Commission." All I know is that they met in West Germany and in the course of their meeting they officially adopted a definition of the expression "New World Order," and all of these individuals approved it, and signed it, saying that they officially adopted this as the definition, for the first time by any prestigious organization of the expression that's being used by our President and Mr. Gorbachev, and Mr. Yeltsin; the expression "New World Order."

Jim French: So, what is their definition?

Lindsey Williams: I will read it. Quote: "A supranational authority to regulate world commerce and industry; an international organization that would control the production and consumption of oil; an international currency that would replace the dollar; a world development fund that would make funds available to free and Communist nations alike; an international police force to enforce the edicts of the New World Order."

Jim French: What are you reading that from?

Lindsey Williams: This was published in the *McAlvany Intelligence Advisory* and Don McAlvany produces one of the most respected financial newsletters in the world today. He got it right from the minutes of the Brandt Commission when they met in West Germany in February of 1991.

FREEMASONRY AND ILLUMINISM VS THE VATICAN

Some researchers believe that the major dynamic in world politics is the centuries old battle between the Vatican (a deposed would-be world government) and a continually shifting coalition of anti-papal forces (possibly coalescing around the Cerberus-like three-headed monster of the British Empire, Freemasonry, and the Rothschild banking empire). Other emerging world forces, such as the Chinese or the radical Islamic world, are generally seen as outside this basic conspiracy between the Neo-British Empire (which is generally thought to contain the U.S., depending on which theory one is listening to at the time) and its struggle with the Vatican.

Some, like Lyndon LaRouche, believe that the British oligarchy is The Conspiracy; others believe that the Freemasons are The Conspiracy; and some, like the editors of the publications *Criminal Politics* and *The Spotlight,* insist that International Bankers are The Conspiracy. This coalition of Presbyterians, Methodists, Lutherans (the majority of Masons) vs. the old Roman Catholic Church seems to show that the object of powerplays for world dominance is more than mere wealth. Is there a religious struggle taking place? Some say this is the age-old battle between Good and Evil.

Is Masonry good or evil? From a liberal, pro-democratic, humanistic view, Masonry champions the cause of Good. It could be argued that the American Revolution was a Masonic plot. The American Revolution was masterminded by a cadre of Masons and the aristocratic liberal intelligentsia of the day, with the aid of anti-monarchists and fellow Masons abroad. Washington, Jefferson and Franklin, for instance, were Masons.

By some accounts Masonry has ruled America pretty much since. At least eight American Presidents have admitted to being Masons (some researchers say the actual number is twice that). The most recent Masons to hold the Presidency were George Bush and Ronald Reagan. Bill Clinton denies being a Mason, but admits to having been a member of a Masonic youth organization.

An argument could be equally made that Masonry espouses Evil—or is Masonry's evil-twin brother, the Illuminati. The Illuminati was officially founded on 1 May, 1776 in Bavaria in what is today Germany. "The true purpose of the Order," wrote Weishaupt, "was to rule the world. To achieve this it was necessary for the Order to destroy all religions, overthrow all governments and abolish private property." He also directed his (seemingly) "anti-monarchist" organization to take control of Bavaria through infiltration.

Some researchers have suggested that the real architect of the American Revolution might have been Adam Weishaupt, the reputed founder of the Ancient and Illuminated Seers of Bavaria—better known as the Illuminati. Weishaupt and his followers and their heirs have also been fingered as the movers behind the French and Russian Revolutions as well. The Illuminati figures very largely indeed in many of the conspiracy theories being passed about these days. Definitely a heavy-weight contender for being the Big Conspiracy if there actually is one.

How much of their goal has been realized since the Illuminati was founded in 1776?? Did they succeed in infiltrating every aspect of society, controlling us in a hundred ways without our knowledge? Or did they wither away to become a vanished, long forgotten plot, alive only in the minds of paranoids and patriots?

Freemasonry is not to be confused with the Illuminati (or is it?). President George Washington, a Mason, declared that "...none of the Lodges in this country are contaminated with the principles ascribed to the society of the Illuminati." The Illuminati are known to have infiltrated the Freemasons in Bavaria by 1782.

It is unknown if they ever did succeed in subverting the Lodges in America. Masons do not air their dirty laundry in public much. They are alleged to have a nasty habit of covering things up, under bodies if need be. Jack the Ripper, for example, is believed by some researchers to have been a Masonic Royal Physician cleaning up some Royal Family dirty business.

By now you must have guessed that Freemasonry is more than just guys in funny hats on little cars in parades; more than children's hospitals and fund-raising circuses. It is one of the oldest secret societies in the world. It has been described as an occult religion with a socio-political agenda. It is decidedly anti-papal, and not particularly Christian. At its core (perhaps) is a secularization of the Jewish Kabbalah, a mystery religion/magic system that is esoteric even to the Jews.

Freemasonry has maintained elements from man's earliest religions. Whether these elements were a survival from earlier forms, or, like so much in the current "New Age," a re-creation, is a matter of speculation. Are its goals purely secular, as the writings of Weishaupt might suggest, or does it plan to replace the religion(s) of the descendants of Abraham, Jacob, Isaac, Moses and Jesus with something else?

Jim Keith in his *Saucers of the Illuminati* suggests that UFOs are a terrestrial suppressed/secret technology being used by the Illuminati today to control and manipulate populations, possibly through staged encounters with "aliens" that are actually intelligence operatives. In his book *Casebook on Alternative 3: UFOs, Secret Societies and World Control*, Keith further explores the connections between UFOs and the conspiracy (which, at the time he wrote that book, seemed to think was international fascism marching under the banner of Illuminism) and how they may be using this "UFO" technology to accomplish a variety of nefarious ends, including a secret space program. In both books he links the Illuminati and Freemasonry as part of a larger

front for the dynastic families whose accumulated wealth forms a military-banking-industrialist front for The Conspiracy.

A vast number of researchers from a wide variety of political and philosophical disciplines have examined Freemasonry and the Illuminati for centuries, both in Europe and the New World. Some of these researchers believe that Masonry has been attempting the establishment of a theocratic New World Order as symbolized by the reverse side of the Great Seal of the United States of America. Theocracy is the rule of a people or a nation by God, or priests claiming divine guidance, such as the Vatican attempted centuries ago.

Some believe that there is one overarching Conspiracy, and its purpose is the creation of a theocratic world king. A number of theocratic worst-case scenarios have been offered, and I will share one with you here. In *Saucers of the Illuminati* Jim Keith offered evidence that the following list is the core belief structure of an elite hyperplot. This he believes to be a secret shared only within the highest degrees of the "order" and only then among a select few. According to Mr. Keith, at least one of the major threads of the anti-Papist segments of the conspiracy, called by him simply the Illuminati, now believes that:

(1) Jesus married Mary Magdalene…

(2) She was pregnant with his seed at the time of the Crucifixion.

(3) The Holy Grail that the Knights Templar were entrusted with safe-keeping was no Last Supper wine goblet, an ordinary cup infused with the "magic" of the savior's presence, but was only a metaphor (or perhaps inner-circle code) for the very bloodline of Jesus: the pregnant Mary and the heirs of Jesus.

(4) The Knights Templar were not destroyed by the Armies of the Pope at the end of the Crusades, but went underground, perhaps forming Scottish Rite Freemasonry in Scotland.

(5) The bloodline of Jesus was mingled with the royal houses of Europe and has survived to this day.

(6) There is a living claimant to the throne of this world, to the throne of David and of Solomon—a direct heir of Jesus who is very much alive and well and ready to ascend to the throne.

(7) Several threads of the conspiracy are planning to rebuild the Temple of Solomon and fulfill their mutual prophecies of the Messiah by installing this claimant on the throne of the New World Order…

And if that does not sound far enough "out

there" for you... Masonic literature talks about rebuilding the Temple of Solomon in the hearts of Masons. The evidence seems to indicate that they also plan to rebuild the actual temple, and do it around the year 2000!

TOWARDS THEOCRACY

The Conspiracy, then, may include members of a ruling elite who are concerned with preserving their wealth and are true believers in religious dogmas, and, possibly, some very weird ones at that. One or more factions of the Conspiracy may have jumped on the fundamentalist bandwagon. Others could be even kinkier. They may practice goddess worship, Satanism, and even human sacrifice!

The liberal, ecumenical-interfaith crowd is actively pushing for a worldwide religious/moral ethic to provide a spiritual underpinning for the New World Order. Perhaps somewhat predictably, some folks on the so-called religious right have decried their efforts as an attempt to establish the Kingdom of the Anti-Christ.

A number of radical fundamentalist Christian sects desperately desire The End: the death and resurrection of mankind into the Kingdom of Heaven. They think we are living in the End Times and they are literally waiting for the heavens to open up and for God himself to usher them home. This is called the "rapture," when the chosen will be instantaneously transported to Heaven. Others believe that giant UFOs will fly them to the place God has reserved for them.

Not all of these Christians are waiting patiently. A few actually think they can cause the End Times to occur by making things here on earth so bad that God is forced to act. Some of these people have achieved high positions. James Watt was once Secretary of the Interior, whose responsibility was for the preservation and allocation of the natural wealth and resources of this nation. He advocated clear-cutting timber and strip mining in our National Forests and other ecologically unconscionable acts because he believed that the Second Coming would happen in our lifetimes, so there was no need to conserve! What if some of these loonies are in control of HAARP?

Is it possible that a Satanically-inspired Conspiracy wishing to commit the ultimate in ritual murder/human sacrifice might actually attempt to "fry" the whole darned planet? This is definitely a possibility. As we have discussed, several applications of HAARP technology could have life threatening consequences on a global scale. Rents could be torn in the protective layers of ionization and/or ozone, irradiating the lands below. As researcher Michael Unum revealed, this may already have happened on a "small" scale. The experiment with creating an "artificial ionosphere" by dumping copper needles into the upper atmosphere may have interfered with the earth's magnetic field, causing earthquakes. Certainly messing with the electrojet has the potential for causing unpredictable events—perhaps making the magnetic poles change positions, or even bringing about a collapse or reversal of the magnetic field. Any such event could be catastrophic for life on earth. Even if some "madman" does not try to use HAARP to destroy earth, could a fundamentalist Christian want to use HAARP to do "just enough" damage to force God's hand?

John D. Rockefeller, Jr., globalist extraordinaire, said, in 1917:

> I see the church molding the thought of the world, as it has never done before, leading in all great movements as it should. I see it literally establishing the Kingdom of God on earth.

If David Rockefeller, Chairman of the Trilateral Commission, is, today, actually attempting to establish a world government, what is meant by a "Kingdom" of God? Was the elder Rockefeller merely waxing metaphorical, or could they, a leading family of the ruling elite, literally want to establish a religious World King?

This makes us want to ask some very serious questions of the interfaith-ecumenical movement and organizations. One prominent organization worthy of such questioning is the Temple of Understanding, a significant recipient of Rockefeller funding. Established in 1959, it is associated with the Cathedral of St. John the Divine which is the seat of the Episcopal Bishop of New York. Curiously, the Cathedral of St. John the Divine was also the site of Nikola Tesla's funeral—another strange connection to HAARP. The Temple of Understanding's founders included Dr. Albert Schweitzer, Jawaharlal Nehru, Eleanor Roosevelt, Orthodox Patriarch Athenagorus, former U.N. Secretary General U-Thant, the Dalai Lama, Anwar Sadat and Pontiffs John XXIII and Paul VI. It is also closely associated with Mikhail Gorbachev's Green Cross.

The Green Cross is a political/spiritual changeling. It advocates "ethical and moral issues relating to ecology." It is a clear penetration of the environmentalist movement by the Conspiracy. I am afraid that I do not have to space here to do this subject justice. Please research the cooption of the ecological movement by the New World Order/Communists. As a lifelong environmental activist, what I know of this perversion sets my blood boiling—and scares the heck out of me!

The interfaith movement seems to be directed at more than just generating cooperation and dialogue between the world's religions, but in actually creating a single world religion parallel to the single world government. It is charged with creating a universal moral code (to be written by Mikhail Gorbachev per the 1992 Earth Summit held in Rio de Janeiro) that will provide the religious/spiritual/moral foundation for the "edicts" of the New World Order. Our Constitution is based (in part) on Biblical moral precepts; the New World Order's "constitution" will be similarly built on this new "universal" moral code—one written by a hardline (oops, "reformed") Communist!

To get a clue as to what that code will be, read *Global Responsibility: In Search of a New World Ethic* by Hans Kung, board member of the Temple of Understanding. Also read up on the Green Cross and "Agenda 21" signed by 172 nations at the Earth Summit in Rio.

It is also possible that the Conspiracy (or a portion thereof) has realized the power inherent in this religious movement and is merely pretending to be working toward the New Age and/or Second Coming/Kingdom of Christ as a guise to shear the sheep. Before there was politics there was religion and before politicians there were priests—different collars, same job. The cynic and the atheist have always seen religion as a trick played on humanity by cosmic con artists. The unscrupulous by definition have no sacred cows, no moral restraints. Why not take advantage of the sheep? It is easy to imagine them thinking, "If the fools want a Second Coming, we'll give 'em one!"

What is the relationship between the religious and the political conspiracies? Is this seeming effort to bring about a world religion a case of parallel development; a case of the political conspiracy using religion as just another propaganda (conditioning) and population control mechanism; or are religionists of one or more persuasions using the political conspiracy to further their agenda? Either way, with HAARP they have an incredible tool for fooling the world.

An example of such potential misuse of this technology can be seen in the effects of the "Persinger Helmet," a brain research tool designed by Dr. Michael Persinger of the Laurentian University of Ontario, Canada. With it he discovered, in the late 1980s, that when specific frequencies are directed into the hippocampus area of the back brain a large percentage of subjects reported UFO abduction experiences, out of body experiences, and a wide range of altered states of consciousness, including "Union with God." The helmet experience, Dr. Persinger says, "involves a widening of emotional meaning, such that things not typically considered significant would now be considered meaningful" and hallucinations are "perceived as extremely real." What could the Conspiracy do with this knowledge and a tool like HAARP to put a "virtual" Persinger Helmet on all of our heads? One appli-

cation that comes readily to mind is the creation of a fake "Rapture."

As we have seen, the military has announced that they will soon have holographic projectors for disorientating enemies. How might the Conspiracy use such? Imagine being able to project into the skies above the peoples of the earth an image of the God, Goddess or Gods of the dominant religion of each region—Shiva, Buddha, Mohammed, Christ… While doing this, ecstatic emotions and/or engineered states of consciousness are also being beamed at the people. Imagine being able make the people hear the words of the projected God spoken inside their own mind. Imagine being able to tell the people that all Gods are the One God, that the day of fulfillment is at hand; and then to merge the images in the air into One God—one of the NWO's design. Seems likely that the Conspiracy could get near instantaneous conversion of an overwhelming majority of the earth's population to any religion of their choosing by such a ploy.

A Tesla System Using the Earth as a Capacitor
by Richard L. Clark

Nikola Tesla engineered his communications and power broadcast systems based on the Earth as a spherical capacitor plate with the ionosphere as the other plate. The frequencies that work best with this system are 12 Hz and its harmonics and the "storm" frequency around 500 KHz. The basic Earth electrostatic system and the basic Tesla designs are shown in the figure below. All lengths or circuits must be one-quarter wavelength or some odd multiple of it.

The elevated capacitor has really two functions, Capacity to Ground (C_g) and Capacity to Ionosphere (C_i). The bottom plate only to ground is C_g, and both plates are C_i. L2 and C3 are a resonant stepdown air core coupling system at the desired frequency. Simple calculations will allow resonant frequency values to be determined from the Tesla Equivalent Circuit diagram. Be extremely careful of the high voltages in this system.

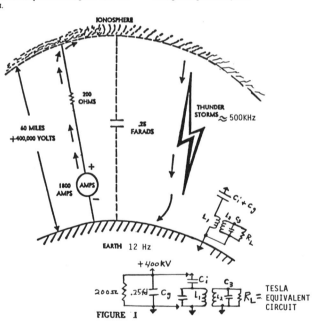

FIGURE 1

Equivalent circuit of earth's electrostatic voltage field.

Chapter Seven:
Criminal Proceedings

THE LAW OF WAR

Although it may appear to be an incongruous concept, the nations of the world have recognized the need to impose restrictions on the waging of war. War will necessarily result in death and injury to humans and the destruction of property; however, in the eyes of the international community, it need not be an unlimited exercise in cruelty and ruthlessness. The necessities of war must be conciliated with the laws of humanity. The resulting restrictions are regarded as the international Law Of Armed Conflict (LOAC), or the law of war.

These concepts... can be found throughout man's history. The ancient Hindu laws of Manu prohibited the use of barbed arrows because they exacerbated the injury upon their removal. The Romans considered the use of poisoned weapons to be unlawful. During the Middle Ages, the Pope condemned the crossbow, noting the appalling injuries it caused...

So wrote Maj. Joseph W. Cook, III; Maj. David P. Fiely; and Maj. Maura T. McGowan in their U.S. Air Force sponsored research paper, "Nonlethal Weapons: Technologies, Legalities, and Potential Policies."

In 1868, the Russian government issued an invitation to the International Military Commission "to examine the expediency of forbidding the use of certain projectiles in time of war between civilized nations." A new type of bullet was the cause of the Russian concern. These new "light explosives" or "inflammable projectiles," when used against human beings, were no more effective than an ordinary rifle bullet; however, they caused greater wounds and thus greatly aggravated the sufferings of the victim. The resulting document, The Declaration of St. Petersburg, prohibited the use of explosive projectiles under 400 grams of weight. It was the first international treaty imposing restrictions on the conduct of war in modern times.

One significance of The Declaration of St. Petersburg is that it develops a line of reasoning governing the legality of weapons. I introduce the concept of legality here because I believe that HAARP is probably a weapon—and possibly an illegal one. Yes, at its most basic level, HAARP is a scientific research tool. However, it also appears to be a weapons system prototype, and possibly much more. I do not know if HAARP, as it sits today, can be used for the weaponry uses we have discussed. I am quite sure, however, that HAARP could be expanded into Bernard Eastlund's monster in relatively short order. The question I am examining is: if this device is, or can be made into a weapon, is it, or the use of it, legal under international law?

The generally accepted line of reasoning governing the legality of weapons is found in the Preamble to The Declaration of St. Petersburg:

> ...Considering [that] the progress of civilization should have the effect of alleviating as much as possible the calamities of war. The only legitimate object which states should endeavor to accomplish during war is to weaken the military forces of the enemy. It is sufficient to disable the greatest possible number of men, and this object would be exceeded by the employment of arms which uselessly aggravate the sufferings of disabled men or render their death inevitable. The use of such weapons would therefore, be contrary to the laws of humanity.

While most cultures around this globe have seen the need to restrain the horrors of war, it was not until the nineteenth century that these sentiments were codified into international law. The Declaration of St. Petersburg was followed in 1899 with The Hague Conventions, the first of which was The Convention with Respect to the Laws and Customs of War on Land, 29 July 1899. It was amended several times during the following decade, such as by the Regulations Annexed to Hague Convention No. IV Respecting the Laws and Customs of War on Land, 18 October 1907.

The Geneva conventions of 1929 and 1949 focused on ameliorating the conditions of civilians, prisoners of war, and the sick and wounded. These can be found in Treaties and Other International Acts Series (TIAS) (Washington, D.C.: US Department of State, 1956), of special interest are the following:

• Geneva Convention for the Amelioration of the Condition of the Wounded and Sick in the Armed Forces in the Field, 12 August 1949, TIAS 3362

• Geneva Convention for the Amelioration of the Condition of the Wounded and Sick and Shipwrecked Members, 12 August 1949, TIAS 3363

• Geneva Convention Relative to the Treatment of Prisoners of War, 12 August 1949, TIAS 3364.

• Geneva Convention Relative to the Treatment of Civilian Persons in Time of War, 12 August 1949, TIAS 3365

The latest amendments to the Law Of Armed Conflict are contained in the 1977 Protocol Additional to the Geneva Conventions, 8 June 1977, which the U.S. has

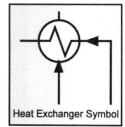

Heat Exchanger Symbol

not yet ratified.

Additionally, a number of international treaties address the legitimacy of specific weapons. These include the following agreements:

• The 1925 Geneva Protocol for the Prohibition of the Use of Asphyxiating, Poisonous, or Other Gases and of Bacteriological Methods of Warfare, 17 June 1925

• Convention on the Prohibition of the Development, Production, and Stockpiling of Bacteriological (Biological) and Toxin Weapons and on Their Destruction, 10 April 1972

• Convention on the Prohibition of Military or Any Other Hostile Use of Environmental Modification Techniques, 10 December 1976

• Convention on Prohibitions or Restrictions on the Use of Certain Conventional Weapons Which May Be Deemed to Be Excessively Injurious or to Have Indiscriminate Effects, 10 October 1980

• Protocol on Non Detectable Fragments, 10 October 1980

• Protocol on Prohibitions or Restrictions on the Use of Mines, Booby Traps, and Other Devices, 10 October 1980.

As well as being a potential violation of the ENMOD Treaty of 10 December, 1976, I believe HAARP also potentially violates the 1980 treaty prohibiting weapons with "indiscriminate effects." The legality of a weapon and the legality of the specific uses of a weapon, are set by these international laws, and other international conventions, international customs, and the general principles of law.

Maj. William J. Neinast, in "U.S. Use of Biological Warfare," *Military Law Review* 24 (1964), wrote: "[I]n considering the use of any weapon, new or old, two questions must be answered. First, can this weapon legally be used? Second, if the first question is answered in the affirmative, is the proposed use of this weapon legal?" HAARP could be a legal weather weapon when used in such a way as to cause temporary effects, such as building up clouds over an Air Force base to increase concealment. However, it could just as easily be used illegally, such as in causing the jet stream to move, inducing a crop-destroying drought and subsequent famine.

These laws, of course, have little to enforce them. Unless an offending nation be sued in international court, or officials of an offending government be brought to trial before an international tribunal, such as at Nuremberg after WWII or as is currently ongoing at The Hague, there is little power to enforce international law.

Here in the U.S. international law is part of our domestic law, as treaties are regarded as the supreme law of the land by the Constitution. This is stated in Article VI, Section 2: "...and all Treaties made, or which shall be made, under the Authority of the United States, shall be the supreme Law of the Land..." Even if the international community is hard-pressed to uphold these laws, the United States is bound by its own Constitution to adhere to these covenants. It is our duty as citizens to ensure that our government does so. Of course, if a treaty violates the Constitution then it is our duty to demand that the United States withdraw from it.

In *U.S. v. List*, the international military tribunal at Nuremberg determined that:

> Military necessity permits a belligerent, subject to the laws of war, to apply any amount and kind of force to compel the complete submission of the enemy with the least possible expenditure of time, life, and money... There must be some reasonable connection between the destruction of property and the overcoming of the enemy.

This means that the rules of international law must be followed even if it results in the loss of an advantage. Kriegsraison, the World War II German doctrine of military necessity, was the belief that the ends justified the means—that a matter of "urgent necessity" could override the LOAC. This principle was rejected in *U.S. v. Krupp*, when the Nuremberg tribunal held that:

> ...[T]o claim that the law of war can wantonly and at the sole discretion of any one belligerent be disregarded when he considered his own situation to be critical means nothing more than to abrogate the laws and customs of war entirely.

There might be some sort of "Kriegsraison" going on in the DOD today. Even if the DOD, Air Force and Navy are guiltless, the Conspiracy almost certainly holds such an attitude. It is quite possible that a conspiracy composed of civilians would not consider itself honor bound to uphold military conventions. Then again, the Conspiracy probably has very little honor to spare.

As Majors Cook, Fiely and McGowan put it in "Nonlethal Weapons: Technologies, Legalities, and Potential Policies":

> International law establishes certain principles governing the prohibition of weapons. Two such principles are unnecessary suffering and indiscriminate effects caused by certain weapons.
>
> Article 23(e) of the 1907 Hague Convention prohibits the use of "arms, projectiles or materials calculated to cause unnecessary suffer-

ing." This concept has been the subject of much concern as there is no precise definition of unnecessary suffering. As stated in Air Force Pamphlet (AFP) 11031, International Law: The Conduct of Armed Conflict, all weapons cause suffering. The St. Petersburg Declaration speaks in terms of arms that uselessly aggravate "the sufferings of disabled men or render their death inevitable."

A primary concern of the Law Of Armed Conflict is the protection of noncombatants. A belligerent may not attack a noncombatant and must cancel an attack on a legitimate military target if the injury to the noncombatant population would be disproportionate. Belligerents cannot employ a "blind" weapon, one that cannot discriminate between noncombatants and combatants.

A weapon that complies with the general principles of the law may not be used in a manner that is restricted by custom or treaty. The Hague Conventions underline that there are restrictions on the conduct of war in Article 22, which provides that "the right of belligerents to adopt means of injuring the enemy is not unlimited."

Weapons may be used only against military objectives. An object is considered to be a military object if its use, nature, location, or purpose make effective contribution to the military action. Some objects are considered dualuse objects. They meet the needs of the civilian population but also effectively contribute to the enemy's military action. These objects may be attacked if there is a military advantage to be gained by their attack. During Desert Storm, the coalition forces bombed bridges across the Euphrates River, not only to restrict the movement of enemy forces but to sever the communications systems. The bridges contained fiberoptic links that provided Saddam Hussein with a communications system to his forces. The attack produced a military advantage for the coalition forces.

The LOAC prohibits attack against noncombatants or civilian property. Again, attacks against military targets may result in injury to protected persons and property. It is the attackers' responsibility to minimize collateral damage against protected persons and property. Places such as buildings dedicated to religion, art, science, charitable purposes, historic monuments, and hospitals are protected from attack. The Hague Convention also prohibits the use of poison, treachery, and perfidy. Emblems of protection such as the Red Cross must be respected. There are rules governing the use of uniforms and certain signals. Assassination is prohibited.

Man is constantly using technology to devise new weapons that international law must address. These weapons range from the very deadly to the nonlethal.

Nonlethal electromagnetic weapons span the spectrum from simple to exotic. Many can be employed (or can have collateral effects) against both personnel and equipment. Blinding and shocking effects are the most common nonlethal results of the use of this class of weapons.

A second factor of assessment is "unnecessary suffering." Several electromagnetic weapons, such as the high intensity light and laser, may produce temporary or permanent blindness. These weapons have been the subject of much discussion. Sweden has been actively condemning the use of lasers as antipersonnel weapons on the grounds that they cause unnecessary suffering.

The controversy surrounding lasers focuses on the legitimacy of deliberately blinding human beings. Exposing a pilot's eyes to a laser may result in the destruction of the entire plane. Intentionally blinding an attacking infantry unit would render them unable to fight. Some scholars, in particular experts from Switzerland and Sweden, argue that intentionally using a laser to permanently blind a combatant is a disproportionate injury to the gained military advantage. The essence of their argument is that The Declaration of St. Petersburg authorized the incapacitation of an opponent only for the duration of the conflict. "Although it is permitted to kill combatants under the law of war, and thus to put them permanently out of action, it is not permitted to use methods or means of warfare exclusively designed to injure soldiers with injuries lasting not only the duration of the conflict but for the rest of their lives." It is their position that intentional irreversible permanent blindness by a laser constitutes "unnecessary suffering."

The U.S. rejects this position. In a memorandum of law, it noted that there was no legal obligation to limit wounding so that the opponent would be temporarily disabled for the period of the hostilities and no longer. Additionally, it noted, "Blinding is no stranger to the battle field." The use of a number of conventional weapons could result in blindness. However, these conventional weapons are more likely to cause death. It is the U.S.' position that lasers do not cause unnecessary suffering but are more humane because the victim is likely to suffer less injury than that caused by conventional weapons.

The injuries suffered as a result of electromagnetic weapons are typically less severe than those injuries resulting from conventional weapons. Although it is possible that a belligerent may be permanently injured or killed as a result of the use of these weapons, there is no evidence that the suffering experienced is greater then that experienced from conventional weapons.

It would appear from the above that the legal position of the U.S. is something along of the lines of "we can do it until there is a clear law specifically against it." If that is the case, then we need to press for an international ruling on HAARP and HAARP-like weapons (like the Russian Woodpecker). Note that it is against the LOAC to use a "blind" weapon, one that cannot tell the difference between combatant and noncombatant. HAARP would most certainly be such a weapon.

We need to drum up public opinion against such use in the U.S. and abroad. Public opinion has stopped the military before—it prevented the laying of ELF antennae in Project Sanguine and it stopped the Vietnam War. Public opinion is a powerful weapon. William Randolf Hearst used it to start the Spanish American War. We need to use it to stop HAARP and the Conspiracy.

A weapon like HAARP in the hands of the Conspiracy can be especially dangerous to the movement to restore this country to the principles of the Constitution. If it comes down to any sort of armed conflict between operatives of the Conspiracy and patriotic "insurgents" it could be decisive. Anyone thinking of taking on the Conspiracy by direct means should keep the following quote from "Nonlethal Weapons: Technologies, Legalities, and Potential Policies" in mind:

> The key to winning a counterinsurgency is winning the hearts and minds of the affected population. In this scenario, any weapon that reduces collateral damage to innocent people or property is advantageous. Insurgents who are interspersed with innocent civilians are especially hard to target. However, it is not even necessary or even desirable to kill the insurgent in order to defeat him. Certain nonlethal weapons might offer solutions to these tactically difficult situations. In Vietnam, for example, the only options available to a patrol under fire from a "friendly" village were (1) return fire and risk generating friendly casualties, or (2) withdraw. Both options have the potential of further alienating a largely friendly population. The ability to incapacitate the insurgents would enable troops to sort out the good from the bad without killing anyone. A secondary advantage of capturing an insurgent rather than killing him is the intelligence that can be garnered from the prisoner, a critical element in defeating an insurgency.
>
> Some nonlethal technologies that offer promise in counterinsurgencies include chemical defoliants and tear gasses, calmative agents, blinding weapons, and acoustical weapons. Of course, as discussed earlier, the weapon chosen must be a legal one. Additionally, such practical issues as portability, training, and effectiveness must also be addressed before relying on such weapons in the hands of troops facing a mortal enemy. Insurgents might be emboldened and able to attract more (though less dedicated) followers if they know that death

is a very unlikely prospect. The insurgency could deteriorate into a game in which the insurgents are incapacitated and captured while counterinsurgents are killed.

Another possible violation of the law of humanity by HAARP can be found in its potential use by spooks and/or the Conspiracy to put words, thoughts, or beliefs into our heads. If one went mad from hearing voices in one's head as a result of being the target of an electromagnetic attack, would that be a violation of the LOAC? Just seeing if HAARP will work comes under the heading of "human experimentation."

THE NUREMBERG CODE

"Is Military Research Hazardous To Veterans' Health? Lessons Spanning Half A Century" was a staff report prepared for the Committee on Veterans' Affairs, U.S. Senate, 8 December, 1994. In it, Committee Chairman John D. Rockefeller IV, wrote:

> During the last few years, the public has become aware of several examples where U.S. Government researchers intentionally exposed Americans to potentially dangerous substances without their knowledge or consent. The Senate Committee on Veterans' Affairs, which I have been privileged to chair from 1993-94, has conducted a comprehensive analysis of the extent to which veterans participated in such research while they were serving in the U.S. military.

Under the heading "III. Findings and conclusions" this staff written document states:

> A. For at least 50 years, DOD has intentionally exposed military personnel to potentially dangerous substances, often in secret
> B. DOD has repeatedly failed to comply with required ethical standards when using human subjects in military research during war or threat of war
> C. DOD incorrectly claims that since their goal was treatment, the use of investigational drugs in the Persian Gulf War was not research
> D. DOD used investigational drugs in the Persian Gulf War in ways that were not effective
> E. DOD did not know whether pyridostigmine bromide would be safe for use by U.S. troops in the Persian Gulf War

F. When U.S. troops were sent to the Persian Gulf in 1994, DOD still did not have proof that pyridostigmine bromide was safe for use as an antidote enhancer

G. Pyridostigmine may be more dangerous in combination with pesticides and other exposures

H. The safety of the botulism vaccine was not established prior to the Persian Gulf War

I. Records of anthrax vaccinations are not suitable to evaluate safety

J. Army regulations exempt informed consent for volunteers in some types of military research

K. DOD and DVA [Department of Veteran's Affairs] have repeatedly failed to provide information and medical followup to those who participate in military research or are ordered to take investigational drugs

L. The Federal Government has failed to support scientific studies that provide information about the reproductive problems experienced by veterans who were intentionally exposed to potentially dangerous substances

M. The Federal Government has failed to support scientific studies that provide timely information for compensation decisions regarding military personnel who were harmed by various exposures

N. Participation in military research is rarely included in military medical records, making it impossible to support a veteran's claim for service-connected disabilities from military research

O. DOD has demonstrated a pattern of misrepresenting the danger of various military exposures that continues today

If the DOD could do that in full public view, live on CNN in the Gulf War, what could they be cooking up in secret? I am totally convinced that if there is a potential to use HAARP in any way for any sort of secret testing on unsuspecting civilians they will find it and do it. It just seems to be in the DOD's nature. Like Lucille Clark said to the HAARP scientists at the first open house, "…tell me I'm wrong."

In "Is Military Research Hazardous To Veterans' Health? Lessons Spanning Half A Century," the writers state:

> During the last 50 years, hundreds of thousands of military personnel have been involved in human experimentation and other intentional exposures conducted by the Department of Defense (DOD), often without a servicemember's knowledge or consent. In

some cases, soldiers who consented to serve as human subjects found themselves participating in experiments quite different from those described at the time they volunteered. For example, thousands of World War II veterans who originally volunteered to "test summer clothing" in exchange for extra leave time, found themselves in gas chambers testing the effects of mustard gas and lewisite. Additionally, soldiers were sometimes ordered by commanding officers to "volunteer" to participate in research or face dire consequences. For example, several Persian Gulf War veterans interviewed by Committee staff reported that they were ordered to take experimental vaccines during Operation Desert Shield or face prison.

...[S]ome of the studies that have been conducted had more questionable motives. For example, the Department of Defense (DOD) conducted numerous "man-break" tests, exposing soldiers to chemical weapons in order to determine the exposure level that would cause a casualty, i.e., "break a man." Similarly, hundreds of soldiers were subjected to hallucinogens in experimental programs conducted by the DOD in participation with, or sponsored by, the CIA. These servicemembers often unwittingly participated as human subjects in tests for drugs intended for mind-control or behavior modification, often without their knowledge or consent. Although the ultimate goal of those experiments was to provide information that would help U.S. military and intelligence efforts, most Americans would agree that the use of soldiers as unwitting guinea pigs in experiments that were designed to harm them, at least temporarily, is not ethical.

Whether the goals of these experiments and exposures were worthy or not, these experiences put hundreds of thousands of U.S. servicemembers at risk, and may have caused lasting harm to many individuals.

Every year, thousands of experiments utilizing human subjects are still being conducted by, or on behalf of, the DOD.

At the time of this writing, (early 1998), over 28,000 Gulf War Veterans have died from Gulf War Syndrome (GWS). Hundreds of their spouses have also died. Hundreds of deformed children have been born as well. The DOD and the VA deny that GWS exists. In galling contempt for the intelligence of servicemembers and the general public, the VA has insisted that GWS is a mental disorder! Uniformly, the VA gives Prozac and similar anti-depressants as the sole "cure" for this "non-disease." Researchers believe that these denials are made to prevent prosecution. The above Senate report makes it clear that

the DOD violated the rights of, and knowingly endangered the lives of, American citizens while serving in the Armed Forces. This is a criminal act, one that would have sent Nazis to the gallows.

Kathy Kasten wrote:

> The Nuremberg Military Tribunal's decision in the case of the *U.S. v Karl Brandt et al.* includes what is now called the Nuremberg Code, a ten point statement delimiting permissible medical experimentation on human subjects. According to this statement, human experimentation is justified only if its results benefit society and it is carried out in accord with basic principles that "satisfy moral, ethical, and legal concepts."

She describes the 10 points of the Nuremberg Code thusly:

> 1. The voluntary consent of the human subject is absolutely essential. This means that the person involved should have legal capacity to give consent; should be situated as to be able to exercise free power of choice, without the intervention of any element of force, fraud, deceit, duress, over-reaching, or other ulterior form of constraint or coercion, and should have sufficient knowledge and comprehension of the elements of the subject matter involved as to enable him to make an understanding and enlightened decision. This latter element requires that before the acceptance of an affirmative decision by the experimental subject there should be made known to him the nature, duration, and purpose of the experiment; the method and means by which it is to be conducted; all inconveniences and hazards reasonably to be expected; and the effects upon his health or person which may possibly come from his participation in the experiment. The duty and responsibility for ascertaining the quality of the consent rests upon each individual who initiates, directs or engages in the experiment. It is a personal duty and responsibility which may not be delegated to another with impunity.
> 2. The experiment should be such as to yield fruitful results for the good of society, unprocurable by other methods or means of study, and not random and unnecessary in nature.
> 3. The experiment should be so designed and based on the results of animal experimentation and a knowledge of the natural history of the disease or other problem under study that the anticipated results will justify the performance of the experiment.
> 4. The experiment should be so conducted as to avoid all unnecessary physical and mental suffering and injury.
> 5. No experiment should be conducted where there is an a priori

reason to believe that death or disabling injury will occur; except, perhaps, in those experiments where the experimental physicians also serve as subjects.

6. The degree of risk to be taken should never exceed that determined by the humanitarian importance of the problem to be solved by the experiment.

7. Proper preparations should be made and adequate facilities provided to protect the experimental subject against even remote possibilities of injury, disability or death.

8. The experiment should be conducted only by scientifically qualified persons. The highest degree of skill and care should be required through all stages of the experiment of those who conduct or engage in the experiment.

9. During the course of the experiment the human subject should be at liberty to bring the experiment to an end if he has reached the physical or mental state where continuation of the experiment seems to him to be impossible.

10. During the course of the experiment the scientist in charge must be prepared to terminate the experiment at any stage, if he has probable cause to believe, in the exercise of the good faith, superior skill and careful judgement required by him that a continuation of the experiment is likely to result in injury, disability, or death to the experimental subject.

It should be absolutely clear that the Senate Committee found the DOD guilty, in administering "investigational drugs," largely without informed consent, of a knowing and deliberate violation of the Nuremberg Code. The DOD not only violated the code, but did it to the detriment of its own people, soldiers in uniform. If it cares so little for maintaining ethical behavior with its own, what chance have we civilians of being treated ethically?

Additionally, evidence is coming forward which shows that chemical and biological weapons were used in the Gulf, despite official claims to the contrary. Many of these internationally banned toxins were supplied to the Iraqis by American firms with the knowledge, permission, and encouragement of the federal government, in criminal disregard for international law. Our soldiers were ordered to blow up stockpiles of U.S.-supplied bio-toxins at the end of the war, unknowingly exposing themselves to hide the actions of criminals in Washington, D.C. Washington continues to deny the use of biologicals in the Gulf to cover up its culpability.

If this is true, which I believe it is, then today, mass murdering war criminals occupy positions of public trust and political power in our government. Their efforts to avoid prosecution have allowed hundreds of thousands of Gulf War Veterans and their families to suffer. Their continuing denials have allowed the communicable GWS disease to spread into the heartland of America. To save their worthless butts they have endangered us all. For more information contact the American Gulf War Veterans Association, 3506 Highway 6, South #117, Sugarland, TX 77478-4401; phone 800 231-7631; or on the web at: www.gulfwarvets.com.

Some New World Order watchers are convinced that the spread of this disease was planned. Some conspiratologists say Gulf War Syndrome was deliberately induced in our trained fighting men and women as a first step to taking over the United States. With the "warrior class" nullified, they argue, it would be easier for the NWO to subjugate unarmed and untrained civilians. Chillingly, there has been much discussion in the "globalist" press in the last few years about what to do with the warrior class once a U.N./NWO scheme of "global governance" has abolished war.

If HAARP experiments are conducted in such a way that we on the ground are impacted by those tests (such as from washes of gamma radiation, much less if it is used to test mind control techniques), it must meet the above 10 points to not be a violation of the Nuremberg Code. First and foremost is "informed consent." It would seem that there is no more likelihood of their telling us about such experimentation now than with the above ground nuclear tests of the 1950s and '60s.

Currently the military is pursuing weapons development goals that are not necessarily compatible with the democratic values of America. HAARP may be an example of such a device. An eye-opening research paper, "Revolution In Military Affairs in Conflicts Short of War" produced by the US Army War College admitted that such weapons were under development, and made a startling recommendation… its authors put forward the idea that, rather than abandon such research, the military should begin a program of re-educating Americans to accept the new technology! If HAARP is a weapon, is it the kind of weapon that we would be proud to use?

This attitude of disrespect by the military for civilian sensibilities is hardly new. Iran/Contra should be kept in mind. The Congress of the U.S. voted to stay out of the civil war in Nicaragua, to support neither the pro-democracy rebels nor the Marxist government. The Reagan White House, particularly North, Poindexter, and Secord, as well as the CIA, disagreed. Rather than abide by the will of the duly elected representatives of the American people and fulfill their oaths to uphold the Constitution, they committed crimes and high crimes (it has to be during a time of declared war for their acts to

have been treason). To further their agenda they committed hundreds of crimes, from lying to Congress to murder. Their blatant disregard for civilian government was a wake-up call—one I fear too few Americans heard.

Iran/Contra is proof that some portions of the military and intelligence communities are completely out of control. "Revolution In Military Affairs" is an affirmation that in fact a revolt is brewing in the U.S. military. Ollie North has been richly rewarded for his treachery. Nearly all of the CIA's players have gone unnamed and unpunished. Some of those who tried to reveal the conspiracy, however, are dead or still in hiding. Iran/Contra was but the tip of this iceberg. If we, the citizenry, do not act soon and force our elected officials to bring the military to task, it is only a matter of time until the next Iran/Contra-like "coup d'etat" occurs.

REDOING THE PAPERWORK

Earlier I mentioned the group Trustees for Alaska. Speaking on behalf of itself, Greenpeace, National Audubon Society, Alaska Center for the Environment, Sierra Club, Alaska Wildlife Alliance, Northern Alaska Environmental Center and National Wildlife Federation, they have requested that the U.S. Air Force prepare a supplement to the July 1993 Final Environmental Impact Statement (FEIS) for the operation of HAARP. They did this by letter to HAARP spokesdroid John Heckscher. I join with many others in requesting that you, too, add your voice. Send your own letter to:

John Heckscher
PL/GPIA
Hanscom AFB, MA. 01731-5000

You can also log on to the official HAARP website and send e-mail comments to him via that link.

The Air Force has admitted that it has a continuing duty to comply with the National Environmental Policy Act (NEPA) by preparing a supplemental EIS should certain conditions be met. The letter to Heckscher from Trustees for Alaska brought up much of the same sort of material as discussed is this book, and in the previous book, *Angels Don't Play This HAARP*. From these "apparent substantial changes in the project and significant new information relevant to environmental concerns about HAARP," they said, "we believe this duty has been triggered." Further, they add:

> Should the Air Force disagree as to the mandatory nature of this duty, we still request that a supplemental EIS be prepared using your discretionary authority to do so. …[T]he Air Force should fund and support an independent review and monitoring effort to alleviate the

public's concerns about the project.

NEPA requires a federal agency to prepare an EIS whenever it undertakes a "major... action significantly affecting the quality of the human environment." As we have seen, the Air Force recognized that HAARP triggered the NEPA duty to prepare an EIS and, in the summer of 1993, in cooperation with the Navy, released the Final Environmental Impact Statement (FEIS) for HAARP. On 18 October, 1993, the Air Force issued its Record of Decision (ROD) which declared the Air Force's intention to proceed with the project. The Council on Environmental Quality (CEQ) is the principal agency responsible for the administration of NEPA. The CEQ regulations require federal agencies to supplement an EIS when:

> ...(i) The agency makes substantial changes in the proposed action that are relevant to environmental concerns; or (ii) There are significant new circumstances or information relevant to environmental concerns and bearing on the proposed action or its impacts.

In addition to the CEQ regulations, each federal agency has its own set of regulations adapting the CEQ regulations to the activities of each agency. Consistent with the CEQ regulations, the Department of Defense regulations require EIS supplementation when:

> ...substantial changes to the proposed action are made relative to the environment of the global commons, or when significant new information or circumstances, relevant to environmental concerns, bears on the proposed action or its environmental effects on the global commons.

As the U.S. Supreme Court has stated, the test for supplementation is based on a "rule of reason":

> If there remains a "major federal action" to occur, and if the new information is sufficient to show that the remaining action will "affect the quality of the human environment" in a significant manner or to a significant extent not already considered, a supplemental... [impact statement] must be prepared. *Marsh v. Oregon Natural Resources Council,* 490 U.S. 360, 373-74 (1989).

Finally, an agency also has the discretion to prepare a supplement to an EIS if it "determines that the purposes of [NEPA] will be furthered by doing so." Trustees for Alaska take all of this as proof that the Air Force must supplement the EIS for HAARP. As discussed earlier in this book, the addition of earth penetrating tomography to HAARP's mission after the FEIS was issued is probably reason enough to trigger a supplemental EIS. Certainly the wealth of new health information on ELF and EMR exposure since the publication of the FEIS should require a new EIS.

As Trustees for Alaska concluded their letter to the Air Force:

> While seemingly benign if one were to look solely to the government's description of the purpose, use and effects of HAARP, information from the popular press, independent scientists and investigative researchers raises flags of caution. This information suggests that HAARP might be a government project with potential impacts on many levels, including far-reaching and little understood biological effects on humans and animals.
>
> Despite the data supporting the claims of these project critics, the Air Force has not analyzed these admittedly Jules Verne-esque qualities or potentials of HAARP. Nevertheless, an evaluation of the history of the technology used in HAARP suggests the possibility of exactly these kind of uses for HAARP. To the extent that the government is either unknowingly or intentionally exploring and implicating these types of uses and effects of HAARP, HAARP represents a potentially significant global threat.
>
> The continuing and serious questions about HAARP reveal that, regardless of the attempts of the Air Force to comply with the law and otherwise inform the public, these efforts have failed. Supplementing the EIS to address these concerns, and establishing an independent review and monitoring program to provide objective evidence of the Air Force's honesty and good faith, would go a long way in changing the current climate of uncertainty and mistrust.

If the Air Force were to comply with this request it might well serve to quell public distrust—it might also let their tiny Bengal tiger out of the bag! I suppose there is a slight chance that they might come clean and reveal that HAARP really is a weapon. More likely they will do exactly what they are doing—stall, deny, and brush off charges of HAARP's danger to the environment. Of course, by doing so they prove the opposition's argument. Keep watching. If they continue to refuse to provide another EIS or if they issue another whitewashed one and refuse to allow meaningful civilian oversight you can be pretty sure that what HAARP's detractors are saying is at least partially true. The trick is not finding out if the government's lying, it is finding out what it is lying about.

SUMMATION

To recap, what do we know about HAARP? When completed, the IRI will be the most powerful high frequency (HF) broadcasting station in the world—"Power 2.8." It will be many times more powerful than any other ionospheric heater in operation anywhere in the world. What's more, it will have a unique focusing and beam steering capacity unlike any of its brethren, thanks to the "genius" of Bernard Eastlund.

We know something of the types of experiments they intend to run with HAARP. They plan to focus a few gigawatts of HF energy at various locations within the ionosphere to see what happens. They also plan to attempt to tune the electrojet, the aurora, to turn it into a "virtual" antenna. With the aurora turned into a rebroadcaster of the signal from HAARP, they plan to irradiate land and sea with extremely low frequency electromagnetic radiation in an effort to verify compliance with counterproliferation treaties and to speak with deeply submerged submarines. If successful they also plan to put this up for civilian use, i.e., hundreds of new radio and TV stations broadcasting from the aurora, adding to the daily dose of environmental EMR exposure.

We know that they have no clue what will happen when they attempt these things. We know this because they have admitted as much. Reputable scientists, as well as concerned citizens, recognize that such tampering with vital natural systems could have a devastating impact on life on this globe. Life here is possible only because of the way the forces of nature balance each other, as seen in the life protecting ozone and ion layers. It is possible that HAARP may have breached that protection already, if a HAARP test did set off the gamma ray detectors at the Nevada Test Site.

We know that HAARP officials, spokesbozos with the Air Force, Navy and DOD, insist that HAARP is entirely safe. How can they say HAARP is safe when they do not know what HAARP will do? To be honest, it is difficult to know if they are lying, or just stupid. Considering the other known clandestine operations that the DOD has been involved in over the years, it is probably correct to believe that once again the government is lying to us.

So, if they are lying to us, to what end? What are they trying to hide? HAARP could be a violation of a number of treaties and conventions. HAARP could also be a violation of our own Constitution—a way for covert operatives to circumvent Bill of Rights protections, such as the Fourth Amendment: "The right of the people to be secure in their persons, houses, papers, and effects, against unreasonable searches and seizures, shall not be violated..." Having spooks put words into one's head, or perhaps extract data from it, is hardly being secure in one's person. Having an eye in the sky detect one's stash of emergency food or weapons is equally a violation of unreasonable search.

Is HAARP a weather or environmental modification device, an advance in Tesla technology, as the authors of the previous HAARP book believed? Is HAARP the ultimate mind control device, as I suspect? Or is HAARP something far kinkier, as the last two chapters showed it could be?

Who, ultimately, is in control of HAARP? Civilian scientists? The Air Force? The Navy? The DOD? Congress? We The People? Or, the Conspiracy? Even if HAARP is under the control of responsible civilian scientists or other men of goodwill, what is to prevent HAARP from being covertly misused by a Conspiracy manipulating them without their knowledge, as Hoagland says NASA personnel are being maneuvered? The New World Order is real and it does desire to bring about a single, one-world government as soon as possible. Could HAARP be their ultimate weapon?

Remember the movie *Doctor Strangelove: Or How I Learned To Stop Worrying And Love The Bomb*, where an insane Air Force General deliberately starts World War III, all the while babbling about POE (Purity Of Essence/Peace On Earth)? We all know that elaborate precautions have been taken to prevent a real life madman from launching nukes, but what has been done to prevent a similar madman—or one of those turban sporting "international terrorists"—from gaining control of HAARP? Have the HAARP folks given any consideration to that? If so, it is not in the literature. And they don't have to storm the facility at Gakona... all they need do is capture a family member of someone who can use HAARP as a weapon. I hope this does not give anyone ideas! There are Satanists in very high positions in the military and ruling elite. For example, Major Michael A. Aquino was a senior officer at the Presidio, a former U.S. Army base in San Francisco, California (now closed and home to Mikhail Gorbachev's Green Cross). Aquino had been a Green Beret, a decorated Vietnam War vet, and a psychological warfare officer who had worked in military intelligence. At the same time that Aquino was stationed at the Presidio, he was the High Priest of the Temple of Set (a spin-off from Anton LaVey's Church of Satan). Literature published by the Temple of Set proclaimed him THE Anti-Christ!

Headlines in the *San Francisco Chronicle* in November 1987 read: "Army Says Constitution Lets Satanist Hold Top Secret Job." Protected by First Amendment rights, he practiced Satanic rituals—while holding a Top Secret clearance—with the knowledge of the military! Aquino traveled to Germany to perform occult rituals in a German castle once used by Nazi SS for black magic ceremonies during the Third Reich. Aquino, in his book, *Crystal Tablet of Set*, wrote that he performed those rituals to recreate an order of Knighthood for followers of Satan! He even encouraged his followers to study the beliefs of the Nazi terrorist group, the Vehm, as well as two fanatical Aryan groups that existed before and during Hitler's reign: the Thule Gesselschaft, and the Ahnenerbe. What if someone like him were to decide to make a lot of points with the Big Guy Downstairs and attempt to sacrifice the whole world?

While that may sound like wild speculation, consider: Major Aquino is an expert in psychological warfare. He co-authored, with Colonel Paul E. Vallely a 12-page (undated) Army report outlining the use of psychotronic weapons, and weapons systems employing the use of mind control. In the military such psychological operations are called "PSYOPS." That report stated:

> ELF (extremely low frequency) waves (up to 100 Hz)... are naturally occurring, but they can also be produced artificially... ELF waves are not normally noticed by the unaided senses, yet their resonant effect upon the human body has been connected to both physiological disorders and emotional distortion. Infrasound vibration (up to 20 Hz) can subliminally influence brain activity to align itself to delta, theta, alpha, or beta wave patterns, inclining an audience toward everything from alertness to passivity. Infrasound could be used tactically, as ELF waves endure for great distances; and it could be used in conjunction with media broadcasts as well.

It almost sounds like he was describing HAARP!

Like all controversial issues, there are at least two sides to the HAARP debate. The writers of "Weather as a Force Multiplier: Owning the Weather in 2025" make some a very compelling points. If HAARP is a weather weapon it might be a good thing—at least as far as maintaining a counterbalance against other nations' similar weapons. If HAARP is a civilian weather control device it could be a tremendous benefit to all mankind. I am sure you have thought of many other reasons why HAARP, as either a military or civilian project, might be good for America and the world. Having SDI on-line might save America's bacon...

On the other hand, the sorts of weapons embodied by HAARP, and the possible conspiratorial uses that those weapons could be put to, make one decidedly less than enthusiastic about supporting such a project. If the potential for ecological disaster is as real as some researchers claim—possibly even ending life on Earth—then HAARP absolutely has to be stopped, and in a hurry.

WHAT CAN YOU DO ABOUT HAARP?

First, promote dialogue on this subject. We, as a nation, need to decide if HAARP is in our best national interests or not. It is my belief that the probable ill effects of HAARP outweigh any possible good. If you agree, you need to act to help pull the plug on this project. Even if you disagree you can help. We need to know what this thing really is for. And we need to be sure that nutcases and the Conspiracy cannot get their hands on it. If you feel HAARP should go forward, insist that sufficient controls are in place to keep it, and us, safe.

Currently, HAARP is funded by Congress, so perhaps we should start there. Senator Stevens of the Defense Committee is the point man for this project. Every effort must be made to reach him and make him realize the dangers in going forward with HAARP. Letters, phone calls, faxes, e-mail, personal contact, etc. are avenues that can be pursued. At the same time we need to pressure the other members of his committee, as well as the Senate and the Congress at large, instructing them, as our elected officials, to stop funding for HAARP—at least until the truth is revealed and the fundamental issues resolved.

We also need to encourage debate on the merits of HAARP in the mainstream and scientific press. We need to get more scientists saying "Hey, wait a minute… there are some problems here…" We need to contact and convince the universities involved in the HAARP project to get out of the program. We need to also put pressure on the State of Alaska to forbid the project to go forward.

HAARP is "overseen" by a huge number of federal, state and local, governmental and civilian agencies and committees. I will include a list of them below. Contact each of these agencies and help them to see the light. Many of these agencies, such as the Council on Environmental Quality, have the power to pull the plug on HAARP. Any of them could be used to develop a negative opinion in others, and in so doing, topple HAARP like a house of cards. For example, the Environmental Protection Agency could be pressured to investigate the filling in of the wetlands at the Gakona site.

The following table lists those agencies that provide active, independent review of HAARP:

National Telecommunications & Information Administration
Federal Aviation Administration
Environmental Protection Agency
Air Force

Navy
Army Corps of Engineers
National Park Service
Fish & Wildlife Service
U.S. Coast Guard
Bureau of Land Management
Bureau of Indian Affairs
(U.S.) Advisory Council on Historic Preservation
Alaska Department of Environmental Conservation
(State of Alaska) Historic Preservation Office
Alaska Fish & Game
Alaska Department of Natural Resources
Alaska Department of Community and Regional Affairs
American Radio Relay League
Aircraft Owners & Pilots Association
Alyeska (the oil company)
ALASCOM (the telephone company)

There is also something called the Resolution Committee. This Committee was established by the Air Force and represents an additional segment of the independent oversight that HAARP must observe. These are the agencies or organizations that are members of this Committee:

- Aircraft Owners & Pilots Association
- ALASCOM
- Alaska Department of Environmental Conservation
- Alaska Fish & Game
- Alyeska Pipeline Services
- American Radio Relay League (ARRL)
- Coast Guard LORAN Station (Tok, AK)
- Community-Appointed Resident (Copper Center, AK)
- Federal Aviation Administration (Anchorage Office)
- Fish & Wildlife (Federal)
- National Park Service
- Joint Frequency Management Office (Elmendorf AFB)

As well as putting pressure on these folks, you can also write letters to your local newspaper, call in to radio and TV talk shows, pressure your local TV news departments, etc. I have mentioned several instances when public outrage, generated by bad press for government agencies, forced officials to hold hearings and discover the truth. Do not underestimate the power of public opinion. Negative public opinion has stopped more wars than bullets. You can even stage media attention-getting events to get to word out. You can also spread the word by buying quantities of this book and passing them out to lawmakers, opinion leaders, friends, family, and others you care about. See discount rates for purchases in quantity on the order form at the back of this book. Organizations ordering in large quantities qualify for special discounts.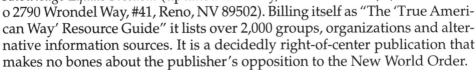

You should join with other concerned citizens to form increasingly effective opposition groups. Many such groups exist today. One way to find kindred spirits is through owning a copy of *Knowledge Equals Freedom* (updated annually, from Knowfree, c/o 2790 Wrondel Way, #41, Reno, NV 89502). Billing itself as "The 'True American Way' Resource Guide" it lists over 2,000 groups, organizations and alternative information sources. It is a decidedly right-of-center publication that makes no bones about the publisher's opposition to the New World Order.

HAARP sits just across the highway from Wrangell—St. Elias National Park and Preserve. This huge hunk of ground is under the "protection" of the United Nations. These "U.N. Biospheres" and "World Heritage Sites" are the work of the Conspiracy, a ploy to shift sovereignty from the "host nation" to the U.N. Would it not be wonderful to use the Conspiracy's own gun, the U.N., against it? Let us put pressure on the U.N. to protect Wrangell-St. Elias, particularly its migratory species, by stopping HAARP!

I am convinced that HAARP has the potential to be an ecological disaster that would compare to the Exxon Valdez spill the way an atomic bomb compares to a Fourth of July sparkler. I hope you have reached a similar conclusion. The more people we alert to this threat, the greater our chances of preventing it.

Now it's up to you. This is, after all, your planet.

ABOUT THE AUTHOR

Jerry E. Smith's career as writer, poet and editor spans three decades. He began in the little magazine field in 1966 when he published his first amateur sci-fi fan magazine (called a fanzine or just "zine") in the Valley Science Fiction Associations's "ValAPA" (Valley Amateur Press Alliance) of Pomona, California. He was active in the zine scene throughout the late '60s and early '70s; appearing regularly in zines and APAs, like the Los Angeles Science Fantasy Society's "APA-L;" culminating with his founding of the Unicorn Society and its Unicorn Amateur Press Alliance ("UnAPA") in Klamath Falls, Oregon, in 1974.

In 1972, at age 22, he moved from Southern California to Klamath Falls, Oregon. There he explored a variety of arts, such as performing both in front of and behind the curtain in plays presented by the Klamath Civic Theater and Klamath Children's Theater (co-authoring the Children's Theater production that he co-starred in). He and Conspiracy/UFO writer Jim Keith have known each other since high school in Pomona. They co-hosted a weekly current affairs radio show on KTEC, broadcasting from the Klamath Falls campus of the Oregon Institute of Technology (OIT) in 1975. In 1973 Mr. Smith worked as the Art Director of the shopper-style newspaper *The Linkville Star*. In 1975 he wore that same hat at *Skyline: Klamath Falls,* whose Editor-In-Chief was Jim Keith. He continued as an editor with Jim Keith's magazine *Dharma Combat* where he has been variously Managing Editor and Art Director since its inception in 1988.

During the 1970s and '80s he wrote hundreds of poems and short stories. Two chapbooks of his poetry, and a few of the shorts, have seen print. In the '90s he got serious about writing; producing a flood of fiction in numerous genres, with a majority of his nearly 100 sales going to men's magazines. He was a regular contributor to the Reno-Sparks area newspaper *The View,* with articles, film reviews and the science-fiction soap opera in print, *Fool's Gold,* which he co-authored with Jim Keith.

1992 saw him take on the position of Executive Director of the National UFO Museum, where in addition to his administrative duties he edited (and wrote for) that organization's quarterly journal, "Notes from the Hangar."

He has placed Op-Ed pieces in local newspapers and regional magazines, such as the article "Telecommunications Bill Raises Constitutional Issues" (which he co-authored with Juanita Cox) in the Summer 1997 issue of the "Sentinel of Freedom" published by the California and Nevada Freedom Coalitions. His first national magazine exposure was the article, "Star Trek:

Sci-fi or Psy-war?," in the Fall 1996 issue of *Paranoia Magazine. HAARP: Ultimate Weapon of the Conspiracy* is his first mass-market non-fiction book.

Mr. Smith is divorced with one son. Religiously, he describes himself as "a cross between a non-practicing Taoist and a quantum physicist who can't do the math." On the other hand, he says his brand of politics is "straight Jeffersonian Libertarian with just a touch of anarchist leanings." While he denies any connection to militias or the extreme right-wing, he is reported to be some sort of survivalist who spends his summers living in a tent while tending a vegetable garden in the Paw-Paw Mountains above Pyramid Lake in Northern Nevada.

He is always interested in reader response. You may write him in care of this publisher (send a self-addressed stamped envelope if you wish to receive a reply), or you can e-mail him at: jerryesmith@mailcity.com

Appendix:
Bernard Eastlund's 1987 Patent

United States Patent [19]

Eastlund

[11] Patent Number: 4,686,605

[45] Date of Patent: Aug. 11, 1987

[54] **METHOD AND APPARATUS FOR ALTERING A REGION IN THE EARTH'S ATMOSPHERE, IONOSPHERE, AND/OR MAGNETOSPHERE**

[75] Inventor: Bernard J. Eastlund, Spring. Tex.

[73] Assignee: APTI, Inc., Los Angeles, Calif.

[21] Appl. No.: 690,333

[22] Filed: **Jan. 10, 1985**

[51] Int. Cl.⁴ H05B 6/64; H05C 3/00; H05H 1/46

[52] U.S. Cl. .... 361/231; 89/1.11; 380/59; 244/158 R

[58] Field of Search .... 361/230, 231; 244/158 R; 376/100; 89/1.11; 380/59

[56] **References Cited**

PUBLICATIONS

Liberty Magazine, (2/35) p. 7 N. Tesla.
New York Times (9/22/40) Section 2, p. 7 W. L. Laurence.
New York Times (12/8/15) p. 8 Col. 3.

Primary Examiner—Salvatore Cangialosi
Attorney, Agent, or Firm—Roderick W. MacDonald

[57] **ABSTRACT**

A method and apparatus for altering at least one selected region which normally exists above the earth's surface. The region is excited by electron cyclotron resonance heating to thereby increase its charged particle density. In one embodiment, circularly polarized electromagnetic radiation is transmitted upward in a direction substantially parallel to and along a field line which extends through the region of plasma to be altered. The radiation is transmitted at a frequency which excites electron cyclotron resonance to heat and accelerate the charged particles. This increase in energy can cause ionization of neutral particles which are then absorbed as part of the region thereby increasing the charged particle density of the region.

15 Claims, 5 Drawing Figures

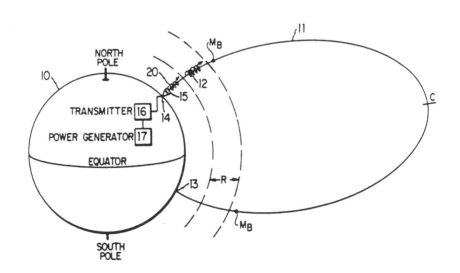

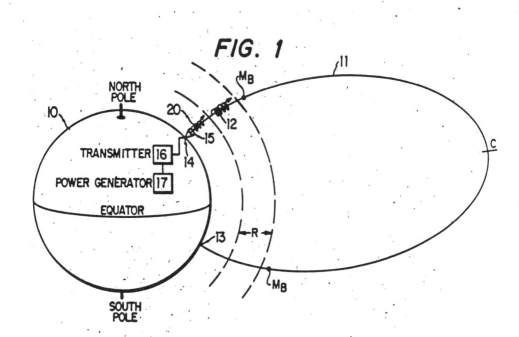

FIG. 1

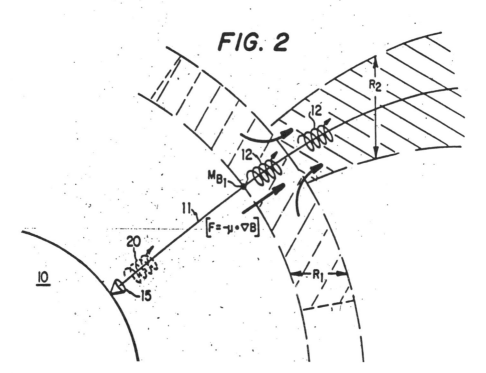

FIG. 2

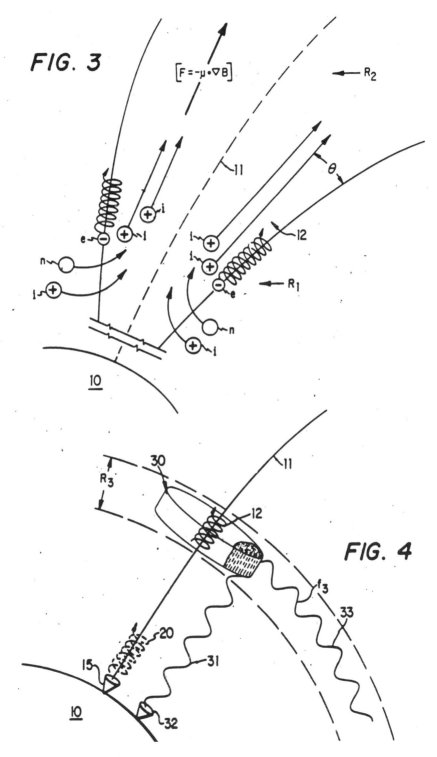

FIG. 3

$[F = -\mu \cdot \nabla B]$

FIG. 4

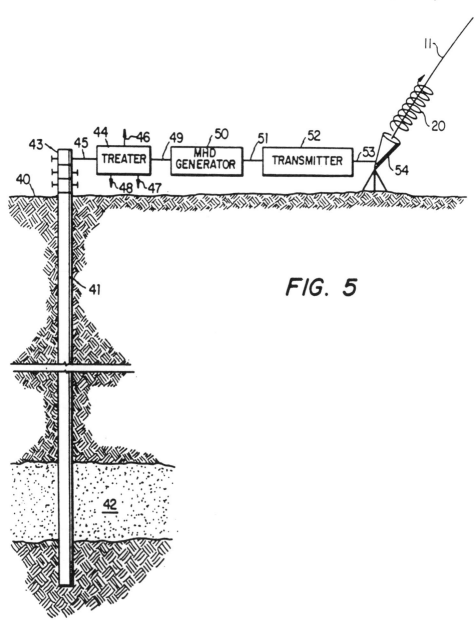

FIG. 5

METHOD AND APPARATUS FOR ALTERING A REGION IN THE EARTH'S ATMOSPHERE, IONOSPHERE, AND/OR MAGNETOSPHERE

DESCRIPTION

1. Technical Field

This invention relates to a method and apparatus for altering at least one selected region normally existing above the earth's surface and more particularly relates to a method and apparatus for altering said at least one region by initially transmitting electromagnetic radiation from the earth's surface essentially parallel to and along naturally-occurring, divergent magnetic field lines which extend from the earth's surface through the region or regions to be altered.

2. Background Art

In the late 1950's, it was discovered that naturally-occurring belts exist at high altitudes above the earth's surface, and it is now established that these belts result from charged electrons and ions becoming trapped along the magnetic lines of force (field lines) of the earth's essentially dipole magnetic field. The trapped electrons and ions are confined along the field lines between two magnetic mirrors which exist at spaced apart points along those field lines. The trapped electrons and ions move in helical paths around their particular field lines and "bounce" back and forth between the magnetic mirrors. These trapped electrons and ions can oscillate along the field lines for long periods of time.

In the past several years, substantial effort has been made to understand and explain the phenomena involved in belts of trapped electrons and ions, and to explore possible ways to control and use these phenomena for beneficial purposes. For example, in the late 1950's and early 1960's both the United States and U.S.S.R. detonated a series of nuclear devices of various yields to generate large numbers of charged particles at various altitudes, e.g., 200 kilometers (km) or greater. This was done in order to establish and study artifical belts of trapped electrons and ions. These experiments established that at least some of the extraneous electrons and ions from the detonated devices did become trapped along field lines in the earth's magnetosphere to form artificial belts which were stable for prolonged periods of time. For a discussion of these experiments see "The Radiation Belt and Magnetosphere", W. N. Hess, Blaisdell Publishing Co., 1968, pps. 1 5 et sec.

Other proposals which have been advanced for altering existing belts of trapped electrons and ions and/or establishing similar artificial belts include injecting charged particles from a satellite carrying a payload of radioactive beta-decay material or alpha emitters; and injecting charged particles from a satellite-borne electron accelerator. Still another approach is described in U.S. Pat. No. 4,042,196 wherein a low energy ionized gas, e.g., hydrogen, is released from a synchronous orbiting satellite near the apex of a radiation belt which is naturally-occurring in the earth's magnetosphere to produce a substantial increase in energetic particle precipitation and, under certain conditions, produce a limit in the number of particles that can be stably trapped. This precipitation effect arises from an enhancement of the whistler-mode and ion-cyclotron mode interactions

that result from the ionized gas or "cold plasma" injection.

It has also been proposed to release large clouds of barium in the magnetosphere so that photoionization will increase the cold plasma density, thereby producing electron precipitation through enhanced whistler-mode interactions.

However, in all of the above-mentioned approaches, the mechanisms involved in triggering the change in the trapped particle phenomena must be actually positioned within the affected zone, e.g., the magnetosphere, before they can be actuated to effect the desired change.

The earth's ionosphere is not considered to be a "trapped" belt since there are few trapped particles therein. The term "trapped" herein refers to situations where the force of gravity on the trapped particles is balanced by magnetic forces rather than hydrostatic or collisional forces. The charged electrons and ions in the ionosphere also follow helical paths around magnetic field lines within the ionosphere but are not trapped between mirrors, as in the case of the trapped belts in the magnetosphere, since the gravitational force on the particles is balanced by collisional or hydrostatic forces.

In recent years, a number of experiments have actually been carried out to modify the ionosphere in some controlled manner to investigate the possibility of a beneficial result. For detailed discussions of these operations see the following papers: (1) Ionospheric Modification Theory; G. Meltz and F. W. Perkins; (2) The Platteville High Power Facility; Carrol et al.; (3) Arecibo Heating Experiments; W. E. Gordon and H. C. Carlson, Jr.; and (4) Ionospheric Heating by Powerful Radio Waves; Meltz et al., all published in Radio Science, Vol. 9, No. 11, November, 1974, at pages 885–888; 889–894; 1041–1047; and 1049–1063, respectively, all of which are incorporated herein by reference. In such experiments, certain regions of the ionosphere are heated to change the electron density and temperature within these regions. This is accomplished by transmitting from earth-based antennae high frequency electromagnetic radiation at a substantial angle to, not parallel to, the ionosphere's magnetic field to heat the ionospheric particles primarily by ohmic heating. The electron temperature of the ionosphere has been raised by hundreds of degrees in these experiments, and electrons with several electron volts of energy have been produced in numbers sufficient to enhance airglow. Electron concentrations have been reduced by a few percent, due to expansion of the plasma as a result of increased temperature.

In the Elmo Bumpy Torus (EBT), a controlled fusion device at the Oak Ridge National Laboratory, all heating is provided by microwaves at the electron cyclotron resonance interaction. A ring of hot electrons is formed at the earth's surface in the magnetic mirror by a combination of electron cyclotron resonance and stochastic heating. In the EBT, the ring electrons are produced with an average "temperature" of 250 kilo electron volts or kev (2.5×10^9K) and a plasma beta between 0.1 and 0.4; see, "A Theoretical Study of Electron—Cyclotron Absorption in Elmo Bumpy Torus", Batchelor and Goldfinger, Nuclear Fusion, Vol. 20, No. 4 (1980) pps. 403–418.

Electron cyclotron resonance heating has been used in experiments on the earth's surface to produce and accelerate plasmas in a diverging magnetic field. Kosmahl et al. showed that power was transferred from the electromagnetic waves and that a fully ionized plasma was accelerated with a divergence angle of roughly 13 degrees. Optimum neutral gas density was 1.7×10^{14} per cubic centimeter; see, "Plasma Acceleration with Microwaves Near Cyclotron Resonance", Kosmahl et al., Journal of Applied Physics, Vol. 38, No. 12, Nov., 1967, pps. 4576–4582.

DISCLOSURE OF THE INVENTION

The present invention provides a method and apparatus for altering at least one selected region which normally exists above the earth's surface. The region is excited by electron cyclotron resonance heating of electrons which are already present and/or artificially created in the region to thereby increase the charged particle energy and ultimately the density of the region.

In one embodiment this is done by transmitting circularly polarized electromagnetic radiation from the earth's surface at or near the location where a naturally-occurring dipole magnetic field (force) line intersects the earth's surface. Right hand circular polarization is used in the northern hemisphere and left hand circular polarization is used in the southern hemisphere. The radiation is deliberately transmitted at the outset in a direction substantially parallel to and along a field line which extends upwardly through the region to be altered. The radiation is transmitted at a frequency which is based on the gyrofrequency of the charged particles and which, when applied to the at least one region, excites electron cyclotron resonance within the region or regions to heat and accelerate the charged particles in their respective helical paths around and along the field line. Sufficient energy is employed to cause ionization of neutral particles (molecules of oxygen, nitrogen and the like, particulates, etc.) which then become a part of the region thereby increasing the charged particle density of the region. This effect can further be enhanced by providing artificial particles, e.g., electrons, ions, etc., directly into the region to be affected from a rocket, satellite, or the like to supplement the particles in the naturally-occurring plasma. These artificial particles are also ionized by the transmitted electromagnetic radiation thereby increasing charged particle density of the resulting plasma in the region.

In another embodiment of the invention, electron cyclotron resonance heating is carried out in the selected region or regions at sufficient power levels to allow a plasma present in the region to generate a mirror force which forces the charged electrons of the altered plasma upward along the force line to an altitude which is higher than the original altitude. In this case the relevant mirror points are at the base of the altered region or regions. The charged electrons drag ions with them as well as other particles that may be present. Sufficient power, e.g., 10^{15} joules, can be applied so that the altered plasma can be trapped on the field line between mirror points and will oscillate in space for prolonged periods of time. By this embodiment, a plume of altered plasma can be established at selected locations for communication modification or other purposes.

In another embodiment, this invention is used to alter at least one selected region of plasma in the ionosphere to establish a defined layer of plasma having an increased charged particle density. Once this layer is established, and while maintaining the transmission of the main beam of circularly polarized electromagnetic radiation, the main beam is modulated and/or at least one second different, modulated electromagnetic radiation beam is transmitted from at least one separate source at a different frequency which will be absorbed in the plasma layer. The amplitude of the frequency of the main beam and/or the second beam or beams is modulated in resonance with at least one known oscillation mode in the selected region or regions to propagate a known frequency wave or waves throughout the ionosphere.

BRIEF DESCRIPTION OF THE DRAWINGS

The actual construction, operation, and apparent advantages of this invention will be better understood by referring to the drawings in which like numerals identify like parts and in which:

FIG. 1 is a simplified schematical view of the earth (not to scale) with a magnetic field (force) line along which the present invention is carried out;

FIG. 2 is one embodiment within the present invention in which a selected region of plasma is raised to a higher altitude;

FIG. 3 is a simplified, idealized representation of a physical phenomenon involved in the present invention; and

FIG. 4 is a schematic view of another embodiment within the present invention.

FIG. 5 is a schematic view of an apparatus embodiment within this invention.

BEST MODES FOR CARRYING OUT THE INVENTION

The earth's magnetic field is somewhat analogous to a dipole bar magnet. As such, the earth's magnetic field contains numerous divergent field or force lines, each line intersecting the earth's surface at points on opposite sides of the Equator. The field lines which intersect the earth's surface near the poles have apexes which lie at the furthest points in the earth's magnetosphere while those closest to the Equator have apexes which reach only the lower portion of the magnetosphere.

At various altitudes above the earth's surface, e.g., in both the ionosphere and the magnetosphere, plasma is naturally present along these field lines. This plasma consists of equal numbers of positively and negatively charged particles (i.e., electrons and ions) which are guided by the field line. It is well established that a charged particle in a magnetic field gyrates about field lines, the center of gyration at any instance being called the "guiding center" of the particle. As the gyrating particle moves along a field line in a uniform field, it will follow a helical path about its guiding center, hence linear motion, and will remain on the field line. Electrons and ions both follow helical paths around a field line but rotate in opposite directions. The frequencies at which the electrons and ions rotate about the field line are called gyromagnetic frequencies or cyclotron frequencies because they are identical with the expression for the angular frequencies of gyration of particles in a cyclotron. The cyclotron frequency of ions in a given magnetic field is less than that of electrons, in inverse proportion to their masses.

If the particles which form the plasma along the earth's field lines continued to move with a constant pitch angle, often designated "alpha", they would soon impact on the earth's surface. Pitch angle alpha is defined as the angle between the direction of the earth's magnetic field and the velocity (V) of the particle. However, in converging force fields, the pitch angle does change in such a way as to allow the particle to

5

turn around and avoid impact. Consider a particle moving along a field line down toward the earth. It moves into a region of increasing magnetic field strength and therefore sine alpha increases. But sine alpha can only increase to 1.0, at which point, the particle turns around and starts moving up along the field line, and alpha decreases. The point at which the particle turns around is called the mirror point, and there alpha equals ninety degrees. This process is repeated at the other end of the field line where the same magnetic field strength value B, namely Bm, exists. The particle again turns around and this is called the "conjugate point" of the original mirror point. The particle is therefore trapped and bounces between the two magnetic mirrors. The particle can continue oscillating in space in this manner for long periods of time. The actual place where a particle will mirror can be calculated from the following:

$$\sin^2 alpha_o = B_o/B_m \qquad (1)$$

wherein:

$alpha_o$ = equatorial pitch angle of particle
B_o = equatorial field strength on a particular field line
B_m = field strength at the mirror point

Recent discoveries have established that there are substantial regions of naturally trapped particles in space which are commonly called "trapped radiation belts". These belts occur at altitudes greater than about 500 km and accordingly lie in the magnetosphere and mostly above the ionosphere.

The ionosphere, while it may overlap some of the trapped-particle belts, is a region in which hydrostatic forces govern its particle distribution in the gravitational field. Particle motion within the ionosphere is governed by both hydrodynamic and electrodynamic forces. While there are few trapped particles in the ionosphere, nevertheless, plasma is present along field lines in the ionosphere. The charged particles which form this plasma move between collisions with other particles along similar helical paths around the field lines and although a particular particle may diffuse downward into the earth's lower atmosphere or lose energy and diverge from its original field line due to collisions with other particles, these charged particles are normally replaced by other available charged particles or by particles that are ionized by collision with said particle. The electron density (N_e) of the plasma will vary with the actual conditions and locations involved. Also, neutral particles, ions, and electrons are present in proximity to the field lines.

The production of enhanced ionization will also alter the distribution of atomic and molecular constituents of the atmosphere, most notably through increased atomic nitrogen concentration. The upper atmosphere is normally rich in atomic oxygen (the dominant atmospheric constituent above 200 km altitude), but atomic nitrogen is normally relatively rare. This can be expected to manifest itself in increased airglow, among other effects.

As known in plasma physics, the characteristics of a plasma can be altered by adding energy to the charged particles or by ionizing or exciting additional particles to increase the density of the plasma. One way to do this is by heating the plasma which can be accomplished in different ways, e.g., ohmic, magnetic compression, shock waves, magnetic pumping, electron cyclotron resonance, and the like.

Since electron cyclotron resonance heating is involved in the present invention, a brief discussion of the

6

same is in order. Increasing the energy of electrons in a plasma by invoking electron cyclotron resonance heating, is based on a principle similar to that utilized to accelerate charged particles in a cyclotron. If a plasma is confined by a static axial magnetic field of strength B, the charged particles will gyrate about the lines of force with a frequency given, in hertz, as $f_g = 1.54 \times 10^3 B/A$, where: B = magnetic field strength in gauss, and A = mass number of the ion.

Suppose a time-varying field of this frequency is superimposed on the static field B confining the plasma, by passage of a radiofrequency current through a coil which is concentric with that producing the axial field, then in each half-cycle of their rotation about the field lines, the charged particles acquire energy from the oscillating electric field associated with the radio frequency. For example, if B is 10,000 gauss, the frequency of the field which is in resonance with protons in a plasma is 15.4 megahertz.

As applied to electrons, electron cyclotron resonance heating requires an oscillating field having a definite frequency determined by the strength of the confining field. The radio-frequency radiation produces time-varying fields (electric and magnetic), and the electric field accelerates the charged particle. The energized electrons share their energy with ions and neutrals by undergoing collisions with these particles, thereby effectively raising the temperature of the electrons, ions, and neutrals. The apportionment of energy among these species is determined by collision frequencies. For a more detailed understanding of the physics involved, see "Controlled Thermonuclear Reactions", Glasstone and Lovberg, D. Van Nostrand Company, Inc., Princeton, N.J., 1960 and "The Radiation Belt and Magnetosphere", Hess, Blaisdell Publishing Company, 1968, both of which are incorporated herein by reference.

Referring now to the drawings, the present invention provides a method and apparatus for altering at least one region of plasma which lies along a field line, particularly when it passes through the ionosphere and/or magnetosphere. FIG. 1 is a simplified illustration of the earth 10 and one of its dipole magnetic force or field lines 11. As will be understood, line 11 may be any one of the numerous naturally existing field lines and the actual geographical locations 13 and 14 of line 11 will be chosen based on a particular operation to be carried out. The actual locations at which field lines intersect the earth's surface is documented and is readily ascertainable by those skilled in the art.

Line 11 passes through region R which lies at an altitude above the earth's surface. A wide range of altitudes are useful given the power that can be employed by the practice of this invention. The electron cyclotron resonance heating effect can be made to act on electrons anywhere above the surface of the earth. These electrons may be already present in the atmosphere, ionosphere, and/or magnetosphere of the earth, or can be artificially generated by a variety of means such as x-ray beams, charged particle beams, lasers, the plasma sheath surrounding an object such as a missile or meteor, and the like. Further, artificial particles, e.g., electrons, ions, etc., can be injected directly into region R from an earth-launched rocket or orbiting satellite carrying, for example, a payload of radioactive beta-decay material; alpha emitters; an electron accelerator; and/or ionized gases such as hydrogen; see U.S. Pat. No. 4,042,196. The altitude can be greater than about 50 km if desired.

e.g., can be from about 50 km to about 800 km, and, accordingly may lie in either the ionosphere or the magnetosphere or both. As explained above, plasma will be present along line 11 within region R and is represented by the helical line 12. Plasma 12 is comprised of charged particles (i.e., electrons and ions) which rotate about opposing helical paths along line 11.

Antenna 15 is positioned as close as is practical to the location 14 where line 11 intersects the earth's surface. Antenna 15 may be of any known construction for high directionality, for example, a phased array, beam spread angle (θ) type. See "The MST Radar at Poker Flat, Alaska", Radio Science, Vol. 15, No. 2, Mar.-Apr. 1980, pps. 213–223, which is incorporated herein by reference. Antenna 15 is coupled to transmitter 16 which generates a beam of high frequency electromagnetic radiation at a wide range of discrete frequencies, e.g., from about 20 to about 1800 kilohertz (kHz).

Transmitter 16 is powered by power generator means 17 which is preferably comprised of one or more large, commercial electrical generators. Some embodiments of the present invention require large amounts of power, e.g., up to 10^9 to 10^{11} watts, in continuous wave or pulsed power. Generation of the needed power is within the state of the art. Although the electrical generators necessary for the practice of the invention can be powered in any known manner, for example, by nuclear reactors, hydroelectric facilities, hydrocarbon fuels, and the like, this invention, because of its very large power requirement in certain applications, is particularly adapted for use with certain types of fuel sources which naturally occur at strategic geographical locations around the earth. For example, large reserves of hydrocarbons (oil and natural gas) exist in Alaska and Canada. In northern Alaska, particularly the North Slope region, large reserves are currently readily available. Alaska and northern Canada also are ideally located geographically as to magnetic latitudes. Alaska provides easy access to magnetic field lines that are especially suited to the practice of this invention, since many field lines which extend to desirable altitudes for this invention intersect the earth in Alaska. Thus, in Alaska, there is a unique combination of large, accessible fuel sources at desirable field line intersections. Further, a particularly desirable fuel source for the generation of very large amounts of electricity is present in Alaska in abundance, this source being natural gas. The presence of very large amounts of clean-burning natural gas in Alaskan latitudes, particularly on the North Slope, and the availability of magnetohydrodynamic (MHD), gas turbine, fuel cell, electrogasdynamic (EGD) electric generators which operate very efficiently with natural gas provide an ideal power source for the unprecedented power requirements of certain of the applications of this invention. For a more detailed discussion of the various means for generating electricity from hydrocarbon fuels, see "Electrical Aspects of Combustion", Lawton and Weinberg, Clarendon Press, 1969. For example, it is possible to generate the electricity directly at the high frequency needed to drive the antenna system. To do this, typically the velocity of flow of the combustion gases (v), past magnetic field perturbation of dimension d (in the case of MHD), follow the rule:

$$v = df$$

where f is the frequency at which electricity is generated. Thus, if $v = 1.78 \times 10^6$ cm/sec and $d = 1$ cm then

electricity would be generated at a frequency of 1.78 mHz.

Put another way, in Alaska, the right type of fuel (natural gas) is naturally present in large amounts and at just the right magnetic latitudes for the most efficient practice of this invention, a truly unique combination of circumstances. Desirable magnetic latitudes for the practice of this invention interest the earth's surface both northerly and southerly of the equator, particularly desirable latitudes being those, both northerly and southerly, which correspond in magnitude with the magnetic latitudes that encompass Alaska.

Referring now to FIG. 2 a first ambodiment is illustrated where a selected region R_1 of plasma 12 is altered by electron cyclotron resonance heating to accelerate the electrons of plasma 12, which are following helical paths along field line 11.

To accomplish this result, electromagnetic radiation is transmitted at the outset, essentially parallel to line 11 via antenna 15 as right hand circularly polarized radiation wave 20. Wave 20 has a frequency which will excite electron cyclotron resonance with plasma 12 at its initial or original altitude. This frequency will vary depending on the electron cyclotron resonance of region R_1 which, in turn, can be determined from available data based on the altitudes of region R_1, the particular field line 11 being used, the strength of the earth's magnetic field, etc. Frequencies of from about 20 to about 7200 kHz, preferably from about 20 to about 1800 kHz can be employed. Also, for any given application, there will be a threshhold (minimum power level) which is needed to produce the desired result. The minimum power level is a function of the level of plasma production and movement required, taking into consideration any loss processes that may be dominant in a particular plasma or propagation path.

As electron cyclotron resonance is established in plasma 12, energy is transferred from the electromagnetic radiation 20 into plasma 12 to heat and accelerate the electrons therein and, subsequently, ions and neutral particles. As this process continues, neutral particles which are present within R_1 are ionized and absorbed into plasma 12 and this increases the electron and ion densities of plasma 12. As the electron energy is raised to values of about 1 kilo electron volt (kev), the generated mirror force (explained below) will direct the excited plasma 12 upward along line 11 to form a plume R_2 at an altitude higher than that of R_1.

Plasma acceleration results from the force on an electron produced by a nonuniform static magnetic field (B). The force, called the mirror force, is given by

$$F = -\mu \nabla B \qquad (2)$$

where μ is the electron magnetic moment and $\nabla \bar{B}$ is the gradient of the magnetic field, μ being further defined as:

$$W_\perp / B = m V_\perp^2 / 2B$$

where $W_\perp$ is the kinetic energy in the direction perpendicular to that of the magnetic field lines and B is the magnetic field strength at the line of force on which the guiding center of the particle is located. The force as represented by equation (2) is the force which is responsible for a particle obeying equation (1).

even the most sophisticated of airplanes and missiles. The ability to employ and transmit over very wide areas of the earth a plurality of electromagnetic waves of varying frequencies and to change same at will in a random manner, provides a unique ability to interfere with all modes of communications, land, sea, and/or air, at the same time. Because of the unique juxtaposition of usable fuel source at the point where desirable field lines intersect the earth's surface, such wide ranging and complete communication interference can be achieved in a resonably short period of time. Because of the mirroring phenomenon discussed hereinabove, it can also be prolonged for substantial time periods so that it would not be a mere transient effect that could simply be waited out by an opposing force. Thus, this invention provides the ability to put unprecedented amounts of power in the earth's atmosphere at strategic locations and to maintain the power injection level, particularly if random pulsing is employed, in a manner far more precise and better controlled than heretofore accomplished by the prior art, particularly by the detonation of nuclear devices of various yeilds at various altitudes. Where the prior art approaches yielded merely transitory effects, the unique combination of fuel and desirable field lines at the point where the fuel occurs allows the establishment of, compared to prior art approaches, precisely controlled and long-lasting effects which cannot, practically speaking, simply be waited out. Further, by knowing the frequencies of the various electromagnetic beams employed in the practice of this invention, it is possible not only to interfere with third party communications but to take advantage of one or more such beams to carry out a communications network even though the rest of the world's communications are disrupted. Put another way, what is used to disrupt another's communications can be employed by one knowledgeable of this invention as a communications network at the same time. In addition, once one's own communication network is established, the far-reaching extent of the effects of this invention could be employed to pick up communication signals of other for intelligence purposes. Thus, it can be seen that the disrupting effects achievable by this invention can be employed to benefit the party who is practicing this invention since knowledge of the various electromagnetic waves being employed and how they will vary in frequency and magnitude can be used to an advantage for positive communication and eavesdropping purposes at the same time. However, this invention is not limited to locations where the fuel source naturally exists or where desirable field lines naturally intersect the earth's surface. For example, fuel, particularly hydrocarbon fuel, can be transported by pipeline and the like to the location where the invention is to be practiced.

FIG. 4 illustrates another embodiment wherein a selected region of plasma R_3 which lies within the earth's ionosphere is altered to increase the density thereof whereby a relatively stable layer 30 of relatively dense plasma is maintained within region R_3. Electromagnetic radiation is transmitted at the outset essentially parallel to field line 11 via antenna 15 as a right circularly polarized wave and at a frequency (e.g., 1.78 megahertz when the magnetic field at the desired altitude is 0.66 gauss) capable of exciting electron cyclotron resonance in plasma 12 at the particular altitude of plasma 12. This causes heating of the particles (electrons, ions, neutrals, and particulates) and ionization of uncharged particles adjacent line 11, all of which

are absorbed into plasma 12 to increase the density thereof. The power transmitted, e.g., 2×10^6 watts up to 2 minutes heating time, is less than that required to generate the mirror force F required to move plasma 12 upward as in the previous embodiment.

While continuing to transmit electromagnetic radiation 20 from antenna 15, a second electromagnetic radiation beam 31, which is at a defined frequency different from the radiation from antenna 15, is transmitted from one or more second sources via antenna 32 into layer 30 and is absorbed into a portion of layer 30 (cross-hatched area in FIG. 4). The electromagnetic radiation wave from antenna 32 is amplitude modulated to match a known mode of oscillation f_3 in layer 30. This creates a resonance in layer 30 which excites a new plasma wave 33 which also has a frequency of f_3 and which then propogates through the ionosphere. Wave 33 can be used to improve or disrupt communications or both depending on what is desired in a particular application. Of course, more than one new wave 33 can be generated and the various new waves can be modulated at will and in a highly nonlinear fashion.

FIG. 5 shows apparatus useful in this invention, particularly when those applications of this invention are employed which require extremely large amounts of power. In FIG. 5 there is shown the earth's surface 40 with a well 41 extending downwardly thereinto until it penetrates hydrocarbon producing reservoir 42. Hydrocarbon reservoir 42 produces natural gas alone or in combination with crude oil. Hydrocarbons are produced from reservoir 42 through well 41 and wellhead 43 to a treating system 44 by way of pipe 45. In treater 44, desirable liquids such as crude oil and gas condensates are separated and recovered by way of pipe 46 while undesirable gases and liquids such as water, H_2S, and the like are separated by way of pipe 47. Desirable gases such as carbon dioxide are separated by way of pipe 48, and the remaining natural gas stream is removed from treater 44 by way of pipe 49 for storage in conventional tankage means (not shown) for future use and/or use in an electrical generator such as a magnetohydrodynamic, gas turbine, fuel cell or EGD generator 50. Any desired number and combination of different types of electric generators can be employed in the practice of this invention. The natural gas is burned in generator 50 to produce substantial quantities of electricity which is then stored and/or passed by way of wire 51 to a transmitter 52 which generates the electromagnetic radiation to be used in the method of this invention. The electromagnetic radiation is then passed by way of wire 53 to antenna 54 which is located at or near the end of field line 11. Antenna 54 sends circularly polarized radiation wave 20 upwards along field line 11 to carry out the various methods of this invention as described hereinabove.

Of course, the fuel source need not be used in its naturally-occurring state but could first be converted to another second energy source form such as hydrogen, hydrazine and the like, and electricity then generated from said second energy source form.

It can be seen from the foregoing that when desirable field line 11 intersects earth's surface 40 at or near a large naturally-occurring hydrocarbon source 42, exceedingly large amounts of power can be very efficiently produced and transmitted in the direction of field lines. This is particularly so when the fuel source is natural gas and magnetohydrodynamic generators are employed. Further, this can all be accomplished in a

Since the magnetic field is divergent in region R_1, it can be shown that the plasma will move upwardly from the heating region as shown in FIG. 1 and further it can be shown that

$$\tfrac{1}{2}M_e V_{e\perp}{}^2(x) \simeq \tfrac{1}{2}M_e V_{e\perp}{}^2(Y) + \tfrac{1}{2}M_i V_{i\parallel}{}^2(Y) \qquad (3)$$

where the left hand side is the initial electron transverse kinetic energy; the first term on the right is the transverse electron kinetic energy at some point (Y) in the expanded field region, while the final term is the ion kinetic energy parallel to B at point (Y). This last term is what constitutes the desired ion flow. It is produced by an electrostatic field set up by electrons which are accelerated according to Equation (2) in the divergent field region and pulls ions along with them. Equation (3) ignores electron kinetic energy parallel to B because $V_{e\parallel} \simeq V_{i\parallel}$, so the bulk of parallel kinetic energy resides in the ions because of their greater masses. For example, if an electromagnetic energy flux of from about 1 to about 10 watts per square centimeter is applied to region R, whose altitude is 115 km, a plasma having a density (N_e) of 10^{12} per cubic centimeter will be generated and moved upward to region R_2 which has an altitude of about 1000 km. The movement of electrons in the plasma is due to the mirror force while the ions are moved by ambipolar diffusion (which results from the electrostatic field). This effectively "lifts" a layer of plasma 12 from the ionosphere and/or magnetosphere to a higher elevation R_2. The total energy required to create a plasma with a base area of 3 square kilometers and a height of 1000 km is about 3×10^{13} joules.

FIG. 3 is an idealized representation of movement of plasma 12 upon excitation by electron cyclotron resonance within the earth's divergent force field. Electrons (e) are accelerated to velocities required to generate the necessary mirror force to cause their upward movement. At the same time neutral particles (n) which are present along line 11 in region R_1 are ionized and become part of plasma 12. As electrons (e) move upward along line 11, they drag ions (i) and neutrals (n) with them but at an angle θ of about 13 degrees to field line 11. Also, any particulates that may be present in region R_1, will be swept upwardly with the plasma. As the charged particles of plasma 12 move upward, other particles such as neutrals within or below R_1, move in to replace the upwardly moving particles. These neutrals, under some conditions, can drag with them charged particles.

For example, as a plasma moves upward, other particles at the same altitude as the plasma move horizontally into the region to replace the rising plasma and to form new plasma. The kinetic energy developed by said other particles as they move horizontally is, for example, on the same order of magnitude as the total zonal kinetic energy of stratospheric winds known to exist.

Referring again to FIG. 2, plasma 12 in region R_1 is moved upward along field line 11. The plasma 12 will then form a plume (cross-hatched area in FIG. 2) which will be relatively stable for prolonged periods of time. The exact period of time will vary widely and be determined by gravitational forces and a combination of radiative and diffusive loss terms. In the previous detailed example, the calculations were based on forming a plume by producing 0+energies of 2 ev/particle. About 10 ev per particle would be required to expand plasma 12 to apex point C (FIG. 1). There at least some of the particles of plasma 12 will be trapped and will oscillate between mirror points along field line 11. This

oscillation will then allow additional heating of the trapped plasma 12 by stochastic heating which is associated with trapped and oscillating particles. See "A New Mechanism for Accelerating Electrons in the Outer Ionosphere" by R. A. Helliwell and T. F. Bell, Journal of Geophysical Research, Vol. 65, No. 6, June, 1960. This is preferably carried out at an altitude of at least 500 km.

The plasma of the typical example might be employed to modify or disrupt microwave transmissions of satellites. If less than total black-out of transmission is desired (e.g., scrambling by phase shifting digital signals), the density of the plasma (N_e) need only be at least about 10^6 per cubic centimeter for a plasma orginating at an altitude of from about 250 to about 400 km and accordingly less energy (i.e., electromagnetic radiation), e.g., 10^8 joules need be provided. Likewise, if the density $N_e$is on the order of 10^8, a properly positioned plume will provide a reflecting surface for VHF waves and can be used to enhance, interfere with, or otherwise modify communication transmissions. It can be seen from the foregoing that by appropriate application of various aspects of this invention at strategic locations and with adequate power sources, a means and method is provided to cause interference with or even total disruption of communications over a very large portion of the earth. This invention could be employed to disrupt not only land based communications, both civilian and military, but also airborne communications and sea communications (both surface and subsurface). This would have significant military implications, particularly as a barrier to or confusing factor for hostile m siles or airplanes. The belt or belts of enhanced ior tion produced by the method and apparatus o invention, particularly if set up over Northern and Canada, could be employed as an early w device, as well as a communications disruption m Further, the simple ability to produce such a situ a practical time period can by itself be a deterrir to hostile action. The ideal combination of suita lines intersecting the earth's surface at the poir substantial fuel sources are available for gene very large quantitites of electromagnetic pov as the North Slope of Alaska, provides the wh to accomplish the foregoing in a practical tin e.g., strategic requirements could necessitate the desired altered regions in time periods of utes or less and this is achievable with this especially when the combination of natur magnetohydrodynamic, gas turbine, fuel EGD electric generators are employed a where the useful field lines intersect the ear One feature of this invention which sati requirement of a weapon system, i.e., conti ing of operability, is that small amounts of generated for operability checking purpos the exploitation of this invention, since the magnetic beam which generates the enh belt of this invention can be modulated its or more additional electromagnetic radia be impinged on the ionized region forme tion as will be described in greater de with respect to FIG. 4, a substantial domly modulated signals of very larg tude can be generated in a highly nonl can cause confusion of or interferen complete disruption of guidance syst relatively small physical area when there is the unique coincidence of fuel source 42 and desirable field line 11. Of course, only one set of equipment is shown in FIG. 5 for sake of simplicity. For a large hydrocarbon reservoir 42, a plurality of wells 41 can be employed to feed one or more storage means and/or treaters and as large a number of generators 55 as needed to power one or more transmitters 52 and one or more antennas 54. Since all of the apparatus 44 through 54 can be employed and used essentially at the sight where naturally-occurring fuel source 42 is located, all the necessary electromagnetic radiation 20 is generated essentially at the same location as fuel source 42. This provides for a maximum amount of usable electromagnetic radiation 20 since there are no significant storage or transportation losses to be incurred. In other words, the apparatus is brought to the sight of the fuel source where desirable field line 11 intersects the earth's surface 40 on or near the geographical location of fuel source 42, fuel source 42 being at a desirable magnetic latitude for the practice of this invention, for example, Alaska.

The generation of electricity by motion of a conducting fluid through a magnetic field, i.e., magnetohydrodynamics (MHD), provides a method of electric power generation without moving mechanical parts and when the conducting fluid is a plasma formed by combustion of a fuel such as natural gas, an idealized combination of apparatus is realized since the very clean-burning natural gas forms the conducting plasma in an efficient manner and the thus formed plasma, when passed through a magnetic field, generates electricity in a very efficient manner. Thus, the use of fuel source 42 to generate a plasma by combustion thereof for the generation of electricity essentially at the site of occurrence of the fuel source is unique and ideal when high power levels are required and desirable field lines 11 intersect the earth's surface 40 at or near the site of fuel source 42. A particular advantage for MHD generators is that they can be made to generate large amounts of power with a small volume, light weight device. For example, a 1000 megawatt MHD generator can be construed using superconducting magnets to weigh roughly 42,000 pounds and can be readily air lifted.

This invention has a phenomenal variety of possible ramifications and potential future developments. As alluded to earlier, missile or aircraft destruction, deflection, or confusion could result, particularly when relativistic particles are employed. Also, large regions of the atmosphere could be lifted to an unexpectedly high altitude so that missiles encounter unexpected and unplanned drag forces with resultant destruction or deflection of same. Weather modification is possible by, for example, altering upper atmosphere wind patterns or altering solar absorption patterns by constructing one or more plumes of atmospheric particles which will act as a lens or focusing device. Also as alluded to earlier, molecular modifications of the atmosphere can take place so that positive environmental effects can be achieved. Besides actually changing the molecular composition of an atmospheric region, a particular molecule or molecules can be chosen for increased presence. For example, ozone, nitrogen, etc. concentrations in the atmosphere could be artificially increased. Similarly, environmental enhancement could be achieved by causing the breakup of various chemical entities such as carbon dioxide, carbon monoxide, nitrous oxides, and the like. Transportation of entities can also be realized when advantage is taken of the drag effects caused by regions of the atmosphere moving up along diverging field lines. Small micron sized particles can be then transported, and, under certain circumstances and with the availability of sufficient energy, larger particles or objects could be similarly affected. Particles with desired characteristics such as tackiness, reflectivity, absorptivity, etc., can be transported for specific purposes or effects. For example, a plume of tacky particles could be established to increase the drag on a missile or satellite passing therethrough. Even plumes of plasma having substantially less charged particle density than described above will produce drag effects on missiles which will affect a lightweight (dummy) missile in a manner substantially different than a heavy (live) missile and this affect can be used to distinguish between the two types of missiles. A moving plume could also serve as a means for supplying a space station or for focusing vast amount of sunlight on selected portions of the earth. Surveys of global scope could also be realized because the earth's natural magnetic field could be significantly altered in a controlled manner by plasma beta effects resulting in, for example, improved magnetotelluric surveys. Electromagnetic pulse defenses are also possible. The earth's magnetic field could be decreased or disrupted at appropriate altitudes to modify or eliminate the magnetic field in high Compton electron generation (e.g., from high altitude nuclear bursts) regions. High intensity, well controlled electrical fields can be provided in selected locations for various purposes. For example, the plasma sheath surrounding a missile or satellite could be used as a trigger for activating such a high intensity field to destroy the missile or satellite. Further, irregularities can be created in the ionosphere which will interfere with the normal operation of various types of radar, e.g., synthetic aperture radar. The present invention can also be used to create artificial belts of trapped particles which in turn can be studied to determine the stability of such parties. Still further, plumes in accordance with the present invention can be formed to simulate and/or perform the same functions as performed by the detonation of a "heave" type nuclear device without actually having to detonate such a device. Thus it can be seen that the ramifications are numerous, far-reaching, and exceedingly varied in usefulness.

I claim:

1. A method for altering at least one region normally existing above the earth's surface with electromagnetic radiation using naturally-occurring and diverging magnetic field lines of the earth comprising transmitting first electromagnetic radiation at a frequency between 20 and 7200 kHz from the earth's surface, said transmitting being conducted essentially at the outset of transmission substantially parallel to and along at least one of said field lines, adjusting the frequency of said first radiation to a value which will excite electron cyclotron resonance at an initial elevation at least 50 km above the earth's surface, whereby in the region in which said electron cyclotron resonance takes place heating, further ionization, and movement of both charged and neutral particles is effected, said cyclotron resonance excitation of said region is continued until the electron concentration of said region reaches a value of at least 10^6 per cubic centimeter and has an ion energy of at least 2 ev.

2. The method of claim 1 including the step of providing artificial particles in said at least one region which are excited by said electron cyclotron resonance.

16

3. The method of claim 2 wherein said artificial particles are provided by injecting same into said at least one region from an orbiting satellite.

4. The method of claim 1 wherein said threshold excitation of electron cyclotron resonance is about 1 watt per cubic centimeter and is sufficient to cause movement of a plasma region along said diverging magnetic field lines to an altitude higher than the altitude at which said excitation was initiated.

5. The method of claim 4 wherein said rising plasma region pulls with it a substantial portion of neutral particles of the atmosphere which exist in or near said plasma region.

6. The method of claim 1 wherein there is provided at least one separate source of second electromagnetic radiation, said second radiation having at least one frequency different from said first radiation, impinging said at least one second radiation on said region while said region is undergoing electron cyclotron resonance excitation caused by said first radiation.

7. The method of claim 6 wherein said second radiation has a frequency which is absorbed by said region.

8. The method of claim 6 wherein said region is plasma in the ionosphere and said second radiation excites plasma waves within said ionosphere.

9. The method of claim 8 wherein said electron concentration reaches a value of at least 10^{12} per cubic centimeter.

10. The method of claim 8 wherein said excitation of electron cyclotron resonance is initially carried out within the ionosphere and is continued for a time sufficient to allow said region to rise above said ionosphere.

11. The method of claim 1 wherein said excitation of electron cyclotron resonance is carried out above about 500 kilometers and for a time of from 0.1 to 1200 seconds such that multiple heating of said plasma region is achieved by means of stochastic heating in the magnetosphere.

12. The method of claim 1 wherein said first electromagnetic radiation is right hand circularly polarized in the northern hemisphere and left hand circularly polarized in the southern hemisphere.

13. The method of claim 1 wherein said electromagnetic radiation is generated at the site of a naturally-occurring hydrocarbon fuel source, said fuel source being located in at least one of northerly or southerly magnetic latitudes.

14. The method of claim 13 wherein said fuel source is natural gas and electricity for generating said electromagnetic radiation is obtained by burning said natural gas in at least one of magnetohydrodynamic, gas turbine, fuel cell, and EGD electric generators located at the site where said natural gas naturally occurs in the earth.

15. The method of claim 14 wherein said site of natural gas is within the magnetic latitudes that encompass Alaska.

* * * * *

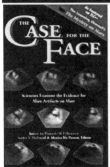

THE FANTASTIC INVENTIONS OF NIKOLA TESLA
Nikola Tesla with additional material by David Hatcher Childress
This book is a readable compendium of patents, diagrams, photos and explanations of the many incredible inventions of the originator of the modern era of electrification. In Tesla's own words are such topics as wireless transmission of power, death rays, and radio-controlled airships. In addition, rare material on German bases in Antarctica and South America, and a secret city built at a remote jungle site in South America by one of Tesla's students, Guglielmo Marconi. Marconi's secret group claims to have built flying saucers in the 1940s and to have gone to Mars in the early 1950s! Incredible photos of these Tesla craft are included. The Ancient Atlantean system of broadcasting energy through a grid system of obelisks and pyramids is discussed, and a fascinating concept comes out of one chapter: that Egyptian engineers had to wear protective metal head-shields while in these power plants, hence the Egyptian Pharoah's head covering as well as the Face on Mars!
•His plan to transmit free electricity into the atmosphere.
•How electrical devices would work using only small antennas mounted on them.
•How his inventions could utilize this free energy in the atmosphere.
•How radio and radar technology can be used as death-ray weapons in Star Wars.
•Tesla's Death Rays, Ozone generators, and more...
342 PAGES. 6X9 PAPERBACK. ILLUSTRATED. BIBLIOGRAPHY AND APPENDIX. $16.95. CODE: FINT

ANGELS DON'T PLAY THIS HAARP
Advances In Tesla Technology
by Jeane Manning and Dr. Nick Begich

According to the authors, the U.S. government has a new ground-based "Star Wars" weapon in the remote bush country of Alaska. This new system, based on Tesla's designs, can disrupt human mental processes, jam all global communications systems, change weather patterns over large areas, cause environmental damage and more. The military calls this atmosphere zapper HAARP for High-frequency Active Auroral Research Program which targets the electrojet—a river of electricity that flows thousands of miles through the sky and down into the polar icecap. The device will be used to X-ray the earth, talk to submarines, more.
233 PAGES. 6X9 PAPERBACK. ILLUSTRATED. $14.95. CODE: ADPH

SECRETS OF COLD WAR TECHNOLOGY
Project HAARP and Beyond
by Gerry Vassilatos
Vassilatos reveals that "Death Ray" technology has been secretly researched and developed since the turn of the century. Included are chapters on such inventors and their devices as H.C. Vion, the developer of auroral energy receivers; Dr. Selim Lemstrom's pre-Tesla experiments; the early beam weapons of Grindell-Mathews, Ulivi, Turpain and others; John Hettenger and his early beam power systems. Learn about Project Argus, Project Teak and Project Orange; EMP experiments in the 60s; why the Air Force directed the construction of a huge Ionospheric "backscatter" telemetry system across the Pacific just after WWII; why Raytheon has collected every patent relevant to HAARP over the past few years; more.
250 PAGES. 6X9 PAPERBACK. ILLUSTRATED. $15.95. CODE: SCWT

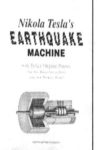

NIKOLA TESLA'S EARTHQUAKE MACHINE WITH TESLA'S ORIGINAL PATENTS
by Dale Pond and Walter Baumgartner
Now, for the first time the secrets of Nikola Tesla's Earthquake Machine are available. Although this book discusses in detail Nikola Tesla's 1894 "Earthquake Oscillator" this book is also about the new technology of sonic vibrations which produce a resonance effect that can be used to cause earthquakes. Discussed are Tesla Oscillators, vibration physics, Amplitude Modulated Additive Synthesis, Tele-Geo-dynamics, Solar Heat Pump apparatus, vortex tube coolers, the Serogodsky Motor, more. Plenty of technical diagrams. Be the first on your block to have a Tesla Earthquake Machine!
175 PAGES. 9X11 PAPERBACK. PHOTOS, ILLUSTRATIONS & DIAGRAMS. BIBLIOGRAPHY & INDEX. $16.95. CODE: TEM

OCCULT ETHER PHYSICS
Tesla's Hidden Space Propulsion System & the Conspiracy To Conceal It
by William Lyne
Space Aliens From the Pentagon author Lyne says that there is a "Secret Physics" with a different set of rules hidden away from us earlier in this century by a powerful elite who fear the technology based on it will strip away their power and wealth. Chapters on: The Occult Ether Theory and Electro-propulsion; Wireless Transmission of Energy; Tesla's Teleforce Discoveries; J.J. Thomson's "Electromagnetic Momentum"; Ether and "Ponderable Matter"; Rotatory Motion and the "Screw Effect"; Tesla's Dynamic Theory of Gravity; Tesla's Secrecy; The Atomic Hydrogen Furnace; more.
106 PAGES. 7X10 PAPERBACK. ILLUSTRATED. REFERENCES. $8.00. CODE: OEP

PRODIGAL GENIUS
The Life of Nikola Tesla
by John O'Neil
First published in 1944, this biography of the great inventor was the first to tell the tale of the brilliant and eccentric personality that was Nikola Tesla. O'Neil knew Tesla, who once remarked to him, "You understand me better than any man alive."
326 PAGES. 6X9 TRADEPAPER. LIST OF PATENTS & INDEX. $14.95. CODE: PRG

NEW BOOKS FROM ADVENTURES UNLIMITED

ANCIENT MICRONESIA
& the Lost City of Nan Madol
by David Hatcher Childress

Micronesia, a vast archipelago of islands west of Hawaii and south of Japan, contains some of the most amazing megalithic ruins in the world. Part of our *Lost Cities of the Pacific* series, this volume explores the incredible conformations on various Micronesian islands, especially the fantastic and little-known ruins of Nan Madol on Pohnpei Island. The huge canal city of Nan Madol contains over 250 million tons of basalt columns over an 11 square-mile area of artificial islands. Much of the huge city is submerged, and underwater structures can be found to an estimated 80 feet. Islanders' legends claim that the basalt rocks, weighing up to 50 tons, were magically levitated into place by the powerful forefathers. Other ruins in Micronesia that are profiled include the Latte Stones of the Marianas, the menhirs of Palau, the megalithic canal city on Kosrae Island, megaliths on Guam, and more.

256 PAGES. 6X9 PAPERBACK. HEAVILY ILLUSTRATED. INCLUDES A COLOR PHOTO SECTION. BIBLIOGRAPHY & INDEX. $16.95. CODE: AMIC

FAR-OUT ADVENTURES
The Best of World Explorer Magazine

This is a thick compilation of the first nine issues of *WORLD EXPLORER* in a large-format paperback. Included are all the articles, cartoons, satire and such features as the Crypto-Corner, the News Round-Up, Letters to the Editor, the Odd-Ball Gallery and the many far-out advertisements. World Explorer has been published periodically by THE WORLD EXPLORERS CLUB for almost eight years now. It is on sale at Barnes & Noble Bookstores and has become a cult magazine among New Agers and Fortean Researchers. Authors include David Hatcher Childress, Joseph Jochmans, John Major Jenkins, Deanna Emerson, Katherine Routledge, Alexander Horvat, John Tierney, Greg Deyermenjian, Dr. Marc Miller, and others. Articles in this book include Smithsonian Gate, Dinosaur Hunting In the Congo, Secret Writings of the Incas, On the Track of the Yeti, Secrets of the Sphinx, Living Pterodactyls, Quest For Atlantis, What Happened To the Great Library of Alexandria?, In Search of Seamonsters, Egyptians In the Pacific, Lost Megaliths of Guatemala, The Mystery of Easter Island, Comacalco: Mayan City of Mystery, and plenty more.

520 PAGES, 8X11 PAPERBACK. ILLUSTRATED. $19.95. CODE: FOA

SECRET CITIES OF OLD SOUTH AMERICA
Atlantis Reprint Series
by Harold T. Wilkins

The reprint of Wilkin's classic book, first published in 1952, claiming that South America was Atlantis. Chapters include Mysteries of a Lost World; Atlantis Unveiled; Red Riddles on the Rocks; South America's Amazons Existed!; The Mystery of El Dorado and Gran Payatiti—the Final Refuge of the Incas; Monstrous Beasts of the Unexplored Swamps & Wilds; Weird Denizens of Antediluvian Forests; New Light on Atlantis from the World's Oldest Book; The Mystery of Old Man Noah and the Arks; and more.

438 PAGES. 6X9 PAPERBACK. HEAVILY ILLUSTRATED. BIBLIOGRAPHY & INDEX. $16.95. CODE: SCOS

ATLANTIS IN AMERICA
Navigators of the Ancient World
by Ivar Zapp and George Erikson

This book is an intensive examination of the archeological sites of the Americas, an examination that reveals civilization has existed here for tens of thousands of years. Zapp is an expert on the enigmatic giant stone spheres of Costa Rica, and maintains that they were sighting stones found throughout the Pacific as well as in Egypt and the Middle East. They were used to teach star-paths and sea to the world-wide navigators of the ancient world. While the Mediterranean and European regions "forgot" world-wide navigation and fought wars the Mesoamericans of diverse races were building vast interconnected cities without walls. This Golden Age of ancient America was merely a myth of suppressed history—until now. Profusely illustrated, chapters are on Navigators of the Ancient World; Pyramids & Megaliths: Older Than You Think; Ancient Ports and Colonies; Cataclysms of the Past; Atlantis: From Myth To Reality; The Serpent and the Cross: The Loss of the City States; Calendars and Star Temples; and more.

360 PAGES. 6X9 PAPERBACK. ILLUSTRATED. BIBLIOGRAPHY & INDEX. $17.95. CODE: AIA

MAPS OF THE ANCIENT SEA KINGS
Evidence of Advanced Civilization in the Ice Age
by Charles H. Hapgood

Charles Hapgood's classic 1966 book on ancient maps produces concrete evidence of an advanced world-wide civilization existing many thousands of years before ancient Egypt. He has found the evidence in the Piri Reis Map that shows Antarctica, the Hadji Ahmed map, the Oronteus Finaeus and other amazing maps. Hapgood concluded that these maps were made from more ancient maps from the various ancient archives around the world, now lost. Not only were these unknown people more advanced in mapmaking than any people prior to the 18th century, it appears they mapped all the continents. The Americas were mapped thousands of years before Columbus. Antarctica was mapped when its coasts were free of ice.

316 PAGES. 7X10 PAPERBACK. ILLUSTRATED. BIBLIOGRAPHY & INDEX. $19.95. CODE: MASK

ANTI-GRAVITY

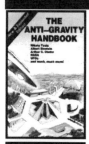

THE ANTI-GRAVITY HANDBOOK
edited by David Hatcher Childress, with Arthur C. Clarke, Nikola Tesla, T.B. Paulicki, Bruce Cathie, Leonard G. Cramp and Albert Einstein

The new expanded compilation of material on Anti-Gravity, Free Energy, Flying Saucer Propulsion, UFOs, Suppressed Technology, NASA Cover-ups and more. Highly illustrated with patents, technical illustrationsand photos. This revised and expanded edition has more material, including photos of Area 51, Nevada, the government's secret testing facility. This classic on weird science is back in a 90s format!
• How to build a flying saucer.
•Arthur C. Clarke on Anti-Gravity.
• Crystals and their role in levitation.
• Secret government research and development.
• Nikola Tesla on how anti-gravity airships could draw power from the atmosphere.
• Bruce Cathie's Anti-Gravity Equation.
• NASA, the Moon and Anti-Gravity.
230 PAGES, 7X10 TRADEPAPER, BIBLIOGRAPHY/INDEX/APPENDIX. HIGHLY ILLUSTRATED WITH 100'S OF PATENTS ILLUSTRATIONS AND PHOTOS. $14.95. CODE: AGH

ANTI–GRAVITY & THE WORLD GRID
edited by David Hatcher Childress

Is the earth surrounded by an intricate network of electromagnetic grid network offering free energy? This compilation of material on ley lines and world power points contains chapters on the geography, mathematics, and light harmonics of the earth grid. Learn the purpose of ley lines and ancient megalithic structures located on the grid. Discover how the grid made the Philadelphia Experiment possible. Explore the Coral Castle and many other mysteries; Including acoustic levitation, Tesla Shields and scalar wave weaponry. Browse through the section on anti-gravity patents, and research resources.
274 PAGES, 150 RARE PHOTOGRAPHS, DIAGRAMS AND DRAWINGS, 7X10 PAPERBACK, $14.95. CODE: AGW

ANTI–GRAVITY & THE UNIFIED FIELD
edited by David Hatcher Childress

Is Einstein's Unified Field Theory the answer to all of our energy problems? Explored in this compilation of material is how gravity, electricity and magnetism manifest from a unified field around us. Why artificial gravity is possible; secrets of UFO propulsion; free energy; Nikola Tesla and anti-gravity airships of the 20's and 30's; flying saucers as superconducting whirls of plasma; anti-mass generators; vortex propulsion; suppressed technology; government cover-ups; gravitational pulse drive, space-craft & more.
240 PAGES. 7X10 PAPERBACK.HEAVILY ILLUSTRATED. $14.95. CODE: AGU

ETHER TECHNOLOGY
A Rational Approach to Gravity Control
by Rho Sigma

This classic book on anti-gravity & free energy is back in print and back in stock. Written by a well-known American scientist under the pseudonym of "Rho Sigma," this book delves into international efforts at gravity control and discoid craft propulsion. Before the Quantum Field, there was "Ether." This small, but informative book has chapters on John Searle and "Searle discs;" T. Townsend Brown and his work on anti-gravity and ether-vortex-turbines. Includes a forward by former NASA astronaut Edgar Mitchell. Don't miss this classic book!
108 PAGES, 6X9 TRADEPAPER, ILLUSTRATED WITH PHOTOS & DIAGRAMS. $12.95. CODE: ETT

UNDERGROUND BASES & TUNNELS
What is the Government Trying to Hide?
by Richard Sauder, Ph.D.

Working from government documents and corporate records, Sauder has compiled an impressive book that digs below the surface of the military's super-secret underground! Go behind the scenes into little-known corners of the public record and discover how corporate America has worked hand-in-glove with the Pentagon for decades, dreaming about, planning, and actually constructing, secret underground bases. This book includes chapters on the locations of the bases, the tunneling technology, various military designs for underground bases, nuclear testing & underground bases, abductions, needles & implants; Is the Military Involvement in "alien" cattle mutilations?, more. 50 page photo & map insert.
201 PAGES. 6X9 PAPERBACK. WELL ILLUSTRATED. $15.95. CODE: UGB

ANTI-GRAVITY

THE FREE-ENERGY DEVICE HANDBOOK
A Compilation of Patents and Reports
by David Hatcher Childress

A large-format compilation of various patents, papers, descriptions and diagrams concerning free-energy devices and systems. *The Free-Energy Device Handbook* is a visual tool for experimenters and researchers into magnetic motors and other "over-unity" devices. With chapters on the Adams Motor, the Hans Coler Generator, cold fusion, superconductors, "N" machines, space-energy generators, Nikola Tesla, T. Townsend Brown, and the latest in free-energy devices. Packed with photos, technical diagrams, patents and fascinating information, this book belongs on every science shelf. With energy and profit being a major political reason for fighting various wars, free-energy devices, if ever allowed to be mass-distributed to consumers, could change the world! Get your copy now before the Department of Energy bans this book!
292 PAGES. 8x10 TRADEPAPER. ILLUSTRATED. BIBLIOGRAPHY. $16.95. CODE: FEH

THE BRIDGE TO INFINITY
Harmonic 371244
by Captain Bruce Cathie

Cathie has popularized the concept that the earth is criss–crossed by an electromagnetic grid system that can be used for anti-gravity, free energy, levitation and more. The book includes a new analysis of the harmonic nature of reality, acoustic levitation, pyramid power, harmonic receiver towers and UFO propulsion. It concludes that today's scientists have at their command a fantastic store of knowledge with which to advance the welfare of the human race.
204 PAGES. 6x9 TRADEPAPER. ILLUSTRATED. $14.95. CODE: BTF

THE ENERGY GRID
Harmonic 695, The Pulse of the Universe
by Captain Bruce Cathie

This is the breakthrough book that explores the incredible potential of the Energy Grid and the Earth's Unified Field all around us. Bruce Cathie's first book *Harmonic 33*, was published in 1968 when he was a commercial pilot in New Zealand. Since then Captain Bruce Cathie has been the premier investigator into the amazing potential of the infinite energy that surrounds our planet every microsecond. Cathie investigates the Harmonics of Light and how the Energy Grid is created. In this amazing book are chapters on UFO propulsion, Nikola Tesla, Unified Equations, the Mysterious Aerials, Pythagoras & the Grid, Nuclear detonation and the Grid, maps of the ancients, an Australian Stonehenge examined, more.
255 PAGES. 6x9 TRADEPAPER. ILLUSTRATED. $15.95. CODE: TEG

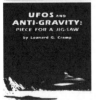

UFOS AND ANTI-GRAVITY
Piece For A Jig-Saw
by Leonard G. Cramp

Leonard G. Cramp's 1966 classic book on flying saucer propulsion and suppressed technology is available again. *UFOS & Anti-Gravity: Piece For A Jig-Saw* is a highly technical look at the UFO phenomena by a trained scientist. Cramp first introduces the idea of 'anti-gravity' and introduces us to the various theories of gravitation. He then examines the technology necessary to build a flying saucer and examines in great detail the technical aspects of such a craft. Cramp's book is a wealth of material and diagrams on flying saucers, anti-gravity, suppressed technology, G-fields and UFOs. Chapters include Crossroads of Aerodymanics, Aerodynamic Saucers, Limitations of Rocketry, Gravitation and the Ether, Gravitational Spaceships, G. Field Lift Effects, The Bi-Field Theory, VTOL and Hovercraft, Analysis of UFO photos, more. "I feel the Air Force has not been giving out all available information on these unidentified flying objects. You cannot disregard so many unimpeachable sources." — John McCormack, Speaker of the U.S. House of Representatives.
388 PAGES. 6x9 PAPERBACK. HEAVILY ILLUSTRATED. $16.95. CODE: UAG

MAN-MADE UFOS 1944—1994
Fifty Years of Suppression
by Renato Vesco & David Hatcher Childress

A comprehensive look at the early "flying saucer technology" of Nazi Germany and the genesis of early man-made UFOs. This book takes us from the work of captured German scientists, to escaped battalions of Germans, secret communities in South America and Antarctica to todays state-of-the-art "Dreamland" flying machines. Heavily illustrated, this astonishing book blows the lid off the "government UFO conspiracy" and explains with technical diagrams the technology involved. Examined in detail are secret underground airfields and factories; German secret weapons; "suction" aircraft; the origin of NASA; gyroscopic stabilizers and engines; the secret Marconi aircraft factory in South America; and more. Not to be missed by students of technology suppression, secret societies, anti-gravity, free energy conspiracy and World War II! Introduction by W.A. Harbinson, author of the Dell novels *GENESIS* and *REVELATION*.
318 PAGES. 6x9 TRADEPAPER. ILLUSTRATED. INDEX & FOOTNOTES. $18.95. CODE: MMU

---

24 HOUR CREDIT CARD ORDERS—CALL: 815-253-6390 FAX: 815-253-6300

email: auphq@frontiernet.net   http://www.azstarnet.com/~aup

NEW BOOKS

HAARP
The Ultimate Weapon of the Conspiracy
by Jerry Smith

The HAARP project in Alaska is one of the most controversial projects ever undertaken by the U.S. Government. Jerry Smith gives us the history of the HAARP project and explains how it can be used as an awesome weapon of destruction. Smith exposes a covert military project and the web of conspiracies behind it. HAARP has many possible scientific and military applications, from raising a planetary defense shield to peering deep into the earth. Smith leads the reader down a trail of solid evidence into ever deeper and scarier conspiracy theories in an attempt to discover the "whos" and "whys" behind HAARP, and discloses a possible plan to rule the world. At best, HAARP is science out-of-control; at worst, HAARP could be the most dangerous device ever created, a futuristic technology that is everything from super-beam weapon to world-wide mind control device. The Star Wars future is now. Topics include Over-the-Horizon Radar and HAARP, Mind Control, ELF and HAARP, The Telsa Connection, The Russian Woodpecker, GWEN & HAARP, Earth Penetrating Tomography, Weather Modification, Secret Science of the Conspiracy, more. Includes the complete 1987 Bernard Eastlund patent for his pulsed super-weapon that he claims was stolen by the HAARP Project.
256 PAGES. 6X9 PAPERBACK. ILLUSTRATED. BIBLIOGRAPHY & INDEX. $14.95. CODE: HARP

LOST CONTINENTS & THE HOLLOW EARTH
I Remember Lemuria and the Shaver Mystery
by David Hatcher Childress & Richard Shaver

Lost Continents & the Hollow Earth is Childress' thorough examination of the early hollow earth books of Richard Shaver and the fascination that fringe fantasy subjects such as lost continents and the hollow earth have had for the American public. Shaver's rare 1948 book *I Remember Lemuria* is reprinted in its entirety, and the book is packed with illustrations from Ray Palmer's *Amazing Stories* issues of the 1940s. Palmer and Shaver told of tunnels running through the earth—tunnels inhabited by the Deros and Teros, humanoids from an ancient spacefaring race that had inhabited the earth, eventually going underground, hundreds of thousands of years ago. Childress discusses the famous hollow earth books and delves deep into whatever reality may be behind the stories of tunnels in the earth. Operation High Jump to Antarctica in 1947 and Admiral Byrd's bizarre statements, tunnel systems in South America and Tibet, the underground world of Agartha, the belief of UFOs coming from the South Pole, more.
412 PAGES. 6X9 PAPERBACK. ILLUSTRATED. $16.95. CODE: LCHE

KUNDALINI TALES
by Richard Sauder, Ph.D.

Underground Bases and Tunnels author Richard Sauder's second book on his personal experiences and provocative research into spontaneous spiritual awakening, out-of-body journeys, encounters with secretive governmental powers, daylight sightings of UFOs, and more. Sauder continues his studies of underground bases with new information on the occult underpinnings of the U.S. space program. The book also contains a breakthrough section that examines actual U.S. patents for devices that manipulate minds and thoughts from a remote distance. Included are chapters on the secret space program and a 130-page appendix of patents and schematic diagrams of secret technology and mind control devices.
296 PAGES. 7X10 PAPERBACK. ILLUSTRATED. BIBLIOGRAPHY. $14.95. CODE: KTAL

LIQUID CONSPIRACY
JFK, LSD, the CIA, Area 51 & UFOs
by George Piccard

Underground author George Piccard on the politics of LSD, mind control, and Kennedy's involvement with Area 51 and UFOs. Reveals JFK's LSD experiences with Mary Pinchot-Meyer. The plot thickens with an ever expanding web of CIA involvement, underground bases with UFOs seen by JFK and Marilyn Monroe (among others) to a vaster conspiracy that affects every government agency from NASA to the Justice Department. This may have been the reason that Marilyn Monroe and actress-columnist Dorothy Killgallen were both murdered. Focusing on the bizarre side of history, *Liquid Conspiracy* takes the reader on a psychedelic tour de force.
264 PAGES. 6X9 PAPERBACK. ILLUSTRATED. $14.95. CODE: LIQC

COSMIC MATRIX
Piece for a Jig-Saw, Part Two
by Leonard G. Cramp

Leonard G. Cramp, a British aerospace engineer, wrote his first book *Space Gravity and the Flying Saucer* in 1954. *Cosmic Matrix* is the long-awaited sequel to his 1966 book *UFOs & Anti-Gravity: Piece For A Jig-Saw*. Cramp has had a long history of examining UFO phenomena and has concluded that UFOs use the highest possible aeronautic science to move in the way they do. Cramp examines anti-gravity effects and theorizes that this super-science used by the craft—described in detail in the book—can lift mankind into a new level of technology, transportation and understanding of the universe. The book takes a close look at gravity control, time travel, and the interlocking web of energy between all planets in our solar system with Leonard's unique technical diagrams. A fantastic voyage into the present and future!
364 PAGES. 6X9 PAPERBACK. ILLUSTRATED. BIBLIOGRAPHY. $16.00. CODE: CMX

24 HOUR CREDIT CARD ORDERS—CALL: 815-253-6390 FAX: 815-253-6300

email: auphq@frontiernet.net   http://www.azstarnet.com/~aup